APACHE
SERVER
FOR
DUMMIES®

APACHE SERVER FOR DUMMIES®

by Ken A. L. Coar

Foreword by Roy T. Fielding
co-founder, The Apache Group

IDG Books Worldwide, Inc.
An International Data Group Company

Foster City, CA ♦ Chicago, IL ♦ Indianapolis, IN ♦ New York, NY

Apache Server For Dummies®

Published by
IDG Books Worldwide, Inc.
An International Data Group Company
919 E. Hillsdale Blvd.
Suite 400
Foster City, CA 94404
`www.idgbooks.com` (IDG Books Worldwide Web site)
`www.dummies.com` (Dummies Press Web site)

Library of Congress Catalog Card No.: 97-80876

ISBN: 0-7645-0291-3

Printed in the United States of America

10 9 8 7 6 5 4 3

1O/SS/QT/QQ/IN

Distributed in the United States by IDG Books Worldwide, Inc.

Distributed by CDG Books Canada Inc. for Canada; by Transworld Publishers Limited in the United Kingdom; by IDG Norge Books for Norway; by IDG Sweden Books for Sweden; by IDG Books Australia Publishing Corporation Pty. Ltd. for Australia and New Zealand; by TransQuest Publishers Pte Ltd. for Singapore, Malaysia, Thailand, Indonesia, and Hong Kong; by Gotop Information Inc. for Taiwan; by ICG Muse, Inc. for Japan; by Intersoft for South Africa; by Eyrolles for France; by International Thomson Publishing for Germany, Austria and Switzerland; by Distribuidora Cuspide for Argentina; by LR International for Brazil; by Galileo Libros for Chile; by Ediciones ZETA S.C.R. Ltda. for Peru; by WS Computer Publishing Corporation, Inc., for the Philippines; by Contemporanea de Ediciones for Venezuela; by Express Computer Distributors for the Caribbean and West Indies; by Micronesia Media Distributor, Inc. for Micronesia; by Chips Computadoras S.A. de C.V. for Mexico; by Editorial Norma de Panama S.A. for Panama; by American Bookshops for Finland.

For general information on IDG Books Worldwide's books in the U.S., please call our Consumer Customer Service department at 800-762-2974. For reseller information, including discounts and premium sales, please call our Reseller Customer Service department at 800-434-3422.

For information on where to purchase IDG Books Worldwide's books outside the U.S., please contact our International Sales department at 317-596-5530 or fax 317-572-4002.

For consumer information on foreign language translations, please contact our Customer Service department at 1-800-434-3422, fax 317-572-4002, or e-mail rights@idgbooks.com.

For information on licensing foreign or domestic rights, please phone +1-650-653-7098.

For sales inquiries and special prices for bulk quantities, please contact our Order Services department at 800-434-3422 or write to the address above.

For information on using IDG Books Worldwide's books in the classroom or for ordering examination copies, please contact our Educational Sales department at 800-434-2086 or fax 317-572-4005.

For press review copies, author interviews, or other publicity information, please contact our Public Relations department at 650-653-7000 or fax 650-653-7500.

For authorization to photocopy items for corporate, personal, or educational use, please contact Copyright Clearance Center, 222 Rosewood Drive, Danvers, MA 01923, or fax 978-750-4470.

IDG BOOKS WORLDWIDE

About the Author

Ken Coar became involved with the World Wide Web when the number of servers across the planet could be counted on the fingers of less than a hundred people, and has remained active in the field ever since. He became interested in the Apache HTTP Server project in 1996, and joined The Apache Group in early 1997. He has published articles in various trade magazines, and is a long-time member of the Digital Computer Users Society (DECUS). He gives presentations around the world on the subjects of the Web technology and computer security.

Ken has been working with computers since he was in the sixth grade — back when computers were barely worthy of the name, and a "program-mable calculator" weighed 40 pounds and took up half the desk. His first useful programming work (he explicitly excludes the sine-wave graph generator that reduced the Selectric to mechanical tears) was used to keep track of student table waiters for the school dining hall. Since then, Ken hasn't looked back — possibly because of what he suspects may be following him.

Ken has worked in the software engineering and system administration fields for the University of Massachusetts, General Dynamics, Digital Equipment Corporation, and Process Software Corporation. He lives in New Hampshire with his wife, four cats, and several computers.

Ken can be reached electronically at `Ken.Coar@MeepZor.Com`

ABOUT IDG BOOKS WORLDWIDE

Welcome to the world of IDG Books Worldwide.

IDG Books Worldwide, Inc., is a subsidiary of International Data Group, the world's largest publisher of computer-related information and the leading global provider of information services on information technology. IDG was founded more than 30 years ago by Patrick J. McGovern and now employs more than 9,000 people worldwide. IDG publishes more than 290 computer publications in over 75 countries. More than 90 million people read one or more IDG publications each month.

Launched in 1990, IDG Books Worldwide is today the #1 publisher of best-selling computer books in the United States. We are proud to have received eight awards from the Computer Press Association in recognition of editorial excellence and three from Computer Currents' First Annual Readers' Choice Awards. Our best-selling ...For Dummies® series has more than 50 million copies in print with translations in 31 languages. IDG Books Worldwide, through a joint venture with IDG's Hi-Tech Beijing, became the first U.S. publisher to publish a computer book in the People's Republic of China. In record time, IDG Books Worldwide has become the first choice for millions of readers around the world who want to learn how to better manage their businesses.

Our mission is simple: Every one of our books is designed to bring extra value and skill-building instructions to the reader. Our books are written by experts who understand and care about our readers. The knowledge base of our editorial staff comes from years of experience in publishing, education, and journalism — experience we use to produce books to carry us into the new millennium. In short, we care about books, so we attract the best people. We devote special attention to details such as audience, interior design, use of icons, and illustrations. And because we use an efficient process of authoring, editing, and desktop publishing our books electronically, we can spend more time ensuring superior content and less time on the technicalities of making books.

You can count on our commitment to deliver high-quality books at competitive prices on topics you want to read about. At IDG Books Worldwide, we continue in the IDG tradition of delivering quality for more than 30 years. You'll find no better book on a subject than one from IDG Books Worldwide.

IDG
BOOKS
WORLDWIDE

John J. Kilcullen

John Kilcullen
Chairman and CEO
IDG Books Worldwide, Inc.

Eighth Annual Computer Press Awards ≥1992

Ninth Annual Computer Press Awards ≥1993

Tenth Annual Computer Press Awards ≥1994

Eleventh Annual Computer Press Awards ≥1995

Dedication

This book is dedicated to the memory of John H. Hughes, teacher and friend — and a shining example of what both should be.

Acknowledgments

I wish to gratefully acknowledge and thank my wonderful wife Cathy, who performed prodigies during the writing of this book. She kept us sane and me at the keyboard, and didn't lose faith even when I was in my crankiest and most procrastinatory moods.

I also want to thank the other members of The Apache Group for the incredibly stimulating environment the project provides, and especially Roy Fielding, Dean Gaudet, and Jim Jagielski for their feedback and support (such as pointing out my goofs).

Much of the research for this book was carried out on hardware my former employer, Process Software Corporation, loaned to me for my Apache work. My thanks to Dean Goodermote, Process' CEO, for his support.

Thanks also are due to the people at IDG Books Worldwide, including Pat O'Brien, Pete Bitar, Kim Darosett, and Heather Dismore, for helping bring some semblance of order out of chaos.

Finally, I also wish to thank the many people who have inspired and supported me during this effort, whether they knew they were doing it or not. A far from complete list includes my sisters Candace and Andrea; my coworkers Cathy Wright, Steve Gonczi, and Kathy Zieman; and my friends, including Mike Jittlov and his family, Lynnell Koehler, John and Deborah Carl, Sandip Sengupta and family, and Joe Coyle and family.

Publisher's Acknowledgments

We're proud of this book; please register your comments through our IDG Books Worldwide Online Registration Form located at http://my2cents.dummies.com.

Some of the people who helped bring this book to market include the following:

Acquisitions, Development, and Editorial

Project Editor: Pat O'Brien

Acquisitions Editor: Pete Bitar

Media Development Manager: Joyce Pepple

Associate Permissions Editor:
Heather H. Dismore

Copy Editor: Kim Darosett

Technical Editor: Dean Gaudet

Editorial Manager: Mary C. Corder

Editorial Assistant: Darren Meiss

Production

Project Coordinator: E. Shawn Aylsworth

Layout and Graphics:
Steve Arany, Lou Boudreau,
Linda M. Boyer, J. Tyler Connor,
Kelly Hardesty, Angela F. Hunckler,
Todd Klemme, Jane E. Martin,
Anna Rohrer, Brent Savage, Janet Seib,
M. Anne Sipahimalani, Deirdre Smith,
Rashell Smith, Kate Snell, Michael A. Sullivan

Proofreaders: Ethel M. Winslow, Kelli Botta,
Michelle Croninger, Joel K. Draper, Brian
Massey, Robert Springer, Janet M. Withers

Indexer: David Heiret

General and Administrative

IDG Books Worldwide, Inc.: John Kilcullen, CEO

IDG Books Technology Publishing Group: Richard Swadley, Senior Vice President and Publisher; Walter Bruce III, Vice President and Associate Publisher; Joseph Wikert, Associate Publisher; Mary Bednarek, Branded Product Development Director; Mary Corder, Editorial Director; Barry Pruett, Publishing Manager; Michelle Baxter, Publishing Manager

IDG Books Consumer Publishing Group: Roland Elgey, Senior Vice President and Publisher; Kathleen A. Welton, Vice President and Publisher; Kevin Thornton, Acquisitions Manager; Kristin A. Cocks, Editorial Director

IDG Books Internet Publishing Group: Brenda McLaughlin, Senior Vice President and Publisher; Diane Graves Steele, Vice President and Associate Publisher; Sofia Marchant, Online Marketing Manager

IDG Books Production for Dummies Press: Debbie Stailey, Associate Director of Production; Cindy L. Phipps, Manager of Project Coordination, Production Proofreading, and Indexing; Tony Augsburger, Manager of Prepress, Reprints, and Systems; Laura Carpenter, Production Control Manager; Shelley Lea, Supervisor of Graphics and Design; Debbie J. Gates, Production Systems Specialist; Robert Springer, Supervisor of Proofreading; Kathie Schutte, Production Supervisor

Dummies Packaging and Book Design: Patty Page, Manager, Promotions Marketing

◆

The publisher would like to give special thanks to Patrick J. McGovern,
without whom this book would not have been possible.

◆

Contents at a Glance

Foreword .... *XXV*

Introduction *1*

Part I: In the Beginning *9*
Chapter 1: What You Need 11
Chapter 2: What Apache Needs 23

Part II: Getting Things Running *31*
Chapter 3: Installing Apache 33
Chapter 4: Basic Configuration 49
Chapter 5: Much Ado about Logging 83
Chapter 6: Authorization and Authentication 97

Part III: Nuts and Bolts *115*
Chapter 7: The Modular Approach 117
Chapter 8: Life Cycle of a Client Request 141

Part IV: Going Further *149*
Chapter 9: [Re]compiling the Software 151
Chapter 10: Examining the Running Server 165
Chapter 11: Document Selection and Content Negotiation 179
Chapter 12: Reacting in Real-Time 201
Chapter 13: Actions, Handlers, and Types 221
Chapter 14: Virtual Hosts 229
Chapter 15: Serving by Proxy 249

Part V: The Part of Tens *263*
Chapter 16: Ten Steps When You Have Problems 265
Chapter 17: Ten Important RFCs 277
Chapter 18: Ten URLs for Web Authors 287
Chapter 19: Ten Apache Answers 295
Chapter 20: Ten Common Error Messages 303

Part VI: Appendixes 311

Appendix A: Troubleshooting 313
Appendix B: About the CD-ROM 323
Appendix C: Server Side Includes .... CD-ROM

Index 333

IDG Books Worldwide End-User License Agreement 354

Installation Instructions 356

Book Registration Information .... Back of Book

Cartoons at a Glance

By Rich Tennant

page 31

page 263

page 311

page 149

page 9

page 115

Fax: 978-546-7747
E-mail: richtennant@the5thwave.com
World Wide Web: www.the5thwave.com

Table of Contents

· ·

Foreword .... *XXV*

Introduction *1*

About This Book 3
How to Use This Book 4
   Conventions 4
Who Are You? 5
How This Book is Organized 6
Icons Used in This Book 6
What Now? 7

Part I: In the Beginning *9*

Chapter 1: What You Need 11

What's Involved in Running Apache? 12
   A system running UNIX 12
   Decisions, decisions: Names and addresses 12
   Network needs 14
   The Internet is optional 14
Skills and Tools You Need 15
   Understanding your system 15
   Editing the configuration files 17
   Superuser access 17
   Filling up your tool belt 18
      A browser, a browser — my caffeine for a browser! 18
      Telnet: what you see is what it said 19
      Packet tracing for fun and profit 20
      Hammers, saws, and compilers 21
      For serious server surgery 22

Chapter 2: What Apache Needs 23

System Requirements 23
   User IDs and groups 24
   Processes: Parents and children 25
   Open sesame! uh, files! 26
   Cycling with Apache — CPU needs 26
   Now, where did I put that? — Memory! 26
   Disk space 27

The Configuration Files 29
    Server-wide configuration files 29
    Per-directory configuration files 30

Part II: Getting Things Running *31*

Chapter 3: Installing Apache **33**

Decisions, Decisions: Source Kit or Binary? 33
    Platforms Supported 35
Kit Contents 36
    The cgi-bin directory 37
    The conf directory 37
    The htdocs directory 37
    What's in htdocs/manual? 38
    The icons directory 38
    The logs directory 38
    The src directory 39
        What's in src/helpers? 39
        What's in src/modules? 40
        What's in src/regex? 40
    The support directory 41
Choosing a Directory Structure 41
Unpacking the Kit 42
    Order in the kit! 42
        The source, the source — my kingdom for the source! 42
        A bit, a byte — a binary for my site 43
Verifying Your Installation 44
    Checking your kits 44
        Verifying PGP signatures 46
        Verifying MD5 signatures 46
        Forgery! What to do? 47
    The operation was a success — but how's the patient? 47

Chapter 4: Basic Configuration **49**

Directives — What's the Score? 49
    Containers for the things contained 50
    A-one, and a-two, and 51
Scopes: Servers, Directories, Locations, and Files 53
    The server-config files 53
    Scope it out! 54
    Quite a lovely <Location> 56
    Lord of the <Files> 56
    Getting wild! 57

Order of the day 58
    Digging through directories 59
    Following the files 59
    Looking at locations 60
Narrowing the field 60
Overrides — The Layered Approach to Directive Validity 61
Root Directories — How It Can Be Told 62
    The ServerRoot 63
    DocumentRoot — Where the wild things are 64
    Permissions 65
Minimal Configuration 68
Command-Line Options 72
    -d — Where's the directory? 72
    -f — What's the file? 72
    -h — What ingredients are there? 72
    -l — Who are the cooks? 74
    -v — What version of Apache? 75
    -X — EXperimental operation 75
Starting, Stopping, and Reloading the Server 75
    Starting over without stopping 76
The Default Server 77
Sleight of Web — Aliases 77
    Script directories 78
Naming Conventions 78
    Plain text 78
    HTML files 79
    Images 80
    Binary files 80
    Scripts — Files that get executed 81

Chapter 5: Much Ado about Logging **83**

Who's That Knocking At My Door? 83
Log Analysis Tools 86
    Analog 86
    GetStats 87
Customizing the Access Log 88
Tracking Usage with Cookies 88
Logging and Advertising 90
Recording Server Errors 93
    Errors from invoked scripts 94
Roll Over, Apache 95

Chapter 6: Authorization and Authentication **97**

Do I Know You? 97
Prove It! 98
Basic Authentication 99
Security-Related Directives 100
    `Allow` — Conditions for entrance 100
    `Deny` — "Don't let them in, Sam" 101
    `Order` — Who's on first? 101
    `AuthType` — Authorization method to use 102
    `AuthName` — Name of the realm 103
    `Require` — Minimum requirements 103
    `Satisfy` — Mix and match 104
Limiting Access by Method 104
The Security Modules 105
    `mod_access` — Allow/deny access by origin host 105
    `mod_auth` — Text-based authorization 106
    `mod_auth_anon` — Authorization anonymous FTP-style 107
    `mod_auth_db` and `mod_auth_dbm` — Database lookup 108
Handling Large User Groups with Databases 109
Security Do's and Don'ts 110
    Do check and prune your databases regularly 110
    Do enable DNS if using host-based access checking 110
    Do protect your log files and back them up 111
    Don't put security files in Webspace 111
    Don't allow local users to access security files 112
    Don't use your system passwd file for web security 112

Part III: Nuts and Bolts *115*

Chapter 7: The Modular Approach **117**

Callbacks, Handlers, and Hooks 117
    Configuration versus request context 118
    The 18 hooks to modular bliss 119
Standard Modules Included with Apache 123
    Miscellaneous modules 123
        `mod_example` 124
        `mod_unique_id` 124
    Real-time processing modules 125
        `mod_actions` 125
        `mod_autoindex` 125
        `mod_cgi` 126
        `mod_imap` 126
        `mod_include` 127

Security modules 127
    mod_access 128
    mod_auth 128
    mod_auth_anon 128
    mod_auth_db **and** mod_auth_dbm 128
    mod_auth_msql 129
    mod_digest 129
Translators 129
    mod_alias 130
    mod_dir 130
    mod_mime 131
    mod_mime_magic 131
    mod_negotiation 131
    mod_rewrite 132
    mod_userdir 132
Decision-makers 133
    mod_setenvif 133
Protocol assists 134
    mod_asis 134
    mod_cern_meta 134
    mod_expires 134
    mod_headers 134
    mod_proxy 135
Management tools 136
    mod_dld 136
    mod_env 136
    mod_info 136
    mod_log_agent 138
    mod_log_config 138
    mod_log_referer 138
    mod_status 139
    mod_usertrack 140
The Apache Module Registry 140

Chapter 8: Life Cycle of a Client Request **141**

Pages versus Requests 141
First, the Autopsy! (Huh?) 142
Getting a Second Opinion (And a Third, and a Fourth . . .) 143
    The post_read_request phase 144
    The translate_handler phase 144
    The header_parse phase 145
    The access_checker phase 145
    The check_user_id phase 145
    The auth_checker phase 146

The Diagnosis: What to Do? 146
  The `type_checker` phase 147
  The `fixer_upper` phase 147
And the Answer Is 147
  The `content-handler` phase 148
Making Notes about the Operation 148
  The `logger` phase 148

Part IV: Going Further *149*

Chapter 9: [Re]compiling the Software 151
Configuring the Configuration File 151
  Selecting build-time configuration options 152
    Extra! Extra! 152
    Compile-time server switches 154
    The rules of the game 156
Modulating the Module List 158
  Order is important! 159
  Hidden dependencies 159
Doing the Build 160
Installing the New Server 160
Porting to a New Platform 161
  Seeking help is okay 162

Chapter 10: Examining the Running Server 165
Under the Microscope 165
It's Alive! 166
Seeing the Directives in Effect 167
What's the Server Doing, Anyway?? 171
  More tricks with the status module 176

Chapter 11: Document Selection and Content Negotiation 179
Advanced Redirection 179
Client Preferences 183
  Variable dimensions 184
  Quality time 187
  Data-driven content typing 190
  Multiviews 191
  When negotiations break down 192
Controlling Cache Eligibility 193
  Setting arbitrary header fields 195
  Calculating the `Expires` date 196
  Caching negotiated resources 198
  The x-bit hack 199

Chapter 12: Reacting in Real-Time 201

Scripts and CGI 201
The CGI environment 202
Envariables passed to scripts 204
Command-line arguments 208
Communicating with the server 209
The head and the body are separated 210
Response header fields that I've known —
and you should too 212
Server buffering of CGI output 213
Do-it-(all)-yourself scripts 215
Dynamic Content with Server-Side Includes 216
A-parsing we will go. 216
The x-bit hack again 217
The who-what-huh of SSI directives 218

Chapter 13: Actions, Handlers, and Types 221

Content Handlers 224
Data Massage from Outside the Server 224
Error Handlers 226

Chapter 14: Virtual Hosts 229

What's a Virtual Host? 230
What's in a [virtual] name? 230
The rules behind virtual hosts 231
Declaring a virtual host 231
Your host for this evening will be. 232
The simplest case: One address and one name 233
A case for name vhosts: One address, two names 233
A time for addresses: Two addresses, two names 235
The combo platter: Two addresses, four names 236
Multiple Hosts by Address 239
Multiple Hosts by Name 243
Listen: Do You Hear What I Hear? 244
Special Considerations — Logging 244
Splitting up the access log 245
Other logging considerations 247
The Default Server Again 247
The _default_ Host 248

Chapter 15: Serving by Proxy 249

What The Proxy Does 249
Here, let me do that for you 250
Let me see if I have that in stock. 251
Configuring clients to use the proxy 253

Establishing the Proxy 253
    Turning the proxy on — And off 254
    Setting up a virtual host for the proxy 254
    "Cascading Proxies, Batman!" 256
    Forbidding proxy access 256
    Using the proxy to connect web sites 257
Cache Me If You Can! 258
    Keeping undesirables out of the cache 259
    The garbage collector 260
    Decisions, decisions: How long to cache? 260
        How old is this thing, anyway? 261
        How about them other types of documents? 262

Part V: The Part of Tens 263

Chapter 16: Ten Steps When You Have Problems 265

Make Sure It's a Problem 266
Reproduce the Condition 266
Get the Exact Symptomology 266
Check the Server Error Log 267
Verify Directive Syntax and Interaction 268
Read the FAQ (Frequently Asked Questions) List 269
Search the Apache Bug Database 269
Check the Apache Newsgroup 272
Verify File Protections and Check for Resource Exhaustion 272
Report the Problem to The Apache Group 273

Chapter 17: Ten Important RFCs 277

Internet Primer: RFC2151 278
RFCs about the Domain Name System 278
    Domain administrator's guide: RFC1032 279
    Domain name concepts: RFC1034 279
    Domain name specification: RFC1035 280
DNS Aliases for Services: RFC2219 280
The MIME Papers: RFCs 2045 through 2049 281
    Message body formats: RFC2045 281
    Internet media types: RFC2046 282
    Non-ASCII headers in MIME: RFC2047 282
    Registering a MIME type: RFC2048 283
    Conformance and examples: RFC2049 283
HTML Version 2.0: RFC1866 283
Uniform Resource Names: 1737 284
URL Definition: RFC1738 285

Relative URLs: RFC1808 285
The HTTP/1.0 Specification: RFC1945 286
The HTTP/1.1 Specification: RFC2068 286

Chapter 18: Ten URLs for Web Authors 287

The Apache Web Site 287
The Latest Apache Documentation 288
The Apache Documentation Searcher 289
The Apache Bug Database 289
The ApacheWeek Electronic Magazine 290
The Apache Module Registry 291
The World Wide Web Consortium 292
The HTML/3.2 Standard 292
The Internet RFC Repository 293
The Netcraft Web Survey 294

Chapter 19: Ten Apache Answers 295

Why don't my virtual hosts work? 295
How come people can see pages I put a `<Limit>` on? 297
Why don't my SSI directives work? 297
Why can't I use SSI directives in my script output? 298
How do I set up a password-protected page? 299
How do I use `/etc/passwd` for web authentication? 300
How do I enable PUT for web publishing? 301
What are these "connection reset by peer" messages in my error log? 301
What does "Premature end of script headers" mean? 302
Why do I get errors trying to compile Apache? 302

Chapter 20: Ten Common Error Messages 303

"Surf's Up!" — Normal Messages 303
  "Server configured — resuming normal operations" 304
  "SIGHUP received. Attempting to restart" 304
  "httpd: caught SIGTERM, shutting down" 305
  "server seems busy, spawning n children
    (you may need to increase StartServers,
    or MinMaxSpareServers)" 305
Whoops! SEGV, the Fatal Apache Error 306
The Generic "Internal Server Error" 307
SSI Parsing Failures 307
"You can't make me talk!" When the client stops talking 308
"Nobody's hearin' nothin'!" When the client stops listening 309
Slips betwixt cup and lip — or betwixt document and client 309

Part VI: Appendixes 311

Appendix A: Troubleshooting 313

Is It Just Me, or . . .? — Is It a Known Problem? 313
Verifying the CGI Environment 314
Finding the Pulse of an Unresponsive Server 315
Checking Communication by Playing Computer 317
Following the Packet Trail 319
    Recording network conversations 320
    Playing back the recording 321

Appendix B: About the CD-ROM 323

Appendix C: Server Side Includes .... CD-ROM

Index 333

IDG Books Worldwide End-User License Agreement 354

Installation Instructions 356

Book Registration Information .... Back of Book

Foreword

● ●

*W*hat is the World Wide Web? Looking at the definitions in the popular press might lead one to believe that the Web is just the latest browser technology: the package of user interface gizmos that allows people to surf through the Internet. Somewhere along the line, the glitz of browsers like NCSA Mosaic, Netscape Navigator, and Microsoft Internet Explorer became the focus of popular interest in the Web. We shouldn't be surprised at that; after all, did you think about the printing press when first opening this book?

In reality, the browser is the least important and easiest to replace of the components that make up the Web. Most important is the information within the Web, followed by the cables, computers, and network protocols that make up the Internet, and then the Server technology that allows information to become part of the Web. This book explains everything you need to know in order to set up a production-quality HTTP server, along with information about how to connect the server to the Internet and the variety of ways to make your own information part of the Web. What's more, Ken manages to describe it all with a sense of humor, and without assuming you already know how the Internet works.

Before delving into the techie aspects of Apache, there is something you need to understand first. The Web is actually a plot to take over the world, and you have been recruited to help. No kidding — that has been the plan all along (it's how the Web got the name "World Wide"). Don't worry, there's no need to hide the kids or lock the door; I am referring to the world of information, not the physical world.

Sometimes, the best way to conquer the world is one person at a time. The secret of the Web is that, no matter how strange the subject or obscure the fact, there is somebody, somewhere in the world that is absolutely fanatical about that subject and ruthlessly collecting those facts. I'm not just talking about the people in your company's Marketing department; the same applies to hobbyists as well. More importantly, there are thousands (and sometimes millions) of others in the world who are not quite so fanatical about the same subject, but nonetheless interested in seeing those facts.

Why, then, has the Web been able to take advantage of these fanatics, while other technologies failed? The answer is Simplicity and the virtues of Free Software. The Web's exponential growth began with the introduction of server software that was free and easy to install. Chief among these was the NCSA httpd (that's shorthand for HTTP server) developed by Rob McCool in 1993. It used the Unix filesystem and user accounts to make providing web information as easy as editing a file, while pioneering dynamic resources through the introduction of CGI. However, development of NCSA httpd stalled after Rob McCool left NCSA for the commercial world. In February 1995, a group of Webmasters gathered together via the Internet for the purpose of coordinating their individual enhancements and bug fixes into a common distribution, founding the Apache HTTP Server Project in the process. The original Apache Group included Brian Behlendorf, Roy T. Fielding, Rob Hartill, David Robinson, Cliff Skolnick, Randy Terbush, Robert S. Thau, and Andrew Wilson.

Using NCSA httpd 1.3 as a base, we added all of the published bug fixes and worthwhile enhancements we could find, tested the result on our own servers, and made the first official public release of the Apache server in April 1995. The early Apache server was a big hit, but we all knew that the codebase needed a general overhaul and redesign. While the rest of the group focused on implementing new features and supporting the rapidly growing Apache user community, Robert Thau designed a new server architecture (code-named Shambhala) which included a modular structure and API for better extensibility, pool-based memory allocation, and an adaptive pre-forking process model. In other words, faster, more reliable, and easier to extend than any other server software available (free or commercial in origin).

The Apache Group continues to grow and improve the Apache server software. We are dedicated to improving the Internet through the definition and implementation of standard protocols like HTTP and the provision of free software to anyone who wants to join the Web. Fortunately for all of us, Ken Coar is a member of the Apache Group and ready to guide you through the intricacies of HTTP server installation and management.

Your mission, should you accept it, is to install and operate the Apache server — the world's most popular software for allowing fanatics to share with the rest of us the information they have collected (or invented) about their favorite subjects. Think of it as the printing press for the information age, and you are about to unleash one small part of the modern Renaissance.

Welcome to the Web!

Roy T. Fielding   University of California, Irvine   October 1997

Introduction

● ●

*W*elcome to the wonderful wide world of providing web-based content! More specifically, welcome to the world-wide community of Apache Web server software users!

Some people think that being a Webmaster and running a web server is like getting a law degree:

✔ It takes a long time.

✔ It costs a lot of money.

✔ When you're done, lots of people hate you.

But with the Apache software and a system to run it, even nice people without much money can be Webmasters!

I can't think of a single invention that has brought information and technology into the hands of the general public more quickly or thoroughly than the World Wide Web. It's sort of like the advent of television — only ten times faster. Back in 1993, there weren't very many people who knew about it (the Web, not television!); mentioning W-W-W in those days typically would get you a blank stare and the question, "Huh? The world-wide *what?*" Nowadays it's on business cards and television advertisements. What a change!

The amazing power of the web technology is the ability to bring different pieces of information, and different *types* of information, together on a single screen. Neat "front ends" and "GUIs" open the doors to information that used to be accessible only to the Gurus and the Keepers of the Arcane Lore.

But you knew all that, right? What does this have to do with the Apache web server software?

The Web is a clear example of that wonderful buzz-term that's been bandied around boardrooms for the last few years: *client/server*. In a client/server environment, the client makes requests for things to happen, and the server does them. In the case of the Web, the client (typically a browser such as Netscape Navigator or Internet Explorer) asks a server for a resource (such as an electronic copy of a magazine article). The server either provides it or tells the client why not.

With the explosive growth of the Web, lots of people smell potential money-making opportunities. Web clients and servers have been leapfrogging each other with what they can do. Modern web browsers do a lot — they handle electronic mail, USENET news groups, and even Web page *design* now. There are many more potential consumers of electronic information than providers, just as there are more readers of books than authors, so a lot of entrepreneurial effort has gone into making the browsers feature-rich. (It doesn't hurt that the browser is what the end-user "touches" — fancy doodads attract customers.) Similarly, Web servers have been steadily enhancing their functionality, though most of their new abilities aren't directly visible to the end-user.

I know, I know — you want to know about Apache. I'm coming to it. . . .

One of the first major web server packages came from the same people that brought us the first major web client package. Those people were the folks at the [U.S.] National Center for Supercomputing Applications, at the University of Illinois in Urbana-Champaign. (NCSA for short.) The client was (and still is) called Mosaic, and the server was (and still is) called NCSA HTTPd. I don't know if they expected the popularity of their work, but the software became *so* popular — "How popular *was* it?" — it was *so* popular that they weren't getting any of their real work done.

Enter Apache. (This is the part for which you've been waiting. Thank you for your patience. If you jumped straight here, subtract 10 Apache Guru Points and go back to the beginning.)

Because U.S. government money funded NCSA, the software they developed was free. Some of the people who wanted to see changes made started communicating with one another and sharing their modifications. These modifications were (and still are) expressed as actual changes to the source code of the server. Anyone who wanted to add the changes could use a tool called `patch`. The result was people using "patched" versions of the server (naturally called "a patchy server") and the name was born. The people who were developing the "patchy server" became known as The Apache Group.

Since the initial formation of the Group, development of the Apache Web server software has continued. At the time of this writing, at least one survey of Web sites on the Internet shows more than 48% (over 695,000) of them to be running one version or another of Apache.

Why is Apache so popular?

- ✔ It's free.
- ✔ There are *lots* of people already running it, more than are running anything else (band-wagon syndrome).

✔ The developers are generally accessible through electronic mail.

✔ It's free.

✔ It's easily tailored, so if you want to change the server it's simple to do.

✔ There's a tremendous pool of people already using it, so there's a good chance someone else has already made the customization you want.

✔ Did I mention that it's free?

The Apache Group currently consists of roughly three dozen regular contributors from around the world, but the membership is extremely informal and subject to change.

Despite initial appearances, the name of the Apache Web server software has nothing to do with the Native American people of the same name.

About This Book

Reading this book should be fun and informative. It's written in good (mostly), plain, straightforward English (except where babbling in tongues like C or sh is required), with lots of examples and instructions. Among other things, the stuff in this book shows you how to

✔ Unpack and install the Apache software on your system.

✔ Design the structure of your web document directories.

✔ Configure Apache to supply local files in response to client requests.

✔ Configure Apache to tell clients to look elsewhere.

✔ Set up the server so clients can ask for a single URL — and get it in the language of the end-user's choice (if it's available).

✔ Design your own custom error messages.

✔ Run multiple web sites from a single system.

✔ Obtain the latest version of the software from the Internet.

✔ Debug problems with your configuration.

✔ Ask for help from other Apache users and The Apache Group.

How to Use This Book

You don't have to read this book from the beginning to the end for it to make sense or be useful. (You may read it like a novel if you like, of course. If you discover a plot, please let me know!) Rather, you can look up specific topics in the Table of Contents or the Index to find the nitty-gritty itty-bitty details.

Conventions

Apache is controlled by instructions contained in text files. That means there are no buttons you can click or menus you can select, and you can't blame "mouse-bounce" for mistakes. You have to get right in there and *type* those instructions yourself. It's more intimate that way, don't you think?

Regardless of whether you agree, one of the points here is that in many situations the difference between upper- and lower-case letters is significant. Since you're going to be typing the instructions yourself, you need to keep this in mind.

Exchanges with the computer appear in a monospaced typeface like this:

```
% ./Configure
```

Monospaced simply means that all the characters are the same width. If two lines each have thirty monospaced letters on them, you can be sure that the thirtieth one in the second line will be right under the thirtieth one in the first line.

When you're exchanging information with the computer, it will type some stuff and you will type some. (That's what makes it an exchange.) To make it clear in the book, the stuff the computer prints will be displayed normally, and the stuff you're supposed to type will be bold, like this:

```
% ./Configure
```

When an example demonstrates a command, any prompt the system is likely to display will be shown. *Don't type the prompt!* If text isn't bold, the *computer* typed it.

Commands and instructions you feed to the computer's command interpreter fall into two basic categories: those that require *superuser authority* (see Chapter 1) and those that don't. If the prompt looks like an octothorpe ("#"), it means you probably have to be running with superuser authority for the command to work. If the prompt is "%" then your identity probably shouldn't matter.

```
% telnet          # can be anyone
# shutdown -r now  # need to be superuser
```

Usually, it's clear when you need to hit the "do-it" key (Enter, or Return, or whatever it may be on your keyboard). In some cases, you may need to type special characters. These are in bracketed smallcaps, like [THIS]. Control characters are represented as [CTRL/X] — for example, [CTRL/C] means Control-C. (Surprise!)

Sometimes you'll need to type something, but exactly what, will be up to you. (For example, the name of your system.) Items for which you need to "fill in the blank" will be presented in *italics,* like this:

```
% ./Configure -f alternate-config-file
```

In some cases, the computer output in the book won't match what you'll see on your screen. To represent variable system output like this, I'll put such output in italics, too. You can tell whether it's something variable the computer said, or something variable *you're* supposed to say, by whether it's bold or not.

```
% uname -a
OS-name system-name system-version hardware-platform
```

Finally, in some of the examples there are embedded comments describing various things. These will be off to the right of the text if possible, *not* in a monospaced font, and preceded by a "#" character (the usual UNIX comment character):

```
% make              # start compilation
```

Don't type these comments!

Who Are You?

In writing this book, I've made some basic assumptions about you (and yes, I know what they say about *assume*ing things). I've assumed that

- You've used UNIX at some point
- You've surfed the Web (at least a little)
- You're familiar with command-line environments (such as UNIX shells or DOS command prompts)
- You know about editing text files (as opposed to using a word processor)
- You feel at least marginally comfortable using a text editor (such as vi or emacs)

How This Book is Organized

Part I describes what you'll need to get going with Apache: your workshop, if you will. Some hand tools (compilers, Telnet, *et cetera*) and a workbench (your system) are absolute necessities, and a power tool or two (browsers, packet tracers) can come in handy. If you're just getting going with Apache, Part I is a good place to start.

Part II describes what it takes to get the Apache software on your system and running in just about its most simple configuration. It covers the basics of Apache directives (which are how you control the server), file structure, the server's logging capabilities, and some of the simpler ways of protecting information. If you want to install Apache but aren't sure how, check out Part II. If you've already installed Apache and it doesn't seem to be running correctly, check here for basic issues that may be causing your trouble.

Part III goes into some (though not a lot of) detail about just *how* Apache works. It describes how the different types of functionality are implemented, and follows a client request through the Garden of the Modules.

Part IV covers more advanced topics, such as customizing the server, providing pages according to the end-user's language choice, and interacting with the end-user with things like order forms and surveys. It also covers the *proxy module,* which acts as a go-between or intermediary for web requests, and *virtual hosts,* which allow you to make a single server look like dozens of different systems. If you're into providing content in a big way, or providing Web hosting services like an ISP (Internet Server Provider), be sure to check out some of the topics in Part IV.

Part V is the ubiquitous "Part of Tens" without which no *...For Dummies* book is complete.

In the Appendixes, you'll find the appendix on Troubleshooting, which gives detailed instructions for identifying problems with the server, and the appendix on Server-Side Includes, which gives lots of details about how to make the Apache Web server tailor pages at display time. (This Appendix is only available on the *Apache Server For Dummies* CD-ROM) There's also an appendix about the software on the CD-ROM that comes with this book.

Icons Used in This Book

Apache doesn't use icons, but *Apache Server For Dummies* does.

Tip points to shortcuts that save you time and trouble.

Warning keeps you from stepping on landmines.

Technical Stuff you can skip, if you want to.

Remember that these friendly reminders can help you make connections.

1.3 helps you recognize tips that apply to Apache 1.3. If you're supporting an older version, it's an important distinction.

What Now?

You've managed to make it through most of the Introduction! (If you jumped straight here, give yourself 10 Apache Guru Points.) Probably the next thing you should do is take a brief rest, and contemplate what section you want to look at next.

Let's get started!

Part I
In the Beginning

The 5th Wave®   By Rich Tennant

"Hold on, that's not a script error, it's just a booger on the screen."

In this part . . .

The two chapters in this part are like the list of ingredients at the beginning of a cookbook recipe: they describe the things you need in order to end up with a successful Apache Web server system.

I'm a complete klutz when it comes to following recipes; I often fail to read ahead or between the lines and don't realize until I come to the "whip egg whites until they form soft peaks" part that I should have dug out the egg-beater. I've avoided inflicting this on you though.

Chapter 1

What You Need

- -

In This Chapter

▶ Understanding the basic hardware and software

▶ Taking an inventory of your system

▶ Going public on the Internet

▶ Getting Apache running

▶ Figuring out if the server is working

▶ Rebuilding the server later

- -

*J*ust as you need blueprints and a piece of land before you can start
building a house, you need a special framework in place before you can
install and run the Apache software. You can get started given the very bare
essentials, like building on a tiny deserted island or in the middle of a forest,
but to actually get your web server to the stage where other people can visit
requires dealing with The System. When you set up your Apache Web server,
you need to do the equivalent of contacting the phone company to get a
phone number, wiring to your house, and a listing in the phone book.

Fortunately, some prefabricated Apache configurations are available. If
prefab isn't available in your neck of the woods, you're going to need special
tools for building the software. The same situation applies if you start with a
prefabricated server, but you want to build an addition or redecorate.

Regardless of how you build your Apache server, you probably need basic
debugging tools — the equivalent of a building inspector — to explain why
the buffers won't flush and the wallpaper keeps falling down.

So, sharpen your pencil, get out your T-square, and get to work!

What's Involved in Running Apache?

When I say "running Apache," I mean having an environment in which you can start the Apache software and have it perform as instructed (which is hopefully the same as expected). A web server in general, and the Apache software in particular, have certain requirements, which I describe in the following sections.

A system running UNIX

Upon writing this book, the Apache software is available only for systems running some version of a UNIX operating system. Numerous UNIX versions (as well as the systems running them) are available, and Apache works on many of them. However, if your version doesn't have formal support, you can relatively easily make Apache run on it.

See Chapter 3 for information about system environments that Apache supports out-of-the-box and how to make Apache support your system if it isn't on the list.

The UNIX operating system is very popular, and you can find different flavors of it, many of them free, for almost any piece of hardware around. So if you've been looking for something to do with that old Intel 386 box that's currently holding your boat in place . . . make it a web server running UNIX and Apache!

Decisions, decisions: Names and addresses

Computers like to work with numbers, which is basically what they do best. Humans (and most other wetware of which I'm aware) tend to prefer symbols. For example, do you look up your friends in the telephone directory by their numbers or by their names? If you want to visit the Dummies Press Web site, are you going to remember www.idgbooks.com or 206.80.51.140? (Probably neither, but if you *had* to memorize one or the other, which would you use? I thought so.) Systems registered on the Internet have at least one *IP address* assigned to them so that they, being computers, can *talk* to each other.

You don't really need to worry about the technical details of IP addresses, because they are just a way of turning the name you like into a number the silly computers can use. However, do keep in mind that an IP address looks like this: nnn.nnn.nnn.nnn — four groups of numbers separated by dots. If you see something that resembles this pattern, you can *usually* say, "Aha! An IP address!" Be careful, though, because you may find other things in Cyberspace that look like that pattern, too.

Because computers are the go-betweens when a person wants to access a web site, something has to translate the web site's name, or *URL* (Uniform Resource Locator), into a number. If you're going to run a web server, you need to be aware of some differences between the server's presence on the network versus your presence as a customer through an ISP (Internet Service Provider), such as AT&T Worldnet.

1. Usually, when you dial in to your ISP, your desktop system becomes a *peer* on the Internet. Being a peer means that your system can communicate with other systems on the Net and vice versa. Because ISPs have ever-changing numbers of customers dialed in at any particular time, they typically keep a pool of IP addresses around, and whenever you connect, they grab one of the addresses and temporarily assign it to you so you can have access.

2. As long as you stay connected, you keep that address. However, as soon as you hang up, the address goes back into the pool and may be given out to someone else moments later. When you dial in again, you probably get a different address than you had before.

3. If all of your ISP's subscribers decide at the same time that they want to see the photographs of the Martian Air Force repelling NASA, they may use up all of the addresses in the dial-in pool — and suddenly you find yourself locked out with a busy signal.

Sharing addresses is fine for a casual Internet user who isn't online 24 hours a day. However, for a web server that's accessible around the world and around the clock, this setup falls a little short. If your address keeps changing and it's not listed anywhere, people have a hard time trying to reach you.

It doesn't have to be this way, of course. Some service providers allow their customers to rent a *permanent* address, which is always assigned to them when they connect and never assigned to anyone else. Having a permanent address often costs you a little extra.

Even if you get a permanent address assigned for your web server and a permanent name to go along with it, anyone who tries to reach it when it's not hooked up to the network gets a "host not reachable" error, or the equivalent.

If you're going to run a web server, and you want people to be able to access it, you need the following:

> ✔ A name for the people to use (such as `WWW.IDGBooks.com`)
>
> ✔ A permanently-assigned IP address, which the computer understands
>
> ✔ A link to the Internet that's up and running when you need it — and, more to the point, when your visitors need it

Many ISPs help you establish a site name, IP address, and Internet link (for a price), but *you* need to come up with the name. You automatically have a name that you can use for testing — `localhost` — but other users cannot use that name to access your system. *Some of the steps for getting a name you can do yourself for less cost, but you're going to end up talking to a service provider in order to get the electrons flowing.* If you build your house out in the woods and call it "ThistleDew," you won't get any mail until you work out an arrangement with the postal service.

Note: See the section "The Internet is Optional," later in this chapter, for more about the `localhost` name.

Network needs

At the very least, you need a system that runs TCP/IP, because that's how web clients and servers communicate. (All versions of UNIX automatically do this.)

If you're going to run Apache in a network with other systems, you need a way to find the other systems and for them to find you. In other words, you need an assigned name (alphabetical) and network address (numerical) and a way to translate between them. Usually, you need an environment running BIND (Berkeley Internet Name Daemon; rhymes with *grind*), which means name servers, resolvers, and so on. Talk to your system or network administrator.

The Internet is optional

Although the full moniker of the Web is *World-Wide Web,* the technology works just as well within the confines of a small corporate network — or even on a single system — so you don't need to actually go out and get an Internet connection before you can start playing with Apache. If you already have a connection, some things are easier, such as sending electronic mail to other Apache users — rather problematic if you aren't on the Net! However, having the connection is by no means a requirement.

Setting up Internet access is often a case of multiple stages of hurry-up-and-wait, particularly if you're looking for access with the conditions a full-time web server needs. You can work with Apache in a stand-alone environment until the network portion is ready, but keep an eye on the long-term view as you set up the server. (In other words, don't hard-code a bunch of things you'll only have to change later.)

Even systems that aren't connected to a network have an address they can call their own. This address is called a *loopback* address, and its numeric value is 127.0.0.1. It's alphabetical name is localhost. The loopback address is sort of like the personal pronoun *I* — everyone can use the term, but it refers to only the person actually speaking. When you access a web server using a URL such as localhost/, you're actually talking to yourself. Webmasters talk to themselves all the time, so therapy isn't indicated.

Skills and Tools You Need

To put up a house you need some essential equipment, such as building materials, hammers, saws, nails, the ability to drive them straight, bandages, antiseptics. . . . (Ever hear the expression, "safe as houses?") Similarly, if you're going to build an Apache Web server, you need to have some specific tools and skills. Fortunately, you can acquire some skills through trial and error, just as you can when you build your first house. If you do something wrong with Apache, your server isn't likely to collapse on your head like a house would.

Understanding your system

Depending on its popularity, a web server may be just one small element of what a system is doing, or it may be that system's entire reason for existence. If your server is going to be pushing at the boundaries of what the system itself is capable of handling, you really need to know that ahead of time so you won't suddenly find yourself in an unexpected crisis situation. Even if you don't push the normal envelope, each system has its own special quirks.

Get familiar with your system. If you ever run into problems and have to ask someone for help, knowing the answers to these questions will be very useful:

- How much memory does your system have?
- How many CPUs does your system have?

- ✔ What is the operating system?

- ✔ How much disk space does your system have? (And how much of that space is the system administrator going to let you use?)

- ✔ Does your system mount filesystems from other hosts in the network (such as with NFS)? If so, will any of your web documents live on those filesystems?

- ✔ Does your system use BIND (see the previous section "Decisions, decisions: names and addresses") to translate host names to IP addresses?

- ✔ Does your system use NIS for distributed user and password information?

You can find the answers to some of these questions from the UNIX utility uname. Try entering the following command and keep the output handy:

```
% uname -a
```

"Why do I need to know all this technical information?" you may ask. The answer is: You don't. But chances are you'll eventually encounter some sort of problem or issue and need to ask someone for help, and knowing some background information saves time (and makes you look better). Even if you don't memorize the answers to the previous questions (give yourself 100 Apache Guru Points if you do), scribble them down somewhere for future reference.

Because of all the various combinations of UNIX environments available, not all of them work the same way. If you can say, "I can't open more than 200 logfiles, and I'm running JozeUNIX 1.3," you may get an immediate response: "You need to add -DLOBOTOMIZE_JOZE to the EXTRA_CFLAGS line in your Configuration file." See? You get your answer quickly, and you look like a pro (whether you are one doesn't matter). If you didn't include that little snippet of information, the problem-solving exchange would have gone on a lot longer.

You find lots of notes in the online Apache documentation about various system limitations and ways to work around them, so if you run into a problem, you can search for keywords relating to your specific environment and save even more time.

Pay particular attention to your document environment. The most common function of a web server is providing files in response to requests from clients. Those files have to live somewhere, and you should know something about their locations and environments. Try to find out answers to the following questions:

✔ Are the files in question on a filesystem mounted from another host?

✔ Are the files readable by the web server?

✔ Are there any symbolic links *(symlinks)* involved when the web server tries to access the files?

If you know the answers to these questions, you're well on the way to heading off the most common problems.

Editing the configuration files

The Apache Web server software is controlled by instructions that you (yes, *you*) put into text files. The server software doesn't provide any fancy graphical interfaces to these files, so you need to get in there and edit them yourself.

Because the configuration files are simple text, just about any editor will do — from ed to vi to Emacs. If you want, you can even copy the files to another system for editing and then copy them back when you're done. Just be careful to ensure that the files remain in UNIX text format; the Apache software can't handle files formatted for fancy word processors.

I rarely edit the configuration files directly on my server because my favorite editor isn't available under UNIX. I actually edit the files over the network from a completely separate system.

If you don't feel comfortable using a text editor or don't know how, you're going to be at a *serious* disadvantage when you try to set up Apache. You need to learn to use an editor (give yourself 20 Apache Guru Points if you do this), or retype the entire file each time you want to make changes, or wait for a graphical interface to become available. Of course, maybe you can get someone else to do the editing for you, but that's cheating — subtract 30 Apache Guru Points.

Superuser access

You don't necessarily need to have Absolute Power on your system in order to run an Apache Web server. However, Absolute Power does make life a lot simpler. If you have *superuser access* (also called *superuser authority*), you can do the following things:

✔ Set up your web server in the standard way, on port 80, which means that people can access your server using `yourhost.com/` rather than having to add the port number (for example, `yourhost.com:2048/`). (People can easily forget the port number.)

✔ Rebuild your operating system's kernel if you have to increase or change parameters. (Most people don't need to do this procedure unless they're running *really* big Web sites.)

✔ Turn on packet filtering when you need to debug or verify things at that level.

✔ Use tools to check accounting records or limit access (for example, the suExec tool).

✔ Fiddle with your system's network interfaces.

✔ Reboot your system to get a clean start when things appear hopelessly wedged. (You don't need to reboot very often.)

Of course, having superuser authority brings its own set of potential problems. UNIX systems assume you know what you're doing if you have superuser authority, so they usually won't stop you — or even grumble — if you inadvertently delete crucial files or make the system un-rebootable. (Of course, they may complain later!) In addition, when running things like a web server from the superuser account, you need to be careful that *whatever-it-is* doesn't take improper advantage of your trust and break things on your behalf or open unsuspected security holes. The Apache Group has been very, very pessimistic about security issues in the server software, so you can feel at least moderately comfortable with starting Apache (as opposed to *running* it) from the `root` account. Apache lets you — nay, *encourages* you — to give it another user identity to which it will switch after it gets going.

Filling up your tool belt

Even the most skilled builder doesn't accomplish much without his or her tools. What tools *you* need depends on whether you're happy with your prefab Apache house — er, server — as it stands or intend to remodel.

A browser, a browser — my caffeine for a browser!

Because you're setting up a Web server, you can probably benefit from being able to see things the way visitors to your web site do. In fact, a web browser is the most basic server verification and debugging tool, because you can usually tell right away whether the server is working correctly. Even if you don't intend to rebuild the software, you should still have a browser.

Remember that the tools your visitors use for browsing the Web may be different from what you use. If you can, keep a collection of browsers around and look at your pages in a variety of ways: with different browsers, window sizes, font and color settings, and so on. Making sure that your site looks good under wildly different conditions wins you 50 Apache Guru Points.

Telnet: what you see is what it said

Unfortunately, you won't be able to find answers to all your problems by staring at a browser window — for example, you may not be able to explain why a particular page keeps showing up in a monospaced typeface rather than proportional.

You may want to try to "play computer" and talk to the server from the perspective of a browser. This technique short-circuits all the filtering and interpretation the real browser would put on the page and lets you see what the server is really saying.

The *protocol,* or network language, that the Web uses is quite simple and text-based. This means that you can use a Telnet application to "play browser." Keep the following points in mind when using a Telnet application:

✔ The Telnet application should support line-mode (meaning that it won't send the stuff you type to the server until you press the Enter key — if it automatically sends every single character as you type it, backspacing to correct typos becomes *very* weird).

✔ Don't try to set the terminal characteristics before you start typing. Some Telnet clients try to negotiate terminal settings (for example, window size, backspace capability, and so on) with the far end before they start listening to you and passing along what you type. When the far end is a web server rather than a Telnet server, this doesn't work very well.

Doing unexpected things, or normal ones in surprising or disconcerting ways, is called "Violating the Principle of Least Astonishment."

Most UNIX operating systems come with a default Telnet application that meets these requirements. If your operating system doesn't, you may need to download a freeware or shareware one from the Internet.

Does my Telnet have the right stuff?

If your UNIX box passes the following test, your Telnet application should be just fine for working with Apache (please note that the first word on the sixth line, "helo," is *supposed* to be spelled that way):

```
% telnet localhost 25
Trying 127.0.0.1...
Connected to localhost.
Escape character is '^]'.
220 YourSystem Sendmail-identification
helo localhostess[del][del][del]
250 YourSystem Hello localhost, pleased to
   meet you
quit
221 YourSystem closing connection
Connection closed by foreign host.
```

What you just did (you *did* do it, didn't you?) is pretend to be a mail application. If you typed the commands without getting any off-the-wall error messages, you know that your Telnet starts in line mode (good!) and doesn't pre-negotiate terminal settings (excellent!).

If you feel more comfortable using some other platform (such as a PC) to test your server, go ahead and try the same set of steps. You can do this test from another system on the network only if your server system has a name and address. Replace the references to localhost in the previous example with the correct information for your server system.

Packet tracing for fun and profit

The network protocol that web browsers and servers use to talk to each other, HTTP (HyperText Transfer Protocol), is pretty simple. However, HTTP is complicated enough that you probably won't be able to keep track of the various options and permutations in your head. In addition, sometimes you may want to know what the client actually said, and you can find that out no better way than by watching the client talk. Being able to watch the client talk is particularly useful when you encounter a client that *thinks* it speaks the language but is actually mangling it a little (and you do find some of these clients out there).

Because you're reading the client's lips in this case, rather than trying to impersonate the client, you need a tool that has that skill. An excellent tool is the *tcpdump* utility, which records network traffic according to rules you define (such as "listen to everything on the network," or "tell me what's going to my web server, but not what it's replying").

If your system doesn't come with a version of tcpdump, you can get one by way of an anonymous FTP from ftp.ee.lbl.gov.

Although tcpdump is excellent for wire-tapping network conversations between computers, sometimes you may have trouble figuring out what it's talking about (tcpdump was written by nerds, after all). An excellent translator to interpret tcpdump's remarks is the tcpshow utility.

You can download the tcpshow tool from the Internet. Sometimes, you can find this tool lurking at `www.cs.berkeley.edu/~daw/mike/`, along with its accompanying `man` page.

You can use these two tools, tcpdump and tcpshow, together or separately. To monitor the network in real-time, you can have tcpdump speak to tcpshow, and have tcpshow display the translation on your screen. Or you can have tcpdump record the traffic for later analysis.

Because tools that listen to the network can be easily abused to invade privacy and the like, many systems require you to have *superuser authority* (see "Superuser access," earlier in this chapter) in order to do it. If you don't have superuser authority, you may not be able to use these tools, so make the system administrator your friend!

Hammers, saws, and compilers

If you find that a prefabricated Apache server isn't available for your environment or that you want to remodel the server you already have, you're going to need the tools it takes to recompile the software from (drum roll, please) . . . The Source.

The Apache server software is written in ANSI-compliant C. Any C compiler that can cope with ANSI-isms should be able to digest the source and produce a usable server image.

The basic tools you needed to rebuild the server software are

- ✔ The Bourne shell interpreter, `sh`
- ✔ The do-it-if-it-needs-doing utility, `make`
- ✔ An ANSI C compiler

With the possible exception of the last tool, almost all UNIX systems come with these essential ingredients. If your system doesn't, free versions are available on the Internet. If you don't have access to the Internet yourself, find some friends that do.

See Chapter 3 and Chapter 9 for more information about the topics that need these tools.

For serious server surgery

In dire situations, you may need to use a debugger to collect information about what's going wrong. If you have the debuggers dbx or gdb or the like, you're all set. But don't give this too much thought until you really need the tool: using these is covered in the Appendix.

If anything prints when you enter either of the following lines, you know you have the corresponding debugger:

```
% which dbx
% which gdb
```

Check your operating system documentation to see what other debugging tools you may have.

Chapter 2

What Apache Needs

In This Chapter

▶ The demands Apache places upon hardware

▶ Consumable resources Apache consumes

▶ Setting up user and group identities

▶ Understanding the two types of Apache configuration files

*Y*our Apache Web server is your trusty assistant. You give the server tasks to do, along with some latitude for handling situations for which you haven't given explicit instructions, and then you let the server loose to do its job without constant supervision. At least that's the idea.

However, to be a good assistant, Apache needs you to give it the necessary resources to do its job. An administrative assistant can't make photocopies if the paper's locked up, a telemarketer can't call your customers without their telephone numbers, and the town clerk can't register your tax payment if he doesn't know how (which doesn't mean that you don't owe it).

It's time to play office manager, and make sure you have an environment that your Apache server feels comfortable in so it can do its job.

System Requirements

The first thing your Apache assistant needs is an environment to work in, kind of like a desk or office. In this section, I explain what the server needs so it can get down to work.

User IDs and groups

Apache accesses files, devices, and directories on UNIX the same way that any other user of the system would — meaning that Apache needs to have some sort of identity. Along with an identity goes a "thing" (sorry, I can't think of a better way to put it without sounding pompous) called *access rights*.

Access rights determine what Apache does and does not have the right to access. If you're going to have Apache run as someone other than yourself, you should choose carefully who it runs as.

If you don't have *superuser* access to your system, you severely limit your ability to give Apache its own unique identity. Without superuser access, Apache can run as though it is you, but not as if it is someone else. In other words, people accessing the Apache server can access documents only if you can access them yourself.

If you've been blessed with Absolute Power . . . ahem, superuser authority, you can set up the Apache server to run with the access rights of just about anyone you like. (Or don't like.)

Because Apache hands out your files to random people on the network, don't have it run as someone with access to information you don't want published far and wide!

Just to make sure that nothing unexpected happens (hah!), I strongly recommend that you create a separate account that the Apache server uses and no one (and nothing) else — except possibly you as Webmaster, but not very often.

So much for the user ID. Choosing a group membership for the Apache server process is a little more involved and requires a little more thought, because you need to consider how the document files will be updated and by whom. A typical access wish list may include the following

- ✔ The server should not be able to serve everything on the system.
- ✔ The server should be able to access documents in only a specific set of directories.
- ✔ Only a select group of people should be able to update the documents.
- ✔ The people who can update the documents should *not* be able to affect the server itself.

The simplest solution is to create a single username that only the Apache server uses, a group for people responsible for the content of your web site, and possibly another group for those charged with managing the server itself.

See Chapter 4 for details about where the web documents live and for more on user ID and group assignments.

Processes: Parents and children

The Apache Web server works kind of like a task force of people or a secretarial pool. When you start up the server, one of the first things it does is create a number of *child* processes — you control how many with configuration directives. Like a good parent, the main process keeps track of what all the children are doing at any particular time.

When a request comes in to the server, the server chooses one of the children that isn't busy and hands it the request for processing. When the child is done with the request, the child goes back into a "ready for more" state.

Each child handles only a certain number of requests before it undergoes a forced retirement. When this retirement happens, the fulfilled child goes away gracefully, and the main process creates a new child to take the retired one's place. One of the reasons for this recycling of children is to avoid any leftover side effects from one request to another (environment variables, memory allocated but not deallocated, and so on). Like the number of children, you, as Webmaster, use configuration directives to control the maximum number of requests each child can handle before it goes away.

The main process always tries to keep some minimum number of children around, but it can create more children if the going gets tough and the traffic gets heavy. After the activity quiets down again (assuming that it does), the number of child processes shrinks back to keep from using up system resources for no good reason.

Similarly, the main process creates more children if the number drops below your minimum setting. This concept causes a lot of confusion; some Webmasters, not understanding where all those processes come from, go through killing them all, and then are surprised when the children get reincarnated almost immediately. The main process is just trying to do its job. If you want to change the number of Apache child processes that use your system as a playground, you need to talk to the parent.

See Chapter 4 for more information about managing the Apache process tree.

Open sesame! uh, files!

The UNIX world treats just about everything as a file: your terminal, a network connection, tape drives — and even real files! Each open file requires the system to allocate some resources to keep track of it (such as who's using it, where the users are in reading through it, and so on). To keep the activity level sane, many operating systems impose limits on the number of open files allowed per process (and sometimes for the entire system).

Apache can be a very heavy consumer of the open file quota. Each active request consumes an open-file slot for the network connection, and each log file takes up one as well. And in processing a request, the server is likely to temporarily open several more files to check for security rules and the like.

You can tell when you run out of available file slots because the server starts misbehaving. No, I can't be more specific because the symptoms depend on the operating system and what the server was trying to do when it hit the wall.

Some tools are available to help you determine whether your problems are due to file descriptor (open-file slot) exhaustion. I include one of the tools, lsof, on the CD-ROM with this book.

Cycling with Apache — CPU needs

Most of the Apache server's work involves reading and writing information, not performing calculations. As a result, the server doesn't get CPU-bound (doing nothing but calculating) very often. If your system suddenly starts losing races with snails, and you can trace the problem to the Apache server processes, usually you have a problem with one of the modules.

A modest 386 Intel box running Linux can typically handle about ten requests per second — without straining the CPU at all. A Pentium-based system with lots of memory can handle hundreds of requests per second. The AltaVista search engine (http://altavista.com/) uses multi-CPU 64-bit Alpha systems with 500MHz clocks and 20GB of main memory, and handles roughly 10 million requests a day. So judge accordingly — if you want to run a honking big Web site, use some honking big hardware. If your desires are more modest, your hardware can be, too.

Now, where did I put that? — Memory!

Although Apache doesn't usually place much of a demand on the CPU (central processing unit), it does have a tendency to use memory in great pulsing gobs. Nowadays most systems use *virtual memory*, which means that you can trade disk space for real memory to a certain extent, but that's a trade that you may want to unmake later. Virtual memory was very tempting when disk space was a lot less expensive than real memory, but prices are more reasonable now.

Your best bet is to make sure you have enough real memory so that you don't need to fake the system out with a disk (or at least not as much). As you may expect, the amount of memory you need depends on what you're doing. The following factors help you determine the amount of memory you need:

✔ What else the system is doing

✔ The number of child processes in your server tree

✔ What modules are linked into the server

✔ Whether you're using parsed HTML and CGI scripts and if so, how much you're using

If you provide for 2MB of real memory for each child process, you should be in pretty good shape for a system with average module usage.

Disk space

The Apache software uses disk space in two different ways:

✔ For static files — namely, the configuration files and the documents you want the server to serve

✔ For dynamic files, such as the various log files (access log, error log, and so on)

The static files that are directly part of Apache itself don't take up very much space. If you allocate 50MB (megabytes) for them, you should have plenty of room.

As for the amount of space your document files require — well, no one can tell you how much space you need! Right? Right! You need to figure out how much space your documents will need.

The dynamic files can pose a bit of a problem because they keep growing, and growing, and. . . . The file that grows at the most predictable rate is the access log; it increases by about 1K (kilobyte) for every 10 requests. You can calculate how much space your access log is going to require based on that rough formula.

In Web terms in general, and Apache terms in particular, a *request* means a single requisition for a particular resource. It does not mean a page. A single browser page often requires a dozen actual requests to get the text, pictures, and so on. Apache treats each of those requests as a unique request.

The error log, unfortunately, is not as obliging as the access log. It can be quiet for days, and then suddenly go nuts and fill your disk in next to nothing flat. Space in this log file is used up at a rate of about 100 bytes per error message. Some messages you can count upon receiving:

- ✔ **Server reload messages:** Any time you start, stop, or reload the server, an entry is added to the error log.

- ✔ **Authentication violations:** If usernames and passwords protect part of your document namespace, you get an entry in the error log every time someone tries to get at the restricted areas but misspells the password or the username.

- ✔ **Document access failures:** If the server replies to a request with an error message, the error log records it. The error message can be anything from `file does not exist` (self-explanatory, I hope) to `file permissions deny server access`.

- ✔ **Network errors:** These errors include normal messages like `lost connection to client`.

- ✔ **Miscellaneous server errors:** These errors should be uncommon, but you may get a few like `premature end of script headers` and `caught SEGV, attempting to dump core` (which means something's seriously broken).

The error log usually contains much more information about *why* the problem occurred than the system ever shows to the end-user who receives the error message. One of the main reasons for the existence of the error log is so that you, the Webmaster, can figure out what's going wrong — and fix it.

Sometimes the error log fills with messages about a problem that isn't really an Apache issue at all, but rather some sort of system or network glitch that indirectly affects Apache.

Apache does come with a script that allows you to *roll over* the log files whenever you like, so if the files start growing at an alarming rate, you can close the current versions and open new ones without interrupting the Web service you're providing.

The following amounts of space are a good starting point for a relatively clean Apache installation:

✔ 50MB for the server and its assorted static files

✔ 10MB for the access log (good enough for about 100,000 requests)

✔ 10MB for the error log (enough for approximately 100,000 errors)

If you add to these figures the amount of space you need for your own documents, you should be able to at least run long enough to figure out how much *more* space you need!

If you allocate on the low side, remember to keep an eye on the amount of space that the log files are using!

The Configuration Files

You tell the Apache server what to do by putting *directives,* instructions, into text files and telling Apache to read them. Some of these files are read only once — when the server starts or is reloaded — and some files are read every single time a related file or directory is requested.

Using the entire word *configuration* seems kinda clunky, especially because you don't use it in conversation with other Apache Webmasters very often. From now on, I use *config* as a reasonable abbreviation. Okay? Thanks; I knew you'd understand.

Server-wide configuration files

The configuration files — which are read once: when the server loads or reloads — are called the *server-wide* config files. They get processed in a sort of global environment, when the server is just setting itself up and hasn't started processing requests yet. These config files define the ways in which the server should handle requests.

If the server can't read one or more of the server-wide config files, it generally fails to start altogether.

When the server is still in the process of setting up, it probably doesn't get around to opening the error log if it encounters a problem with the server-wide configuration files. So you don't miss out on any problems, error messages are sent to the standard error device, stderr (also called *diagnostic output*), during this phase of operation. Therefore, the errors probably show up on your terminal or your system console, depending on the circumstances.

The server-wide configuration files are usually very small (just a few kilobytes at most) and aren't accessed very frequently.

Per-directory configuration files

While the server-wide configuration files are usually read infrequently — such as when the server starts or reloads — other configuration files get read more often.

These other files are called *per-directory* configuration files, or sometimes .htaccess files because that's what they're usually named.

You can change the name Apache uses for the per-directory configuration files with the `AccessFileName` directive.

Just like the server-wide config files, per-directory config files are text files, and they contain directives, although some directives aren't permitted except at the server-wide level.

These per-directory files are typically even smaller, by a good margin, than the server-wide config files — but they have the potential to be accessed *much* more often.

See Chapter 4 for details about when and how the per-directory config files are accessed.

Part II
Getting Things Running

"That's right, Daddy will double your allowance if you install his Apache Server software."

In this part . . .

When you want to turn lumber, wires, and nails into a house you can live in, you usually work from a set of blueprints. When you want to make a cake from flour, eggs, and sugar, you use a recipe. And when you want to turn a set of files into a running web server, you follow a similar set of instructions.

This part contains chapters that describe how to unpack the Apache Web server software, get it up and running, and add controls to it so you can see who's visiting and limit access to particular areas if you want to. Go ahead — it's easy!

Chapter 3

Installing Apache

. . . .

In This Chapter

▶ Installing source kits *versus* binary kits

▶ Choosing a directory tree for your server

▶ Understanding what's in the Apache software kit

▶ Installing the software

▶ Verifying the kits and your installation

. . . .

To *run* Apache, you must first *install* Apache. This chapter describes how you install the Apache Web server software, from locating and unpacking the kit to making sure all the files are where they're supposed to be.

The process consists of a series of steps which are simple when taken one at a time. Taken as a whole, though, the installation process may seem daunting — and undaunting you is what this chapter is all about.

Decisions, Decisions: Source Kit or Binary?

Apache kits come in two flavors: with a compiled binary you can use immediately, and without. Both flavors include a bunch of ingredients, such as support utilities, the source code to the server (which you need if you're going to change any of its basic operation), and the "standard" modules which are most commonly used and are supported by The Apache Group. If you're getting started with the Apache Web server, begin with a pre-built binary if at all possible and save the icky compilation stuff for later.

Your Apache kit should include the source code whether you have a pre-built binary or a source-only kit. If you don't have the source (you can check by looking for a `src/http_core.c` file in your kit), you know your Apache kit came from somewhere other than The Apache Group and it may have been modified in other ways as well.

The Apache kit on the CD-ROM that's intended to be installed under Windows does *not* include the source code. That's only because it's a *beta* release (still under development); when the final Windows version of 1.3 is released, it should include all of the source code as an installation option. If you're only going to install the server on a Windows machine, and not under UNIX, see the sidebar in the "Unpacking the Kit" section of this chapter for details.

In order to avoid a lot of duplication, the CD-ROM that accompanies this book contains a generic source kit (which doesn't contain a pre-compiled binary server) and a set of pre-built server binaries and the tailored scripts to build 'em.

To see if a pre-built server is available for your system, look in the ASFD/ apache/kits directory on the accompanying CD-ROM. If you see a filename that looks like it may be distantly related to your system, that's good. (If you find one that indicates it's a close relative, even better!)

In order to view the contents of the accompanying CD-ROM, you need to mount it on your system. Someone with *superuser authority* (see Chapter 1) probably needs to mount it. If that person is you, you need to know the name of your CD-ROM drive. Assuming the name is something like /dev/rz6, you can mount the CD-ROM with a command like

```
# mount -r /dev/rz6c /mnt
```

If you don't have access to the CD-ROM, or you're reading this book a long time after it was published, you can check out the Apache Web site at http://www.apache.org/dist/ to see the latest official Apache kits.

The Apache Group puts a lot of effort into making the software workable on dozens of different system platforms (see Table 3-1), and when a new release comes out, the Group usually puts together some pre-built binary images for a subset of those platforms. Many of the supported platforms are only supported because another user figured out how to make Apache work on that platform, and then forwarded the details to the Group. In other words, just because Apache is supported on XYZ doesn't mean that a pre-built binary is available for XYZ.

Many of the members of The Apache Group have more than one system available to them; so they can make sure the software builds and works on each one. For example, I have systems running DIGITAL UNIX and Red Hat Linux in my lab, so I always verify that Apache works on both of them. The most common UNIX platforms available in the world are well-represented among the hardware available to the Group members, so you have a good chance of finding a pre-built server image for your specific hardware and operating system platform. The first part of the decision about whether to use a binary or not becomes: "*Is* there a binary for my system?"

If you don't find one, you need to build a server image after you unpack the generic source kit. No big deal — unless your platform isn't directly supported, in which case you have to do a *port* (see Chapter 9) after unpacking the kit.

"Porting" software means making it work on a system or in an environment where it currently *doesn't* work. Making a Macintosh application work on Windows NT would be called *porting* it, and the finished version that worked on Windows would be called the "Windows *port*" of the application.

The term *image* is frequently used to refer to a program that has been compiled (as opposed to a script, which isn't) and can be run. The name comes from Ye Olden Dayes, when you created one of these programs by compiling it into memory and then saving the *image* of the memory contents into a disk file. Then you could copy that picture of memory contents back into memory any time you wanted and use the program. Even though copies of programs aren't made this way (much) any more, the term still hangs around.

Assuming that you luck out and find a binary available for your WidgetMaster Nine Thousand, the next question you should ask (although the answer isn't nearly as important) is, "Did the person who built this binary include My Favourite Modules?" (Modules are pieces of software that can be added to or removed from the server. Each module supports some small capability, such as the ability to correct misspellings or to figure out which version of a document is best based upon the user's choice of language.) If you're installing Apache for the first time and don't know what your favourite modules are yet, don't worry — whatever modules are included in your binary should be enough to get you going. Keep this question in the back of your mind and haul it out into the light of day again when you read Chapter 9. (If you never read Chapter 9, don't worry about the space this question takes up in your brain — it's a small question.)

Even if you have to build the server image yourself, the default configuration gives you all you need for a full-function Web server. The parts that the default setup doesn't include are advanced. I cover them in Part IV — read when ready, Gridley!

Platforms supported

The actual number of operating systems that Apache supports (those systems that the Apache Configurate script knows about) is somewhere in the neighborhood of five dozen. Apache supports some systems less than others (meaning that Apache runs, but may compile with some warning messages), which is simply a result of what systems are available to the folks within The Apache Group. The most common platforms supported by the configuration script include A/UX 3.1.*, AIX, Apollo Domain, BSDI, Convex, DGUX, DIGITAL UNIX (*née* OSF/1), FreeBSD, HP-UX, Linux, MachTen, Maxion, MPE/iX, NeXT, OpenBSD, OS/2, Paragon OSF/1, SGI IRIX, Solaris, SunOS, Tandem, ULTRIX, UnixWare, and UXP/DS

Many of the platforms are known to work with Apache because members of The Apache Group actually do their development work on them.

If you don't see your system listed, don't give up hope: I may not have mentioned it, or it may have been added after I made up that list. The worst case is that your platform isn't supported, and you need to port Apache to it yourself. See Chapter 9 for more on making Apache work on your system.

To see which of these applies to your situation, you need to ask the server configuration script to tell you if it recognizes your system. Go visit the "Kit Contents" through "Unpacking the Software" sections in this chapter, unpack the /mnt/ASFD/apache/kits-1.3b3/apache.tar kit, and then come back. I'll wait.

Back already? Good, good. Now that you unpacked the source kit, enter the following commands (assuming you unpacked into /usr/local/web):

```
% cd /usr/local/web/apache/src
% helpers/GuessOS
```

If the GuessOS script recognizes your system, it says so. If it doesn't, it also should say so — only louder. If the script doesn't know what system you're using, you're going to have to port the server to your environment; remember to go to Chapter 9 when you get done with this chapter.

Kit Contents

The Apache server kit comes as a compressed tar archive file, allowing the directory hierarchy to be maintained, which is important. (A tar archive file, also called a *tarchive*, is to UNIX what a ZIP file is to Windows. It's a way to package a bunch of files and folders into a single bundle.)

Some versions of tar have been known to complain about "checksum errors" when asked to digest Apache kit archive files. In all cases reported to The Apache Group thus far, these errors have not been a problem — only that particular version of tar was getting confused — and the archive files have been valid. If you do encounter this error, you need to verify your kit's integrity. See "Verifying Your Installation" later in this chapter.

The contents of an Apache kit archive file is a directory tree that looks like the following:

```
apache-+-/cgi-bin
       +-/conf
       +-/htdocs-/manual-+-/images
       |                 +-/misc
       |                 +-/mod
       +-/icons
       +-/logs
       +-/src----+-/helpers
```

```
 |         +-/modules-+-/example
 |         |          +-/proxy
 |         +-/regex
+-/support
```

The directory tree was changed for the 1.3 version of the Apache Web server project. If you unpack the `kits-1.3b3/apache.tar` package on your system, instead of the `kits-1.2.4/apache.tar` package, the directory tree will look like the following:

```
apache-+-/cgi-bin
       +-/conf
       +-/htdocs-/manual-+-/images
       |                 +-/info
       |                 +-/misc
       |                 +-/mod
       |                 +-/vhosts
       +-/icons
       +-/logs
       +-/src—+-/ap
              +-/helpers
              +-/main
              +-/modules-+-/example
              |          +-/extra
              |          +-/proxy
              |          +-/standard
              |
              +-/os—+-/emx
              |     +-/unix
              |     +-/win32
              |
              +-/regex
              +-/support
              +-/test
```

Throughout this book, I make numerous references to the various subdirectories, such as "the `src` directory" or "look in `src/modules` for ...".

The following sections describe what's actually *in* these directories.

The `cgi-bin` *directory*

The `cgi-bin` directory in the distribution contains a sample *CGI* scripts (see Chapter 12) to help you verify that your server executes scripts properly.

This directory is boring, but feel free to add your own scripts to it later.

The conf *directory*

This directory is important. It contains the "seed" configuration files you should use as templates when setting up Apache for your specific environment, and it's the canonical place where "live" server-wide configuration files (the ones the server actually uses) are kept.

Canonical is an Hackish term which means "usual," "expected," "accustomed," or sometimes "proper" or "appropriate." For example, "Driving on the right side of the road is canonical in the U.S.; exceptions often occur due to excessive driver lubrication."

The htdocs *directory*

The htdocs subdirectory provides a sort of "jumping-off place" for you to put your Web documents. As distributed, this subdirectory contains a file that you can use to verify that your Apache Web server is working, as well as a whole bunch of documentation (the entire online manual) about Apache.

What's in htdocs/manual*?*

The htdocs directory (directory tree, actually) contains The Apache Manual.

The kit includes all the documentation about the Apache server, in Web-readable form, and this documentation lives under this directory.

What you get in this directory is the documentation for the specific version of Apache that you install. If you look at the Web locations, you're likely to find documentation for versions either older or newer than yours. However, the documentation on your system is correct for your version of Apache.

You can find the online documentation for the latest formally released version of Apache on the Web at http://www.apache.org/docs/. You can read this documentation to see if you want to upgrade your server.

The icons *directory*

This directory contains a bunch of GIF (Graphics Interchange Format) icons that the server uses, largely when displaying auto-generated directory listings. The module that uses the icons expects to find these files in the local /icons/ Web location, and the template config files point the Web location to this directory; so, be careful about changing this location.

You can put your own icons in this directory. Beware of actually *replacing* any of the files that came with the kit — if you do, your next upgrade-in-place will wipe out your changes.

The logs *directory*

As supplied in the kit, the logs directory is actually empty. However, the kit provides the directory to give you a workable server environment right out of the box. The template config files contain directives that put the access and error logs in this directory.

Problems are known to occur if you store your Apache log files on a remote filesystem accessed through NFS (Network File System). Two of the biggest problems: an NFS problem can give your server terminal constipation, and "append" writes (trying to add something to the end of the file) are not atomic — meaning that lines in the log files may be garbled if multiple children try to write to them at once.

Constipation is another technical term. It means that one application is trying to pass a message along to another application, and the second application isn't listening. Its companion term, *starvation,* means that an application is waiting to be told but no other applications are talking. These are two special cases of a more general condition called a *deadly embrace,* which describes multiple applications waiting for each other and unwilling to admit that anything's wrong. You hear these terms frequently in discussions about how computers talk to each other — or don't.

The src *directory*

Here's the meat of the server, where all the Most Important Ingredients live. If you start with a pre-compiled binary, the files in this directory should be preset to values that let you regenerate the pre-built server image itself. You can find the files that actually make up the guts of the server — the *source code* — lurking in this directory.

You find three basic types of files in this directory:

- ✔ **Configuration files:** Control how the server is built from the *source files*
- ✔ **Source files:** Compiled according to the instructions in the configuration files in order to produce the *result files*
- ✔ **Result files:** Examples include the intermediate .o object files and the actual httpd server image itself.

"Configuration files," within the context of this directory, are different from the ones that you use to instruct a server in its duties. The configuration files in the `src` directory tree are used only when you actually (re)build the server, and they involve compilation instructions. You use the *server config* files at run-time to control the server's actions. The only quality the different config files have in common is their name, which is confusing enough. Just ask yourself whether you're *building* or *running* the server, which should help you keep the two sets of files straight.

What's in `src/helpers`?

In the `src/helpers` directory reside some of the scripts and tools that the server-build configuration process uses. This directory is full of little scripts to figure out what your system is, what libraries are available, whether your C compiler is compatible with Apache, and so on.

Generally, you don't need to directly use anything in this directory or worry about it at all. Treat this directory as one of the Great Mysteries of Life, and you should be fine.

You should not depend directly on anything in the `src/helpers` directory; its contents are subject to change without notice between versions of Apache, as the build scripts are asked to do more and different things.

What's in `src/modules`?

The `src/modules` directory provides a place for you to store modules that you're writing or that come from some other source than the main Apache kit.

As distributed, this directory contains two subdirectories, `proxy` and `example`. These subdirectories contain the proxy module, which is used for caching and request forwarding, and the example module, which demonstrates many of the features of the *API* (Application Programming Interface) for use by anyone ambitious enough to want to write their own Apache modules.

Actually, the proxy module is built from several separate source files, which is one reason it has its own subdirectory. No reason to clutter up the main source directory with a bunch of files you may not use.

If you want to add "other" modules (modules obtained from somewhere other than The Apache Group) to your Apache server, I suggest creating a subdirectory for each of the modules under `src/modules`.

Under no circumstances should you fiddle with the files in the `src/modules` directory itself! Not that it would do you any good; the server build procedure automatically generates the files, so you lose any changes you make here.

As part of the directory restructuring that was done for version 1.3 of the Apache Web server, all of the different modules were put into the `src/modules/standard` directory. A different empty directory, called `src/modules/extra`, is provided for you to use when building your own modules.

What's in `src/regex`?

A lot of the power of Apache comes from its ability to use *regular expressions* in various ways, such as for file matching and URL patterns. Regular expressions allow you to compare names against rules you devise, such as "The letter 'A' followed by three more letters and then the digit '7'," or "Any name ending in '.GIF'." However, not all UNIX systems have an RE (regular expression) library that's reliable, so Apache includes one (called the Spencer library from the name of its creator) in this directory.

Even though this directory contains the Spencer regex (regular expression) library, it has been modified slightly for use with the Apache Web server software. The Apache scripts know how to deal with the modified contents; never try to fiddle with them yourself.

The Apache build scripts know which operating systems have good RE libraries and which ones don't, and they use the Spencer library only if they need to.

The `support` *directory*

This directory contains various tools to help you work with Apache. Some of the tools are actually obsolete now or superseded by other functionality, some are state-of-the-art, and some are rather stale. For the most part, Apache provides this directory "as is" and without warranty (not that any of the rest of Apache has a warranty), and you use the stuff here at your own risk.

Choosing a Directory Structure

After you're familiar with the Apache server's directory tree (see the "Kit Contents" section in this chapter if you're not), you need to figure out where you're going to put the directory tree on your system.

You can shuffle and relocate the various Apache directories within reason (but don't disturb the tree under `src`, or you won't be able to rebuild the software), but the simplest thing to do is to simply restore the tree as is under some directory that makes sense to you.

Be aware that if you change the directory tree, you have to redo it (or *undo* it) the next time you upgrade the Apache software in the same location. The files that are specific to your environment — `conf/*.conf` — are not part of the kit, and they remain undisturbed if you upgrade the software. A good bet is to leave the tree as it comes out of the `tar` file. The `src/Configuration` file may or may not be included in Apache kits, so an even better solution is to unpack any future Apache kits into new directories, and *copy* your changes into the new directory. That way you don't have to worry about something in the kit destroying your customizations.

The tree (as distributed) is intended to help you get Apache running quickly. The template server config files (`conf/*.conf-dist`) contain assumptions about the locations of things like the icons and the document directory, and you need to change these assumptions by editing the server config files if you alter the directory structure.

The Apache Web server kits contain a single directory tree; all files in them are under that single top-level directory. You can unpack the directory tree wherever you like, just as you can unpack a Windows ZIP archive anywhere.

To make it simple, throughout this book I'll assume your Apache Web server directory tree is under the directory `/usr/local/web`. That location is a pretty good place because the top level of the tree is named `apache`, which allows you to run other servers (such as NCSA) alongside Apache just by putting them in parallel subdirectories (for example, `/usr/local/web/ncsa`).

Unpacking the Kit

You know where you want to put the Apache kit contents, right? If not, check out the section "Choosing a Directory Structure" in this chapter.

You can find the kits provided on the accompanying CD-ROM in the `ASFD/apache/kits` directory. If you don't have access to the CD-ROM, but do have access to the Web, you can pick up the latest kits from `http://www.apache.org/dist/`.

If you're installing the Apache Web server package from the CD-ROM on a Windows NT or Windows 95 system, *see the instructions in the sidebar!* The Windows version of Apache that's on the CD-ROM is still being tested and developed, and isn't well documented. See the Apache Web site at `http://www.apache.org/` for the latest details on the Windows version. Once you've read the sidebar, you're basically done with this chapter — but I recommend that you read it through anyway.

Order in the kit!

If you're unpacking (installing) a kit from the CD-ROM that came with this book, the first step is to unpack the full source kit. If a system-specific binary is available that you want to use, unpack it after you unpack the full source kit.

If you're working with a kit from the Apache Web site, the two steps may have been reduced to one for you, depending on whether you're using a binary or a source kit. The binary kit includes the stuff needed to make the kit system-specific.

Installing Apache on Windows NT and Windows 95

Installing the Apache Web server software on a Windows NT or Windows 95 system is very simple: you just run the installation application. The instructions that follow apply to the 1.3beta3 version of the software which is on the CD-ROM. Because this version is still under development, the installation steps may change in the future.

Warning! Since the Windows release of Apache that's included on the CD-ROM is still a test version, it isn't very complete nor very well documented!

1. Insert the CD-ROM into the drive on your system.

2. Using Windows Explorer, navigate to the `D:\ASFD\apache\kits-1.3b3` folder. (If your CD-ROM uses a different drive letter than D:, use that instead.)

3. Double-click on the `apache_win32.exe` application to install the basic Apache Web server kit. It will ask where to install Apache; I recommend either "`C:\Apache`" or "`C:\Program Files\Apache`".

   This directory will be your *ServerRoot*, under which all of your Apache configuration files will be put (see Chapter 4 for more information about the ServerRoot).

4. After the installation is complete, double-click on the `apache_win32_ext.exe` file in the Windows Explorer window to install the online documentation and the icons the server will use when showing directory lists to browsers. Install this package in the same directory where you installed the Apache server kit itself.

There! You're done! The installation should have created a program group called Apache, so you can start up the Web server (later! After you've finished editing the configuration files!) by choosing Start⇨Programs⇨Apache⇨ Apache WebServer.

If you were brave and actually installed the 1.3beta3 Windows version of Apache, give yourself 45 Apache Guru Points!

As you read other portions of this book (which are almost entirely UNIX-oriented), remember that UNIX uses forward-slashes (/) to separate directories or folders. Windows uses sloshes (backward-slashes, \) to separate folders. And everywhere the text refers to "`/usr/local/web/apache`" you should *think* "`C:\Apache`" instead (or whatever directory you used when you installed the kit).

The source, the source — my kingdom for the source!

After you mount your CD-ROM (I assume it's on `/mnt`) and pick out the directory where you want to unpack the source kit (I assume `/usr/local/web`), use the following commands to do the unpacking:

```
% cd /usr/local/web
% tar xf /mnt/ASFD/apache/kits-1.3b3/apache.tar
% mv apache_1.3b3 apache
```

The CD-ROM includes both the 1.2.4 and 1.3b3 versions of Apache. I recommend the 1.3b3 version even though it hasn't been completely tested. If you want to use the 1.2.4 release, use the following commands:

```
% cd /usr/local/web
% tar xf /mnt/ASFD/apache/kits-1.2.4/apache.tar
% mv apache_1.2.4 apache
```

Ta-daaah! That's it — you unpacked the source kit. After unpacking the source kit, you should have a directory tree starting at /usr/local/web/apache. You can rename the apache directory if you like; it doesn't necessarily need to have that name. However, the rest of the book assumes that you haven't renamed it, so make any adjustments to filenames or directory paths as you read the book.

A bit, a byte — a binary for my site

If the CD-ROM includes a binary for your system, find it in the ASFD/apache/kits directory — the name of the file should look like the name of your operating system. If you don't find a binary for your system, you compile it yourself — see the next section and then proceed to Chapter 9.

To unpack a binary kit, you need to be in the src directory of your Apache tree. Use the following commands (replace the sysname portion with the correct name for your system's kit).

```
% cd /usr/local/web/apache/src
% tar xvf /mnt/ASFD/apache/kits-1.3b3/ap-sysname.tar
```

These commands put the platform-specific files (Configuration and httpd) in place, and you should be able to use or recreate the server binary.

Verifying Your Installation

Verifying the installation of your kit requires two elements:

- ✔ Verifying that the kit you used contained the files it should have
- ✔ Verifying that the kit unpacked correctly

You check the kits themselves by waving a magic wand over them and making sure the rabbits you get are the correct color. All right, so it isn't magic, it's Technology, and it's called *checksumming*.

Checksumming a file involves taking all the information in the file and performing a calculation on it. It can be as simple as treating each byte as a number and just adding them together, but it's usually much more complicated. The result of the calculation is the *checksum*. The idea is that if the same calculation is done on two different files, and the checksums are the same, the files are alike.

You can verify that the installation went well by checking to see if it "looks right."

Checking your kits

For the first part of verifying your installation, you need something that can verify the checksums of the kits (assuming you got the kits from either the accompanying CD-ROM or from the Apache Web site). The checksums are generated using two different methods: *MD5 hashing* and *PGP signatures*. To verify the Apache kit, you need a tool that can do one method or the other.

The steps described in this and the following section can be considered optional, or for the severely paranoid or security-conscious. It is perfectly all right to charge ahead with the kit you already unpacked without doing any of this "signature-checking" stuff. Become familiar with it, however, because you may want to be more cautious when the time comes to really start publishing on the Internet with your server — it would probably be a good idea to have as much confidence as you can in the kit you built it from.

For every kit, you find two accompanying files ending in `.md5` and `.asc` — that is, for the `apache.tar` kit, you have an `apache.tar.md5` file and an `apache.tar.asc` file, containing the MD5 hash and the PGP signature of the person who built the kit.

The PGP signatures of the Apache Group members are available in the `apache/KEYS` file in the distribution after you unpack it and also in `ASFD/apache/KEYS` on the CD-ROM itself. It's not entirely safe to trust the copy on the CD-ROM — you should get the keys from some other source than the object they were used to sign — so, you should either use the MD5 hash to verify the kit or use the published PGP `KEYS` file at `http://www.apache.org/dist/KEYS`.

To load the Apache Group members' PGP keys into your keyring, put a copy of the `KEYS` file into your system's `/tmp` directory, and then issue the following command (assuming you have PGP 2.6 installed, of course):

```
% pgp < /tmp/KEYS
```

Verifying PGP signatures

You don't *have* to do this to work with the kit you installed.

To verify the integrity of your kits using the PGP signatures, enter the following commands, modifying them for each kit file you unpacked:

```
% cd /mnt/ASFD/apache/kits-1.3b3
% pgp apache.tar.asc apache.tar
```

TIP

I've got a secret! Encryption on the Web

An awful lot of information traverses the Web, and if it the information was your own, you would probably consider much of it private or personal. So, how do you protect your information? *Encryption* is one answer: Make the information unreadable by anyone except the people you want to read it.

Unfortunately, some governments regard encryption technology as a very sensitive subject and put limits on their citizens' ability to use it. As a result, encryption isn't freely available to everyone — at least not legally.

One use of the technology that's generally considered benign is *authentication* — verifying on the receiving end that you got what the sender sent you. You can't figure out the contents from the authentication information, just that the contents are unaltered.

The two methods to verify Apache kits — MD5 hashing and PGP signatures — are examples of this encryption technology.

MD5 hashing uses a method of examining a file that produces a unique number, or *checksum,* for the file. Just about any other combination of the same number of bits and bytes produces a different checksum — so if the file sizes and the checksums are the same, you can be 99.99% sure the files are, too.

PGP signatures do pretty much the same thing that MD5 hashing does, except they also factor in the identity of the person generating the checksum. The result is that you can say, "When signed by this individual, the checksum is this value." Because the checksum is unique for each signer, the chances of duplication are even more remote than with the MD5 method.

Unfortunately, because PGP can do a lot more than generate authentication signatures, governments treat it under the more stringent rules.

Which methods you can use to verify your Apache kits depends on who and where you are.

You can purchase PGP (Pretty Good Privacy) from PGP, Inc.; see their Web page at http://www.pgp.com/ for more information. A free version of PGP is available from the Massachusetts Institute of Technology; you can find a pointer to that Web page at the PGP site as well. **Note that PGP is subject to U.S. Export Control restrictions.** See the PGP Web site for details.

You don't need to do anything nearly as complicated as checking legal issues to use the MD5 signatures. If your system has an MD5 utility already installed, just use it.

If you don't have an MD5 processor installed, you can find an MD5 checksum tool on the accompanying CD-ROM in the ASFD/apache/tools directory.

These commands blather several lines of output on your screen. About half-way through these lines, you should see something like the following:

```
File has signature.  Public key is required to check signature.
File 'apache.$00' has signature, but with no text.
Text is assumed to be in file 'apache.tar'.
.
Good signature from user "Jim Jagielski <jim@jaguNET.com>".
Signature made 1997/08/07 09:04 GMT
```

(The name of the signer doesn't really matter if the signer is listed in the KEYS file.)

The important thing is that you see the `Good signature` message, so you received whatever the signer put the "seal of approval" on.

If you get a message like:

```
WARNING: Bad signature, doesn't match file contents!
```

don't trust the kit! It doesn't match what the signer signed!

The latest and greatest Apache software kits are available from the Apache Web site at `http://www.apache.org/`. If you don't have Internet or Web access, make friends with someone who does so you can get the kits.

Verifying MD5 signatures

You don't *have* to verify your Apache Web server kit to start using it.

To verify the integrity of your kits by comparing the MD5 checksums, enter the following commands to generate the checksum and compare it to the one on the CD-ROM:

```
% cd /mnt/ASFD/apache/kits-1.3b3
% md5 apache.tar > /tmp/src.md5
% diff apache.tar.md5 /tmp/src.md5
```

If you don't have the `md5` tool installed on your system, you can install it from the `ASFD/apache/tools` directory on the CD-ROM. You can use the following command to see if you already have one installed; if it prints anything you have an `md5` tool on your system:

```
% which md5
```

If you restored a binary kit on top of your source kit, repeat the previous commands with the appropriate changes for the different file names.

The MD5 mechanism is not as secure as the PGP one for testing the kits on the CD-ROM, because the `.md5` files for these kits are *only* on the CD-ROM itself. Someone could have altered the kits and generated new `.md5` files. You wouldn't be able to tell. With PGP signatures, the key factor is the identity of the signer, which can be kept and obtained separately from the file or kit being signed.

Forgery! What to do?

If the signatures of your kits don't match the expected results, you have three possible explanations:

✔ You checked the signatures against the wrong files.

✔ The kits have been compromised — changed from what they're supposed to be — and you shouldn't use them.

✔ The kits and signature files weren't matched up properly when they were prepared.

Double-check the first possibility before going any farther; step through and make sure you're using the right file names.

If you're sure the signatures don't match the kit files, the two basic paths you can take from here are:

✔ Get a new copy of the kit.

✔ Go ahead and use the kit anyway.

If you go ahead and use a kit that doesn't match its signature or checksum, you're taking a chance. Someone may have planted a security hole in the kit.

The operation was a success — but how's the patient?

The easiest way to make sure that you unpacked your kit correctly is to make sure the documentation pages work as they should. To see these pages, you need a browser.

You don't need to have the Web server up and running to check the documentation pages, because they should still be accessible through the `file:` URL scheme, which doesn't use the network. The URL you want is

```
file:/usr/local/web/apache/htdocs/index.html
```

If you've installed the `apache_win32.exe` and `apache_win32_ext.exe` packages on your Windows system, use your favorite browser to open the file (*not* URL!) "`C:\Apache\htdocs\index.html`".

If you're using a GUI (graphical user interface) browser, you should see a screen that says "It Worked!". This screen represents the "success" page that comes with Apache, which indicate that things appear to be installed properly. You look at this screen again with the benefit of the server itself in Chapter 4, but for now just follow the links through the documentation. Everything should work correctly, with the links taking you from page to page. If you encounter a lot of broken links, possibly your kit wasn't unpacked correctly, or the kit itself wasn't prepared properly. Double-check the unpacking steps and redo the installation if necessary.

If the links all work the way they should, congratulations! You've installed the Apache server software, and it should be ready to be configured for use.

Chapter 4
Basic Configuration

In This Chapter

▶ Applying directives

▶ Desgning containers

▶ Writing rules

▶ Defining scope

With the Apache software installed on your system, you've taken the first step toward becoming that most trendy of cybercitizens, a Webmaster. The Apache software isn't going to do much just sitting on the disk, though, any more than an orchestra does without music or direction. This chapter describes the basic instructions you need to give your Apache performer before it can start spinning your web. Get your baton ready, *maestro!* You're about to go on!

Directives — What's the Score?

The Apache software can perform a lot of features, but it runs on a computer — which means it only does what it's told to do. Similarly, an orchestra doesn't make up its music; it plays only what the conductor directs it to play. You can direct your Apache server by using instructions called (wait for it) . . . directives.

A *directive* is a single line of text starting with a keyword. The keyword may stand alone, or it may require you to add other commands on the line as well. Consider the following example:

```
CacheNegotiatedDocs
ScriptAlias /cgi-bin /usr/local/web/apache_1.3.0/cgi-bin
```

The first directive has no *arguments,* or parameters, and the second has two. Arguments are separated from the directive keyword and from each other by white space. If an argument needs to include white space, you have to enclose it in quotation marks like this:

```
TransferLog "|rlog myhost"
```

You can spell out directive keywords in uppercase, lowercase, or a mixture of the two; usually, people spell them by capitalizing the first letter of each word, as in the previous example. However, the following configuration lines have exactly the same effect as they would if the directives were spelled in all lowercase or all uppercase:

```
cAcHeNeGoTiAtEdDoCs
sCRIPTaLIAS /cgi-bin /usr/local/web/apache/cgi-bin
```

If you find this format easier to read, go for it — but I use the first format (each word capitalized) in this book. When you write a book about this stuff, spell the directive keywords however you like.

Although you can mix and match the case of directive keywords to suit your fancy, you can't assume you can do that with the directive arguments. In almost all cases, the arguments are extremely case-sensitive!

The Apache Web server ignores any extra white space between arguments — or even in front of the directive keyword — so you can indent your configuration lines in whatever manner pleases you. The only exceptions are comment lines, which always *must* begin with an octothorpe (#) in column 1.

Containers for the things contained

Apache has a special category of directives called *containers,* which are actually pairs of directives: a start-directive and an end-directive. Following the HTML tag model (which is used by Web page authors), these directives usually look like this:

```
<keyword[ arguments]>    # container start-directive
</keyword>               # end-directive
```

The brokets ("broken brackets" or "angle brackets" — "<" and ">") and slashes are part of the directive keyword. You can't insert any spaces or stuff like that anywhere between the broket and the end of the keyword. Well, you can — but the directive won't work.

You place arguments to container directives inside the closing broket, but you must otherwise follow the normal directive rules (use quotes if it contains white space, recognize that it's probably case-sensitive, and so on).

Here are some example container directives (note that the directive arguments are inside the closing broket):

```
<Directory /foo>
</Directory>
<Location /~*>
</Location>
<VirtualHost _default_>
</VirtualHost>
```

The rules about capitalization of the directive keyword still apply here; however, so do the rules about case-sensitivity and the directive arguments.

Although Apache container directives look like HTML tags . . . they aren't. That means you can't bunch multiple directives up on a single line; the rule is "one directive per line." This directive won't work:

```
<Directory /foo>DirectoryIndex zed.html</Directory>
```

Syntactically speaking . . .

When Apache processes its directives, one of the first things it does is check to see if the syntax is correct; actually using the directive comes later. (When you read a sentence, you first check to see if you can understand it — wondering if what it says makes sense later.)

Apache uses a bunch of syntax rules, and every directive has exactly one rule that applies to it. Every directive line must match that directive's syntax rule. The rules may not be obvious to you from looking at the directives, but using syntax rules makes it easy and fast for the software to check the validity of the directive. If a directive is supposed to have one argument, and you give it two, Apache can quickly spot the error and say, "Bzzzt! Wrong!"

Here are the most basic rules for directives. Each description includes the internal nickname for the rule and the name of a directive to which the rule applies (if there is one).

- ✔ **NO_ARGS:** No Arguments
  These directives stand entirely by themselves on the line, and complain bitterly if you try to give them an argument. Example: `CacheNegotiatedDocs`.

- ✔ **TAKE1:** One Argument
  As you may expect, you can give these directives a single parameter — no more, no less. Example: `User`.

- ✔ **TAKE2:** Two Arguments
  You wanna take a guess? Right; you must supply exactly two arguments. Example: `ScriptAlias`.

- ✔ **TAKE3:** Three Arguments
  Anything other than three parameters results in a configuration error. Example: None, not currently used.

These descriptions don't quite cover all eventualities, so here are some additional combinations. Not all of them are used by directives built into the Apache software; some of them have been defined for completeness or because it was thought they may be useful someday, either to the basic Apache Web server software or to people who write additional plug-in modules for the server:

✔ **TAKE12: One or Two Arguments**
Need I say more? You can give directives that fall into this category either one or two parameters (but never three, five, or none). What these directives do may differ slightly depending on how many arguments they have, so read the description of the directive (in the online documentation at <http://www.apache.org/docs/mod/directives.html>) carefully. Example: RLimitCPU.

✔ **TAKE23: Two or Three Arguments**
Directives of this type always have at least two arguments and may have three. As with the TAKE12 directives, the number of arguments may subtly change the meaning. Example: Header.

✔ **TAKE13: One or Three Arguments**
Under no circumstances would this kind of directive have only two arguments — at least no circumstances in which it would work. Example: None, not currently used.

✔ **TAKE123: One, Two, or Three Arguments**
This type of directive takes at least one and at most three parameters. Example: None, not currently used.

Sometimes you need to give Apache an arbitrary list of items that need to be treated the same way. The following categories cover this situation:

✔ **ITERATE: One Repeating Argument**
Directives that use this syntax apply the same functionality to each item in an arbitrarily long list of arguments. You can look at an ITERATE directive as though it is a series of TAKE1 directives, each with a successive argument from the list. Example: IndexIgnore.

✔ **ITERATE2: One Constant and One Repeating Argument**
This directive syntax is an odd one and probably the best way to view it is as a series of TAKE2 directives. For each TAKE2 directive, the first argument would be the same, but the second argument would be a successive value from the list. For example, an ITERATE2 "KeyWord A B C D" would be similar to TAKE2 "KeyWord A B", "KeyWord A C", and "KeyWord A D". Example: AddIcon.

Finally, here are two other oddball categories for how directives can handle their arguments:

> ✔ **FLAG:** One Flag Argument
> Directives that turn functionality on or off fall into this category.
> The single argument is either the word on or off and isn't case-sensi-
> tive. Example: FancyIndexing.
>
> ✔ **RAW_ARGS:** None of the Above
> Some directives just don't fall into any of the preceding categories, so
> Apache allows them to make up their own rules. Example:
> AllowOverride.

Scopes: Servers, Directories, Locations, and Files

Apache is really rich and full-featured with its ability to twiddle with details.
The Apache Web server gives you lots of opportunities to tailor how it should
handle its requests, starting at the most general level— the server-wide
configuration — and zooming in closer and closer to the actual end resource.

The server-config files

Because of its origins (from NCSA HTTPd, remember? Did you skip that part
of the introduction? If you did, and you don't know where Apache came
from, subtract 10 Apache Guru Points and go back to the introduction and
read it!), the Apache server knows about three different server-wide configuration files:

✔ **The server configuration file,** httpd.conf: This file typically contains
directives that affect how the server runs, such as the user and group
IDs it should use, the location of the other files, and so on. Because the
server configuration file is the main file that the server starts with,
Apache doesn't include any directive that says where to find it — the
location is passed on the command line when the server starts (see the
"Starting, Stopping, and Reloading the Server" section in this chapter).

✔ **The resource configuration file,** srm.conf: This file usually contains
things that define where documents are found, how to translate Web
addresses to file names, and so on. The ResourceConfig directive tells
the server where to find this file (which needs to be put in the server
configuration file).

✔ **The security configuration file,** access.conf: This file is intended to
contain instructions about who's supposed to be able to access what
information and how they need to prove they're permitted to do so. Like
the resource configuration file, you can tell the server where to find this
file with the AccessConfig directive in the server configuration file.

If you don't rename any of these files, Apache looks for them by the names in the previous list (`httpd.conf`, `srm.conf`, and `access.conf`) in the `conf` subdirectory under the ServerRoot (the top level of your Apache directory tree, `/usr/local/web/apache`).

Apache no longer restricts the functions of the various server-wide configuration files; any one of these files can contain any directive. (The sole exceptions are the `AccessConfig` and `ResourceConfig` directives, which need to be in the server configuration file for obvious reasons.) In fact, you can get by with only a single configuration file containing everything (many Apache Webmasters do this, in fact) and tell the server the other files are obsolete with lines like the following:

```
ResourceConfig /dev/null
AccessConfig   /dev/null
```

Even though you can store your server's configuration directives in multiple files (`httpd.conf`, `srm.conf`, and `access.conf`), you need to remember that the server doesn't treat them any differently. That is, when the server processes the directives in the `srm.conf` file, it remembers everything it did when it read the `httpd.conf` file. And when the server goes through the `access.conf` file, it hasn't forgotten a single word of what it found in the `httpd.conf` and `srm.conf` files. This can lead to confusion; for example, if you have a `<Directory />` block in the `httpd.conf` file, and another `<Directory />` block in the `srm.conf` file, which one will the Apache server use? (The one in the `httpd.conf` file — you can see my point.)

Scope it out!

The ability to have a configuration file specifically for an individual directory is mostly meant for flexibility and convenience. You don't have to use the configuration file; everything you can do with *per*-directory config files you can do in the server config files with *scoping*.

What's scoping? It's a way to say, "The following applies only to X," where X is a directory, or a set of files, or a URL location. You define a scope using the appropriate container directives (see the "Containers for the things contained" section in this chapter), as in the following example

```
<Directory />
    AllowOverride None
    Options None
    Order deny,allow
    Deny from all
</Directory>
```

The directives in the example tell the server, "For any request that translates to a file in the / directory or in a subdirectory somewhere under it, return an error and don't allow any access." That container is actually a good thing to have in your server config files, just to protect against accidental access to documents that may otherwise be unintentionally granted.

The `<Directory>` and `<Location>` scopes include not only the paths you specify, but all the subordinate ones as well. In other words, the directives in the `<Directory />` container in the previous example also apply to `/usr/foo` because it's a descendent of the / directory. The `<Files>` scoping container refers to a filename pattern, not a hierarchical path, and applies only to files that specifically match the argument — wherever they may be found within the scope.

Apache evaluates scopes from the more general to the more specific. If you follow the previous `<Directory>` container block with two blocks like this:

```
<Directory /usr/local/web/apache/cgi-bin>
    AllowOverride All
    Options ExecCGI
    Order allow,deny
    Allow from all
</Directory>
<Directory /usr/local/web/apache/htdocs>
    AllowOverride All
    Options IncludesNoExec
    Order allow,deny
    Allow from all
</Directory>
```

you override the very restrictive settings in the first block — but only for these two directories (`/usr/local/web/apache/cgi-bin` and `/usr/local/web/apache/htdocs`) and their descendants.

The last two `<Directory>` blocks (in the preceding example) allow CGI scripts to function if they come from `ServerRoot/cgi-bin`, and allow the server to give clients files that it finds in the `DocumentRoot` tree — including performing SSI parsing on them first. (See Chapter 12 for more information about scripts and real-time document processing.)

The directory that's the top of your tree of Web documents is called the *DocumentRoot*. Similarly, the directory that sits at the top of the tree of Apache Web server control files is called the *ServerRoot*. If you've installed the Apache software according to the instructions in this book, your DocumentRoot is `/usr/local/web/apache/htdocs`, and `/usr/local/web/apache` is your ServerRoot.

Depending on how simple or complicated your environment is, you may be able to get away with as few as three or four blocks. Each block handles one of the following tasks:

- Lock down the entire filesystem by default
- Allow access to the DocumentRoot tree
- Allow server-wide CGI scripts to run
- Allow access to *per*-user directories (for example, `http://host/~user/`)

"But I'm sure I've seen directives that weren't inside one of these containers you're talking about!" You're right, you have — good eyes. Outside of containers is the environment called the *server,* or global, scope. Directives found in that scope supply defaults for everything in the server's environment; the containers are actually just narrowing the scope from there and modifying those defaults.

Quite a lovely `<Location>`

The `<Location>` container directive is pretty much just like the `<Directory>` container described in the preceding section, with one very important difference. The `<Directory>` container defines a scope that is tied tightly to the directory structure on your Web server's disks. The `<Location>` container refers strictly to URL paths, whether the server ends up translating them to files or not.

To put it another way, the `<Directory>` container refers to a place in filespace, and the `<Location>` refers to a place in Web-space. Web-space is a sort of formless, virtual limbo, where resources may be related to concrete documents on a disk somewhere — or may not.

A mnemonic device that may help you remember the difference between these two scoping mechanisms is, "Directories on disk, but Locations in limbo."

The argument to the `<Location>` directive is a Web path relative to your server. In the following example, if the name of your server is `Nice.And.Com` then the scope specified by `<Location /with/Gusts>` matches the URL:

```
http://Nice.And.Com/with/Gusts
```

Because Web-space locations may or may not translate to real filespace paths, the server may or may not be able to find `.htaccess` files to process. For this reason, specifying any maybe-not-real resource paths in `<Location>` scopes in your server config files is a good idea. If they do translate to filespace, you can use the `.htaccess` files to further refine the processing.

.htaccess files, also called *per*-directory configuration files, are described in Chapter 2.

Lord of the `<Files>`

While `<Directory>` refers to filesystem paths and `<Location>` to URL paths, the `<Files>` container provides controls over files that are named a certain way (such as any file names ending in .gif, or starting with the letter a, and so on), regardless of where the server may find them.

Like the other container directives mentioned in the preceding sections, the `<Files>` container takes an argument. In this case, though, the argument isn't a path — it's a file name:

```
<Files .htaccess>
    Order deny,allow
    Deny from all
</Files>
```

The previous block ensures that the server doesn't hand out any private configuration files named .htaccess that it finds in the same scope as the `<Files>` block.

You can nest `<Files>` blocks within `<Directory>` (but not `<Location>`) blocks, in which case they apply to all files in that scope that match. As usual, more-specific matches override less-specific ones.

Unlike other scoping containers, you can use the `<Files>` directive in .htaccess files.

Getting wild! Using wildcards and matching patterns

"But wait a minute! What if I want to allow access only to directories beginning with a?" Have I got a deal for you: pattern matching!

Pattern matching involves checking a name (such as a file name or directory name) to see if it matches a specific pattern. The pattern can be simple, such as checking to see if the name ends in .gif, or it can be really complicated, like seeing if the third letter of the name is X and the seventeenth letter is g.

If you've used UNIX or Windows before, you should be familiar with basic wildcards like *.doc or Marketing.*. Those are simple patterns.

The <Files>, <Location>, and <Directory> container directives can recognize UNIX shell-style *wildcards* (? and *) in their arguments. The ? matches any single character, and the * matches zero or more characters (any characters). For example, if you want to put a limit on all files whose names contain the string payroll, you can use the following wildcard pattern in a <Files> block:

```
<Files *payroll*>
    Order allow,deny
    Deny from all
</Files>
```

Similarly, if you want to allow the server to hand out documents from users' public_html subdirectories, but not their home directories, you can conceivably do it with something like this:

```
<Directory /usr/users>
    Order deny,allow
    Deny from all
</Directory>
<Directory /usr/users/*/public_html>
    Order allow,deny
    Allow from all
</Directory>
```

In Apache 1.2, the wildcard characters can match any character, even the / path separator; a*b would match both axb and a/b. Apache 1.3 is back in line with the usual shell rules — that is, the slash isn't matched.

But what if the payroll files in the previous example don't all contain the string payroll in their names? What if some files are named *cheque-run* and others are named *salary*? Does that mean you have to duplicate the <Files> container for each of these files?

No, it does not. Thanks to the wonders of technology (and The Apache Group), you can specify much more complex patterns using what are called *regular expressions* (REs or regexes). Using regular expressions, all of those payroll files could be matched by the single pattern (payroll)|(cheque-run)| (salary).

Providing details about regular expressions and RE syntax is definitely beyond the scope of this book. If you don't know about them, go read up on the subject (may I recommend *UNIX For Dummies*?) and give yourself 10 Apache Guru Points. If you're already familiar with REs, you don't get any points — sorry.

To signal that you want Apache to treat an argument as an RE pattern rather than a shell pattern, you actually insert an argument between the directive name and the pattern. The argument is simply the tilde character, ~. To include those additional name fragments from payroll, you can use this pattern:

```
<Files ~ (payroll)|(cheque-run)|(salary)>
    Order allow,deny
    Deny from all
</Files>
```

In Apache 1.3, the alternate syntaxes for extended regular-expression pattern matching have been moved to new directives: <FilesMatch>, <DirectoryMatch>, and <LocationMatch>. These directives are equivalent to their older counterparts <Files ~ **pattern**>, <Directory ~ **pattern**>, and <Location ~ **pattern**>, which still exist.

Order of the day

With all the different ways to define scope (see the section "Scopes: Servers, Directories, Locations, and Files" in this chapter), knowing how the Apache server applies all the rules is useful. Because so many Web documents actually come from files, Apache evaluates the scopes that relate to files first. Here's the basic sequence that Apache follows:

1. **Checks the** <Directory> **blocks to see if any of them are ancestors of the specified document.**

2. **Examines the** <Files> **blocks to see if any of them match the actual file name.**

3. **Finally, checks the** <Location> **blocks to see if any of them cover the Web-space resource.**

This list is very oversimplified, and each step actually has secret instructions about how to proceed. I describe these secret instructions in the sections that follow; try to contain your excitement, won't you?

This scope-evaluating process is made more complicated by the way the server looks for and processes .htaccess files.

Digging through directories

The server's sequence for processing <Directory> blocks, broken down into excruciating detail, goes through a series of steps. The entire sequence is repeated for each component of the path in the request; that is, for a request for "/a/b/c/d.html", the server will follow these steps for "/", then "/a", then "/a/b", and finally "/a/b/c". This portion of the path that's being checked is called the *prefix*.

The following list describes how the Apache 1.2 server handles `<Directory>` containers. The sequence is different for version 1.3 of the server, and the 1.3 process is described next. Here are the steps the Apache 1.2 server performs for all the possible prefixes in the request's path:

1. **Compares the prefix against each `<Directory>` container that was loaded from the server config files. The containers are checked in the same order as they appeared in the config files at the time the server was loaded.**

2. **If the container uses a regular expression, checks to see if it matches against the request, and evaluates the directives in the container immediately (called *merging* them) if it does. Then marks this regular-expression container as having been merged so it won't be merged more than once *per* request (which may otherwise happen if the pattern matches more than one of the prefixes).**

3. **If the container doesn't use a regular expression, and the container's directory is the same as the prefix, merges the directives in the container.**

4. **Looks for a `.htaccess` file in the prefix directory and merges the file's contents if the file exists.**

Well, maybe that wasn't so excruciating after all.

In the previous steps, "merging" directives means merging their meaning with any directives that the sever has already evaluated.

The way the Apache Web server handles `<Directory>` containers is different for version 1.3. Here are the steps the 1.3 server follows to evaluate which `<Directory>` containers apply to a request:

1. **Compares the prefix against each `<Directory>` container that was loaded from the server config files that *doesn't* use a regular expression and has the same number of components as the prefix (for example, "/a/b" has two components, "/a" and "/b"). The containers are checked in the same order as they appeared in the config files at the time the server was loaded.**

2. **If the container's directory matches the prefix, the container's directives are merged.**

3. **Looks for a `.htaccess` file in the prefix directory and merges the file's contents if the file exists.**

4. **Repeat Steps 1, 2, and 3 for each possible prefix in the request path (that is, for a request path of "/a/b/c/d.html", the preceding steps would be performed for "/a", "/a/b", and "/a/b/c").**

5. **Finally, check all regular-expression `<Directory>` containers and merge the directives in any that match the full directory path from the request (for example, "/a/b/c" from a request path of "/a/b/c/ d.html").**

Following the files

After evaluating the global scope and ⟨Directory⟩ blocks and processing the unscoped .htaccess directives as much as possible, the server looks for ⟨Files⟩ blocks to apply. As with the other scope containers, the server evaluates them in the order they were encountered.

The server considers ⟨Files⟩ blocks to match even if no actual file is available. That is, if you have a ⟨Files⟩ block that prevents the server from handing out GIF images, you get a "forbidden" error if you ask for a .gif — even if no such file exists!

Don't forget you can use the ⟨Files⟩ container directive in *per*-directory .htaccess files.

Looking at locations

The last set of scoping directives Apache examines are the ⟨Location⟩ blocks. Apache checks these blocks in the order they occur in the server config files, and if it finds any that are logical ancestors of the requested resource, it processes the directives in the container.

Narrowing the field

The server checks the *per*-directory config files every time it manages to map a request onto the on-disk filesystem. It checks every directory in the path to the file for an .htaccess file, and merges the contents of any files that it finds into a collection of current settings that it applies to the request. For example, if your server is asked 100 times for something that turns out to be the file /usr/local/web/htdocs/thisfile.html, it's going to look 500 times for *per*-directory config files, starting at the top of the directory tree and working its way downward:

- ✔ At the top level, for /.htaccess
- ✔ Next, for /usr/.htaccess
- ✔ Next, for /usr/local/.htaccess
- ✔ Next it looks for /usr/local/web/.htaccess
- ✔ Finally, it tries to process /usr/local/web/htdocs/.htaccess

The default name of the *per*-directory configuration file is .htaccess, but you can change it with the AccessFileName directive. For the sake of simplicity, I assume throughout the book that you haven't altered this name and that you refer to these files as .htaccess files.

If each of the files in the previous search actually exists, that's a lot of activity! Which is a pretty good reason to not use .htaccess files excessively, and put as much configuration information as you can into ⟨Directory⟩ and ⟨Location⟩ blocks in the server config files.

Overrides — the Layered Approach to Directive Validity

Not all directives can appear in all possible locations (see Chapter 2). For example, having the .htaccess file in a particular directory try and configure aspects of the whole server doesn't make any sense. Where it can appear is another attribute of a directive's definition — some directives can only be used in the server config files, and some can be used in the server files *and* .htaccess files.

If a directive can appear in .htaccess files at all, the server would process it only if the server administrator (that's you!) allows the directive to override any server-wide settings. You define what aspects of server processing can be overridden with the AllowOverride directive like this:

```
<Directory /usr/local/web/apache/htdocs>
    AllowOverride AuthConfig
</Directory>
```

This example specifically says that .htaccess files under the DocumentRoot can fiddle with the authorization and access controls to the files in their directory trees.

Table 4-1 illustrates the possible locations where directives may or may not be usable, depending upon the directive definition. The description of each directive indicates where it can be used.

You can find the latest version of the Apache Web server documentation online at the following Web location:

```
http://www.apache.org/docs/mod/directives.html
```

Because the AllowOverride directive itself is only allowed inside <Directory> and <Location> containers in the server config files, .htaccess files can't change the override settings.

The different overrides include:

- **All:** If this override is active, then there are no restrictions on what directives may be used at the current and lower scope — unless a lower level chooses to be more restrictive.

- **None:** As you may expect, this override is the opposite of the All keyword. It says that the server should not honor any .htaccess directives within the current scope. Again, a more specific container for a sub-scope may open this up and allow .htaccess files to override settings within that sub-scope.

✔ **AuthConfig:** This override controls directives that have to do with authentication and authorization — asking the user who he/she is and to prove it. If the override is active, .htaccess files can ask these sorts of questions.

✔ **FileInfo:** The FileInfo override controls directives that deal with how the server processes files, such as defining their content type based on a private suffix.

✔ **Indexes:** This override controls directives that have to do with providing lists of directory contents or translating image coordinates to file names.

✔ **Limit:** You use directives controlled by the Limit override to restrict access to documents, such as "only allow clients from my system to see these."

✔ **Options:** This override controls directives that deal with the options available in a directory (currently only the XBitHack and Options directives).

Table 4-1	Places Where Directives Can Appear			
Restriction Name	*Server Config Files (Only Inside* <Directory> *and* <Location> *Containers)*	*Server Config Files (Only Outside* <Directory> *and* <Location> *Containers)*	*Server Config Files Anywhere)*	*.htaccess Files*
RSRC_CONF		✔		
ACCESS_CONF	✔			
OR_AUTHCFG	✔			✔ if within scope of an AllowOverride AuthConfig
OR_LIMIT	✔			✔ if within scope of an AllowOverride Limit
OR_OPTIONS			✔	✔ if within scope of an AllowOverride Options
OR_FILEINFO			✔	✔ if within scope of an AllowOverride FileInfo
OR_INDEXES			✔	✔ if within scope of an AllowOverride Indexes

Root Directories — How It Can Be Told

Like a server at a restaurant, a Web server's existence usually centers around handling customer requests. A waiter stands between the customer and the kitchen and has instructions about what's on the menu, where to seat customers, and so on. The waiter doesn't do the cooking, but does know (hopefully!) where the kitchen is.

Similarly, the Web server doesn't usually control the content of what it gives to clients, but it does have a "sheet" of instructions and a supply of resources (like a waiter's napkins and silverware) to help it accomplish its job. The Apache "server station" — where you find the server's instructions and records — is called the *ServerRoot;* the "kitchen" — where Apache keeps the documents — is known as the *DocumentRoot.*

The ServerRoot

The ServerRoot area actually consists of a tree of directories containing accounting logs, configuration files, some standard documents (such as file icons and the online Apache server documentation), management tools, and useful CGI scripts (see Chapter 12 for more information about CGI scripts).

Remember the directory structure in the Apache source kit? (If you don't, check out Chapter 3.) The top-level directory, apache, is your ServerRoot.

The server accesses the various subdirectories in the ServerRoot tree in different ways and to different degrees. Some subdirectories are very inactive, such as the one that contains the support tools, which is rarely accessed. Some don't change much, but the server accesses them a lot — such as the directory that contains the file icons. Others are extremely active and the server constantly updates them — for example, the directory where the server logs the accounting information. And some fall in between, such as the configuration directory — which you change only when you want to twiddle the server's controls and that the server reads only when it reacts to your twiddling.

Like the cash register or safe at a restaurant, the ServerRoot area shouldn't be available to the customers. Make sure your files aren't too permissive! See the "Permissions" section later in this chapter for more information.

Surprisingly enough, the Apache directive that tells the server the location of the ServerRoot is called ServerRoot.

ServerRoot shortcuts

References to subdirectories of the Server-Root in the configuration files themselves usually omit the parent directory from the file specification and just refer to the subdirectories as `conf`, `icons`, and so on — the server understands this shortcut format. However, when you talk to another human being (assuming you're one yourself, of course — I have no proof that this book isn't read by extraterrestrial life forms. If you're an ET, please let The Apache Group know!) . . . as I was saying, if you're communicating with another sentient being verbally, you may need to add the phrase "relative to the ServerRoot" to make sure you're understood. If you want to add this phrase in an e-mail message, the usual syntax is something like `{ServerRoot}/conf/httpd.conf`.

Several of the Apache configuration directives that tell the server where to find files understand that if you don't give an absolute path (that is, leave off the leading "/" character), the location is relative to the ServerRoot. For example,

```
ServerRoot      /usr/local/web/apache
AccessFileName conf/access.conf
```

tells the server that it can find the configuration file that contains access control information (the AccessFile) in the directory fully qualified (that is, with the complete directory path included) as `/usr/local/web/server/conf/access.conf`.

Allowing the use of ServerRoot-relative shortcuts means that picking up the ServerRoot tree and moving it somewhere else requires a whole lot less editing, making the task much easier.

When you set up your server, one of the most important subdirectories under the ServerRoot is `conf`. The `conf` directory contains the files that actually give the server its instructions: the server configuration files. Usually, Apache configuration files are named with a `.conf` ending; as supplied as part of the Apache package, though, the `conf` directory contains only `.conf-dist` files to be used as templates for the *real* configuration files you develop for your server. See the "Minimal Configuration" section later in this chapter for details.

DocumentRoot — where the wild things are

If your Web site is like a restaurant, the Web server is like a waiter, and the ServerRoot is the server station, the DocumentRoot is its kitchen. The DocumentRoot directive tells the server how to translate the document portion of a URL into the actual file directories on the disk.

TECHNICAL STUFF

Translating URLs to files

A Web URL actually denotes a *resource*, not a file. The most common occurrence, however, is for URLs to map directly to files on the host system's disks (that is, every URL on your Web site translates to an actual file on your hard drives). Unless you take explicit steps to change the behaviour, Apache tries to turn a URL into a reference to a file under the DocumentRoot.

In a URL such as the following

`http://www.apache.org/docs/FAQ.html`

the underlined portion is what Apache translates. The value of the DocumentRoot would be inserted at the first / — that is, if DocumentRoot is set to "/usr/local/ webdocs" the previous URL would actually result in the server handing the client the file "/usr/local/webdocs/docs/ FAQ.html".

Lots of things can (and do) change this default behaviour of URL/filename translation. You can read about some of these things, such as *aliases* and *redirects*, in the "Sleight of Web — Aliases" section in this chapter, and other translation methods in Chapter 11.

While you can easily move your Document-Root around, remember that if you change the structure of the directory tree, you're actually changing the URLs of the documents. So plan your DocumentRoot directory tree with care. (Advanced rewriting techniques can bail you out, if you've dug a hole from which you have to escape. See Chapter 11 for details.)

Like the waiter in the restaurant, the server usually just carries things from the kitchen (the DocumentRoot and its subdirectories) to the customer (the client). Sometimes the server adds garnish or handles special orders (see Chapter 12 for more on modifying documents at request time), but mostly it carries plates . . . er, documents. The menu and the kitchen can be tiny or huge; the individual meals may be snacks or seven-course dinners, but the server handles them all with aplomb. It doesn't even get surly if you don't tip.

Some Apache directives interpret their arguments as being relative to the DocumentRoot the way others do the ServerRoot, but the document namespace of a server is usually much more complicated than the server's configuration directories. There aren't any simple rules about which directives refer to full file or directory names and which ones are relative to the DocumentRoot — the way file names are handled is specific to each and every directive. It's made even more complicated by the fact that the Web namespace isn't identical to the filesystem layout — what's the shortcut to a document that isn't a file? The moral is: Carefully read the description of each directive you use and don't make assumptions!

Permissions

Because of some of the things a Web server needs to do, it usually starts under the `root` user ID. Nothing exists to keep the `root` superuser from doing whatever it wants, though, so most Webmasters prefer to have the server running as `root` to be a temporary condition. The Apache software supports this desire and can change its identity after it gets going.

Because the Apache server is probably going to be running as some user other than `root`, you need to make sure it can access the files it needs — and no more. In other words, you let it use the cash register — but you don't give it the combination to the office safe. You let it pick up dishes from the kitchen — but you make sure it's not allowed to cook.

In most cases, you want some user other than the server to own the DocumentRoot and ServerRoot files, and you want the file permissions to allow the server only read and possibly execute access. The sole exception to this general rule is the accounting information — the server needs to be able to record its activities (and errors).

You may even want to go so far as to ensure that only the owner of the files has write access, and only the server has read access, and all others have no access at all. In other words, the only way anyone can access your Web-related files is either by being the owner or by going through the Apache Web server — if an end-user can log on to your system as anyone else (except `root`, of course), it doesn't help him or her access your Web documents. Setting up the ownership and permissions this way can be a little complicated to manage because it means all the changes need to be done from the owning account. You either end up with a very overworked person, or else (if multiple people use the owner user ID) no accountability as to who did what.

That's a pretty severe case and illustrates the truism that "security costs — one way or another." A much more workable solution is to have the DocumentRoot directories and files owned and writable by a particular group and only readable by everyone else. That way, you can put the people you want to have manage the content into that group, and the server can't change anything because it isn't a member — it gets the read-only access. Of course, this setup means that anyone who can log on to your system can *read* the files, but that's certainly less hazardous than letting J. Random Person modify them.

The ServerRoot area is a little more complicated. You generally don't want just anyone to be able to look around in there. However, the server needs to be able to access files in the ServerRoot in order to do its job — but you don't want it to be able to change anything. (Except the accounting and log files.) The simplest solution is to have everything owned by `root` and in the group used by the server. You give the owner read-write access, the group read-only access (except the accounting and log files), and everyone else no access at all. Then the owner can make changes, the server can read what it needs to read, and no one without a need-to-know can see the files. The disadvantage to this arrangement is that the root user (or one with superuser authority) needs to make all the changes to the server. But after your server is up and running, you probably won't need to make changes very often. You have to be root to stop, start, and otherwise manage the server anyway, so maybe this setup fits your needs for the long term.

With the exception of the log files and accounting information, the server itself typically doesn't need anything more than read or execute access to the ServerRoot.

Scheming to protect

You can set up an environment that allows multiple people to manage your site's Web content, without being able to interfere (much) with the Apache Web server, by taking the following steps:

1. **Create a new, unique group for managing Web documents (for example, wwwdoc).**

2. **Create a new, unique group for the server (for example, httpd).**

3. **Create a new, unique username for the server (for example, apache) and make the group from Step 2 (httpd) its default group.**

4. **Edit the /etc/group file (or the equivalent on your system), and add the usernames of the people who should be able to modify the Web documents to the group from Step 1 (wwwdoc).**

5. **Make the directories where the server stuff lives (the ServerRoot) owned by root and by the root's group. Allow only read access to the group, and don't allow any access at all to anyone else.**

6. **Make the directories containing the Web documents, and the documents themselves, owned by the group from Step 1 (wwwdoc), read-write to the owner and the group, and no access to the rest of the universe.**

Who owns the document files doesn't really matter because this scheme provides for access through group membership. By setting the file ownership to yourself or a project leader or something like that, you ensure that someone would be able to get at the documents if the staff is all out golfing.

The ownership of the server files is a little more tricky, because the server is doing things on behalf of unknown people on the network. You want to make sure that the server can do what it's supposed to do, but not be tricked into doing anything it oughtn't.

Different flavors of UNIX use different names for the root user's default group. Some systems call the group root, or wheel, or system. You can find out what *your* system calls root's default group by using the following command when logged in as root (the first name listed is the default group):

```
# groups
```
The following commands should set up the necessary ownership and protection for you, based upon the default installation tree:

```
# cd /usr/local/web/apache
# chown -R root .
# chgrp -R root .            # Use root's default group instead of 'root'
# chmod -R u=rwx,g=r,o= *
# chmod u=rwx,g=rx,o=rx . cgi-bin cgi-bin/*
# chgrp -R wwwdocs htdocs
# chmod -R u=rwx,g=rwx,o=rx htdocs
```

Yes, there's nothing but a space after that last "=" symbol in the fourth line. It means "no access."

You can substitute "775" for the "u=rwx,g=rwx,o=rx", and "740" for the "u=rwx,g=r,o=" bit. If you're not familiar with file permissions represented as octal numbers, learn about them in any book about UNIX system administration and then give yourself 10 Apache Guru Points. Lots of things refer to UNIX file permissions in terms of the octal representation, so you really ought to know about it.

What did those commands do?

✔ It made the ServerRoot, the DocumentRoot, and all that they contain owned by root and root's default group.

✔ It made the ServerRoot files modifiable *only* by root, but readable by members of root's default group and inaccessible to anyone else.

✔ It made the ServerRoot directory itself, the cgi-bin directory under it, and the files in the cgi-bin directory readable by everyone so the server can find the documents and execute the scripts.

✔ It made the DocumentRoot files modifiable by root and members of the wwwdoc group and inaccessible to anyone else.

If you changed your DocumentRoot to something other than the htdocs directory under the ServerRoot, you need to expand on the first and the last two lines of the previous example to make sure the directory is protected correctly.

Minimal Configuration

Don't forget that the run-time server config files, which live in the conf directory, are different from the configuration files used to build the server from source code, which live in the src directory.

To set up a minimum configuration for a working, stand-alone server, you have to set up some basic directives, and you should define some other ones.

✔ ServerType

This directive tells the server whether it's going to run as a *daemon,* always lurking around the system, or whether it's an *inetd* application that starts only on demand.

The inetd value for the ServerType directive is deprecated as of Apache 1.3, which means "don't use it unless you have to." The steps involved in getting the server running can take a significant amount of time (depending on the complexity of your environment), which means inetd isn't the most efficient mode of operation. Various optimizations and default settings aren't available in inetd mode, which sometimes leads to confusing error messages and unexpected results. So few people actually run Apache this way that The Apache Group has decided not to expend any more effort on it.

✔ ServerRoot and DocumentRoot

I cover these directives earlier in this chapter. Unless you choose to move things around, the value of the ServerRoot would be the directory where you unpacked the Apache distribution kit. The DocumentRoot is up to you; for your initial setup, you probably want to set it to /usr/local/web/apache/htdocs, which is doubly good because that's the assumption I make in this book.

✔ User

This directive defines the username that the server changes its identity to after it starts as root, which is key in determining what files it can access. I recommend that you create a new account (such as apache) just for the Apache server.

✔ Group

Like the User directive, this one defines what sort of access the Apache server has to the files on your system. Also like the User directive, I recommend that you create a new group (such as httpd) just for Apache. You can give this group a numeric value by preceding it with an octothorpe "#" (also called the "pound sign" — but amaze your friends by calling it an octothorpe!) followed by the GID (group ID) number. I don't recommend using a GID number instead of a group name, though, because it sometimes causes problems — not all versions of UNIX deal correctly with the numeric format. Because you're not a computer (unless you're an AI [artificial intelligence], in which case why are you reading this book?), the name should be more meaningful than the number, so go ahead and use it.

Be sure that the group you specify exists in the /etc/group file or your system's equivalent. If it doesn't, your server will probably fail to start, and die with a cryptic message before it even gets going.

✔ TransferLog

The TransferLog directive tells the server where it should record information about all the requests it receives from clients. The argument is the name of the file (commonly logs/access_log), and if it doesn't start with a slash, the server considers it to be relative to the ServerRoot.

Chapter 5 contains lots of information about logging, including how to tailor your log files so you can see precisely what you want to see if you don't like the default formats.

✔ ErrorLog
Like TransferLog, the ErrorLog directive takes a file name as its argument, which the server treats as relative to the ServerRoot if it doesn't begin with a slash ("/"). The server writes things to this file only when it has some sort of problem; for example, if a client asks for a document that doesn't exist, the server writes an error message to the error log. This file may not show much activity because it's tied to the volume of problems, not the volume of requests. That's a good thing, because it means everything is working pretty much the way it should.

The server error log is your friend! Any time the server seems to be misbehaving, one of the first things you should do is look in the error log for an explanation. You may not find one, but you usually do — so always define this directive.

✔ Port
This directive tells the server which TCP port it should listen on. The default port for Web activity is 80. If you use any value less than 1024, you have to start Apache as root — and if you use any port other than 80, you need to always specify the port number in URLs for your server.

✔ ServerName
The ServerName is how the server identifies itself when it has to report an error to a client and also is how it knows someone's talking to it if a client is speaking in tongues . . . er, HTTP/1.1. You should set this directive to the actual *FQHN* (fully qualified host name) of your server system, such as www.apache.org. It's not case-sensitive, so please yourself about the capitalization — what you type is what clients see if there's an error.

To allow your server to start before the BIND (Berkeley Internet Name Daemon, the service that translates host names to IP addresses and IP addresses to host names) service is running or if BIND is having trouble resolving names or addresses, you should put definitions for all of your server's names in your system's /etc/hosts file or equivalent.

✔ PidFile
The PidFile directive tells the server where to store the process ID number of the parent process. You use this file when the server is running to communicate with it and control it. The usual place is in the logs subdirectory, but you can put it any place the server's user ID has write access.

✔ ServerAdmin
Like the ServerName directive, the server uses this one when it has to display an error message. It usually advises the client to send mail to {ServerAdmin} to report the problem, so use a valid e-mail address.

Now make a configuration with some appropriate values for these directives. The first thing you need to do is copy the distribution configuration
files — which you use as starting points — to working copies. The segments
that follow make the following assumptions, which run pretty much through
the book:

- You unpacked the Apache kit into the tree at /usr/local/web/apache
  (your ServerRoot).
- You're using the htdocs directory under the ServerRoot as your
  DocumentRoot.
- You created one username (apache) and two groups (httpd and
  wwwdocs) to use with the Apache server.

Make copies of the template configuration files. You edit the copies in order
to make any changes you want, and they're used to configure the server. Use
these commands to make the configuration files for *your* server:

```
# cd /usr/local/web/apache
# cd conf
# cp httpd.conf-dist httpd.conf
# cp srm.conf-dist srm.conf
# cp access.conf-dist access.conf
```

Now, edit the httpd.conf file and make changes to set the directives (that I
discuss earlier in this section) as follows:

```
ServerRoot     /usr/local/web/apache
DocumentRoot   /usr/local/web/apache/htdocs
Port           80
ServerName     localhost
ServerAdmin    webmaster@localhost
User           apache
Group          httpd
PidFile        logs/httpd.pid
TransferLog    logs/access_log
ErrorLog       logs/error_log
PidFile        logs/httpd.pid
```

Note that these directives are actually scattered throughout the
httpd.conf file, so modify them where you find them. The spacing is
completely irrelevant; I added white space in the preceding section just to
make it slightly more readable.

Great! Now set the protections on the ServerRoot directory tree and create
the accounting files in such a way that the server can actually write to them:

```
# cd /usr/local/web/apache
# touch logs/access_log logs/error_log logs/httpd.pid
```

```
# chown -R root logs
# chgrp -R root logs          # Use root's default group instead of 'root'
# chmod -R 740 logs
```

You should now have a basic configuration that gets the server up and running. It has a document namespace (even though it's virtually empty), it can read its configuration files, and it can write accounting information.

Okay, start the Apache Web server up:

```
# cd /usr/local/web/apache
# ./httpd -X -d .
```

If all goes well, nothing should happen. (Well, the prompt shouldn't come back, which means that the server is running in single-process mode and didn't find any errors in the configuration files.) If nothing happens, congratulations! You've got a running Apache Web server! Give yourself 100 Apache Guru Points (unless you've done this before). Oh, and hit Ctrl+C to abort the server that's tying up your session.

Command-Line Options

As with most UNIX utilities, you can exercise some degree of control over the Apache server through the command line you use to start it. Because it's a very complex beast and picks up its instructions from the configuration files, the actual list of what you can do from the command line is somewhat limited.

-d — where's the directory?

The -d command line option tells the Apache server where to find the ServerRoot and that it has the canonical (there's that word again! If you're just joining the class, *canonical* means "usual.") structure. The server assumes that the primary configuration file conf/httpd.conf is under the specified directory.

The -d option requires an argument: the value of the ServerRoot. For example:

```
# ./httpd -d /usr/local/web/apache
```

-f — what's the file?

Under some circumstances, you may not want to use the standard directory layout under your ServerRoot. You can change how the server finds the primary configuration file with the -f command line option, which takes a *file* name as an argument rather than a *directory* name. The server treats this file as the primary configuration file (like the `conf/httpd.conf` file that you use when `-d` is specified).

```
# ./httpd -f /usr/local/web/apache/conf/httpd.conf
```

-h — *what ingredients are there?*

Because you can add and remove functionality from the Apache Web server when you build it, the set of directives that are available for use can change correspondingly. And if you use a directive in your server config files that isn't available, the server won't start.

You can use the `-h` command line option to get a listing of exactly what directives are available for any particular server image:

```
% ./httpd -h
<Directory
        Container for directives affecting resources located in the specified
        directories
        http_core.c
        Allowed in *.conf only outside <Directory> or <Location>
</Directory>
        Marks end of <Directory>
        http_core.c
        Allowed in *.conf only inside <Directory> or <Location>
<Location
        Container for directives affecting resources accessed through the
        specified URL paths
        http_core.c
        Allowed in *.conf only outside <Directory> or <Location>
</Location>
        Marks end of <Location>
        http_core.c
        Allowed in *.conf only inside <Directory> or <Location>
                :
                :
```

This listing can go on for quite a while; remember, a typical server knows over a gross of directives.

The description of each directive includes a one-line abstract, the name of the module(s) that declares the directive, and a brief blurb about where the directive can be used.

Because this command line only tells about the server's built-in capabilities, it doesn't try to actually start up the server, nor does it cause problems for any server that's currently running.

If you look closely at the partial output in the previous example, you notice that the container start directives (`<Directory>` and `<Location>`) are missing the closing broket. Give yourself 20 Apache Guru Points if you can figure out why. Give up? It's because the directive name is the *first* part of the statement. Since those container directives require arbitrary arguments before the closing broket, the closing broket itself can't be part of the directive name.

`-l` — *who are the cooks?*

Because most of the power of Apache comes from the compiled-in modules, you can never really be sure just what has been included in a particular binary image. Well, that's not strictly true — the `-l` command line option makes me a liar. The command

```
% ./httpd -l
```

displays a list of what modules were included when the `./httpd` server image was built. For example, here's the output from an actual execution of this command:

```
% ./httpd -l
Compiled-in modules:
  http_core.c
  mod_env.c
  mod_log_config.c
  mod_mime.c
  mod_negotiation.c
  mod_status.c
  mod_info.c
  mod_include.c
  mod_autoindex.c
  mod_dir.c
  mod_cgi.c
  mod_asis.c
  mod_imap.c
  mod_actions.c
  mod_userdir.c
  mod_alias.c
  mod_rewrite.c
  mod_access.c
  mod_auth.c
  mod_auth_id.c
  mod_auth_anon.c
  mod_digest.c
  mod_expires.c
```

(contintued)

(continued)

```
mod_headers.c
mod_usertrack.c
mod_example.c
mod_setenvif.c
```

The -l command line option is only for displaying information and doesn't actually try to start the server or interact with a running one — it just displays the output, and it's done.

-v — what version of Apache?

The -v command line option displays the Apache *server version,* which comes from values set when the server is compiled. This option doesn't actually run the server, it just prints this display — so you can use it without fear that you would start up a new server or interfere with one already running. Here's an example:

```
# ./httpd -v
Server version Apache/1.2.4.
```

-X — eXperimental operation

By using the -X (note that it's a *capital* X) command line option, you tell the Apache software to not reincarnate itself as a daemon and to not create the herd of children it would otherwise do. This option is very, very useful for debugging, because you know exactly which process is handling a particular request. Because only the single process is running and handling client requests, this is not a good option to set by default.

Starting, Stopping, and Reloading the Server

Like many UNIX daemons, the Apache Web server software reincarnates itself in daemon mode if it isn't started that way (which basically means that you don't have to put a "&" at the end of the command line to get the server going). So starting the server is really very simple: Just start the httpd application with the right command line options and from the right account:

```
# ./httpd -d /usr/local/web/apache
```

If problems occur with the server configuration files, the error messages are displayed on the standard error stream of whatever started (or tried to start) the server. If you're starting the server in a noninteractive way (such as through an automatic background job rather than from a terminal or window), you may not see those messages, and the only way you would know something is wrong is because the server ain't there.

After the server is running, you communicate with it by using *signals,* which are sent with the UNIX kill command.

So starting the server is easy. Ah, but stopping the server is slightly more complicated. Remember all those child processes (potentially hundreds of them)? Wading through and killing each of those children can be a significant chore — particularly if the main process kept re-creating them to keep within its parameters. (See Chapter 2 for a discussion about how the Apache Web server uses child processes.)

To shut down the Apache server, you send a SIGTERM signal to the Apache main process, and it takes care of shutting down all the children before committing suicide itself.

Never try to shut down your Apache server by killing all the processes running the httpd image or by sending the SIGKILL signal. Only shut down Apache by signaling the master process and only with SIGTERM.

Remember the PidFile directive (described earlier in this chapter)? Here's where it comes into play:

```
# cd /usr/local/web/apache
# kill -TERM `cat logs/httpd.pid`
```

Starting over without stopping

When running in Standalone mode (highly recommended!), the Apache server has two basic states: running and not running. Because the server reads through the server config files only when it starts up, you need to kill it and restart it any time you want to make a change.

Well, not really; that would be too annoying. You can tell the server to re-read the server config files by sending it more signals, so it keeps running but with the new settings. This process is called *restarting* or *reloading* the server.

There are two flavors of server restart:

- **Graceful restart:** Triggered by sending the server the SIGUSR1 signal. Graceful restarts allow all currently-active requests that the server children are processing to complete before the children reload the configuration files.

- **Graceless restart:** Triggered with the SIGHUP signal, which tells the server to stop whatever it's doing and reload the configuration right now.

  Apache 1.2 introduced graceful restart as a reliable feature.

If any problems occur with the configuration files, they get handled the same way they do at server startup: Error messages are displayed on the standard error device of the process that started (*not* restarted) the server. If that process is long gone, the error messages are lost, and again the only way you know about the problem is because the server isn't running.

The Default Server

Remember the idea of *global scope* that I introduce earlier in this chapter in the "Scope it out!" section? (If you don't, shame on you! If you do, great — but I'm afraid it's not worth any Apache Guru Points.) All the directives in the server config files that aren't inside ⟨VirtualHost⟩ containers (see Chapter 14) apply to what's called the *default server,* or sometimes the *main server.* If you don't have any ⟨VirtualHost⟩ directives, the default server is all you have, so don't worry about it. If you do, or intend to, have any ⟨VirtualHost⟩ containers, remember that the environment defined by the default server provides defaults for the virtual servers.

Sound confusing? I'm not surprised, because it kind of *is* confusing. For now, just remember the term *default server* so you can say "Ah!" and look wise if anyone mentions it. Read Chapter 14, and you can actually *be* wise.

Sleight of Web — Aliases

Keeping all your documents under a single directory tree can make things simple — at least you know where they are — but if the tree gets very deep, you start running into issues with confusing structure and naming conventions, not to mention really-long-names-that-no-one-likes-to-type.

There's a way around this, fortunately. The Apache Web server software allows you to define *aliases,* which are Web-space shortcut names to locations on your disks. For example, you may have the WidgetMaster project files in the following directory on your system:

```
{DocumentRoot}/engineering/products/research/widgetmaster
```

That's a lot of typing! You can shorten the Web path (URL) to this directory to something like wmaster with the following directive in your server config files:

```
Alias /wmaster /usr/local/web/apache/htdocs/engineering/products/research/
               widgetmaster
```

With this directive in place, you can hit the project plan with a URL like this:

```
http://yourhost/wmaster/project_plan.html
```

A lot simpler, eh? Any time the server recognizes the alias at the very beginning of a requested path, it does this substitution before proceeding.

The server substitutes aliases very early in the processing cycle, long before any `<Directory>` or `<Location>` containers are evaluated.

Script directories

The Apache Web server recognizes a special class of directory called a *ScriptAliased* directory (from the directive used to declare it). The server treats files in ScriptAliased directories specially — rather than delivering them to the client, the Apache server tries to run them like a program and send their output to the client.

The `ScriptAlias` directive is very similar to — in fact, is almost identical to — the `Alias` directive (see the preceding section):

```
ScriptAlias /cgi-bin/ /usr/local/web/apache/cgi-bin/
```

The server substitutes this directive the same way as for a normal `Alias` — as soon as it spots a match at the front of the path requested — but it runs the actual file in the directory rather than copying it to the client.

Naming Conventions

This section doesn't really have a lot to do with Apache in particular, but just in case you're using this book to set up your first Web server, I include some file extensions so you can at least make an educated guess about what a file is from its name.

Recognizing file extensions is particularly important because the Apache server is going to make educated guesses based on the name, too. If it can't figure out what a file is, it typically treats the file as plain text — but you can override this default treatment with the `DefaultType` directive.

Because Apache is primarily a UNIX-based Web server and UNIX has case-sensitive filenames, you need to remember that `picture.gif` and `picture.GIF` are two entirely different files — with two entirely different suffixes.

Plain text

Unless you change it with the `DefaultType` directive, the server uses the *plain text* format to send clients any files it can't figure out. What this typically means to your end-users is that they see the file's contents displayed in a monospaced typeface, similar to what I use in this book to represent computer output. Of course, depending on the browser and the actual file content, this font may be less than optimal — nasty not-meant-for-reading files (such as program binaries) may get displayed by mistake.

You can avoid this sort of problem by changing the default type your server sends when all else fails. If you include the following line in your server config files somewhere, any file the server doesn't understand is sent to the clients as a binary file — which hopefully won't mess up their sessions or windows. Of course, configuration mistakes on your part mean more work for your users (because they have to untangle the tagged-as-binary file to figure out what it really is), but at least you're not just dumping gibberish on their screen. The following directive makes the Apache Web server tell clients "this file is binary" if it doesn't know what the file really is:

```
DefaultType application/octet-stream
```

Here are the file extensions that the server usually treats as plain text regardless of the default type:

- ✔ `.txt`, `.text`: A file with these types of name endings are fairly shouting, "Read me!" You don't see `.text` very often, but `.txt` is very common indeed.

- ✔ `.c`, `.h`, `.cxx`, `.f`: Files with these endings are typically program source code, which is readable and best presented in the monospaced format.

HTML files

HTML (HyperText Markup Language) files are those that contain HTML. What a surprise, eh? HTML is the language of the Web and is basically text with some built-in information about formatting or cross-references.

Of course, there's HTML *and* HTML; lots of files actually contain HTML with some additional kick to them, such as SSI (Server-Side Include) instructions.

The most common extensions for HTML files are:

- ✔ `.html`: Standard HTML files on systems that can have more than three characters after the dot.

- ✔ `.shtml`: Files containing HTML enhanced with SSI (Server-Side Include) instructions (which are described in Chapter 12).

- ✔ `.htm`: Files containing HTML, and that typically came from some system that *doesn't* support more than 3-character file extensions (such as Windows NT).

- ✔ `.htp`: Files containing SSI-enhanced HTML and coming from systems with short extension names.

To find out more about HTML, may I suggest *HTML For Dummies* (IDG Books Worldwide, Inc.)? A light meal, very filling, with a pleasing presentation. It's low in cholesterol, too.

Images

Another kind of file that you often find breeding on Web servers is the *graphical image*. This type of file comes in various varieties:

- ✔ `.gif`: Pronounced "jiff" or "giff," this is one of the most common image formats on the Internet. Until recently, GIF files typically contained just static single-frame images — but the GIF format is capable of handling multi-frame picture sequences. Most of those cute little animated icons you see on the Web these days are multi-frame GIF files.

- ✔ `.jpg`, `.jpeg`: Pronounced "JAY-peg," this is another very common Web image format. JPEG images generally take up less space than GIF files (that is, they load faster), but discussions about which is better sometimes escalate to the point at which armor is advisable. I don't know anything about this stuff, so I have no opinion.

- ✔ `.mpg`, `.mpeg`, `.qt`, `.avi`, `.mov`: The first two are pronounced "EM-peg," but the rest are always spelled out. These are multi-frame image sequences. Depending on the format and the author's whim, they sometimes include a sound track. They originated in different spheres (AVI on Windows and QT on Macintosh, for example), so interoperability may be an issue — not all formats will work with all browsers.

Binary files

Binary files contain stuff that probably won't do your screen any good if you display them there. By definition, these files contain binary patterns of ones and zeroes that may (but probably won't) represent characters that you can print (called *printable characters*). The usual content-type for this kind of file is `"application/octet-stream"` — which means it's a bunch of bits (some multiple of eight, the standard byte size, thus the "octet") whose meaning is application-specific. Translation: "It's a bunch of ones and zeroes that means something to somebody, but we're not sure what or whom."

- ✔ `.bin`: Almost universally recognized as meaning "this is a binary file."

- ✔ `.au`: A sound file, containing . . . well, sounds.

- ✔ `.wav`: Another kind of sound file, typically from or for Windows-based clients.

- ✔ `.rmt`, `.mid`, `.midi`: Still more sound files, except these contain instructions for creating sounds rather than recordings of the sounds themselves.

- ✔ `.exe`: Usually means the file is an application program, but who knows for what kind of system. It's definitely binary, though.

- ✔ `.a, .o, .obj`: Intermediate files produced when turning source code into programs.

- ✔ `.tar`: Packages of other files, rather like a ZIP archive on Windows or a StuffIt archive on Macintosh. These files are usually produced on UNIX systems, and there's no telling what may be inside — but there's sure to be control information for taking them apart, and so they're definitely binary files.

- ✔ `.Z`: A file that has been compressed using the UNIX `compress` command (or something which does the same thing). Absolutely binary.

- ✔ `.gz`: Like `.Z`, except it was compressed with the `gzip` (or equivalent) command, which typically squashes things even smaller. These files are therefore even more binary.

Scripts — files that get executed

There are files and files; some contain data (like an image or a sound), and some contain programs or applications. Where Web servers are concerned, programs that the server may be asked to run are called *scripts*. The Apache Web server figures out what files are scripts from the file names:

- ✔ **(no extension):** If the server finds a file in a `ScriptAliased` location (see the "Sleight of Web — Aliases" section in this chapter), it treats the file as a script regardless of the suffix. So, files in these directories often have no suffix at all. Elsewhere, they're usually treated as "dunno, let's use the default type."

- ✔ `.cgi`: Pronounced "see-jee-eye," this is a common suffix for a script that uses the CGI protocol to communicate with the server and the client. A `.cgi` file may or may not be binary, but it can be run like an application regardless.

- ✔ `.pl`: This is a common ending for a script written in Perl. However, it's also the internationally defined two-letter abbreviation for Poland, so a `.pl` file may be a document written in Polish.

- ✔ `.exe`: I mention this type in the section "Binary files." It's still a binary file, but one that can be executed somewhere — although maybe not on your system. It's uncommon on UNIX systems, which don't use this naming convention.

- ✔ `.dll`: This is another binary file, with its origins somewhere in the Windows/Windows 95/Windows NT world.

- ✔ `.com`: This could be a shell script from an OpenVMS system, or it may be like an `.exe` from a Windows system — you can't tell from the name. But it's almost certainly executable somewhere.

Chapter 5

Much Ado about Logging

In This Chapter

▶ Keeping track of client requests

▶ How Apache lets you know when things Aren't Right

▶ Tailoring your transaction logs to include stuff *you* want

▶ Cookies as a way of tracking individuals

▶ Webmastering, advertising, and social responsibility

Webmasters are fascinated by the question: "Who's looking at my site?" They tend to be even more fascinated by the answer. The Apache Web server software gives you lots of ways to discover and record this type of information, kind of like having a collection of video cameras that cover all parts of a store. You can use all the cameras, some of them, or none of them, and you can either look at the tapes or ignore them — but the cameras are always there and ready if you want them.

Who's That Knocking At My Door?

You've decided that you want to at least do some logging of your web site's activity. Because Apache is *feature-rich,* let me cover some background before I hit you with a blizzard of geekspeak.

As with many things in life, a web request falls into one of two categories:

✔ It worked

✔ It didn't

You can call the second category an *error,* because the client didn't get what it requested. This term is appropriate, because Apache keeps track of errors in what's called the *error log.* Catchy, no?

In either case, two collections of information are available:

- ✔ Stuff about the request from the client
- ✔ Stuff about the response from the server

Apache allows you to record just about all this information if you're of a mind to do so. By default, it maintains an *access log,* which is a record of what was requested and by whom and whether it was delivered. Every request receives a record in the access log, whether it succeeded or not.

Apache also maintains the error log, which goes into more detail about the requests that failed and tells you why they didn't work. For example, if a client gets a "forbidden" message when trying to access a page, that's all it sees — but the error log tells the Webmaster whether the cause was a file permission problem, a configuration rule, or something else that kept the user out.

The basic directives for controlling these two very important files are `TransferLog` and `ErrorLog`. The `TransferLog` directive tells Apache where to put the records of all the client transactions, and `ErrorLog` instructs it where to put the evidence when boo-boos happen. Both directives can take values relative to the ServerRoot; in fact, the base Apache kit contains a directory under the ServerRoot just for log files.

```
TransferLog logs/access_log
ErrorLog    logs/error_log
```

If you have multiple servers running or multiple virtual hosts (see Chapter 14), keeping their logfiles separate is a good idea.

The usual information in a request log entry contains the following bits of information:

- ✔ Name or IP address of the client system
- ✔ RFC1413 identify of the user making the request, or "-" if that isn't available
- ✔ Username supplied if the resource required one for access
- ✔ Local system time of the event
- ✔ Actual HTTP request from the client (enclosed in full quotation marks)
- ✔ 3-digit status code the server returned to the client
- ✔ Number of bytes of content (not including any response header information) that the server sent to the client

Here's an excerpt from a transaction log:

```
ida.aolux.com - - [23/Aug/1997:18:48:42 -0400]
                "GET /pix/apache_pb HTTP/1.0" 401 350
ida.aolux.com - coar [23/Aug/1997:18:48:51 -0400]
                "GET /pix/apache_pb HTTP/1.0" 404 166
ida.aolux.com - - [23/Aug/1997:18:49:20 -0400]
                "GET /icons/apache_pb HTTP/1.0" 200 2326
DDD-23.some-isp.com - - [23/Aug/1997:18:50:45 -0400]
                "GET / HTTP/1.0" 401 350
DDD-23.some-isp.com - nobody [23/Aug/1997:18:50:58 -0400]
                "GET / HTTP/1.0" 401 350
DDD-23.some-isp.com - coar [23/Aug/1997:18:51:05 -0400]
                "GET / HTTP/1.0" 200 747
DDD-23.some-isp.com - - [23/Aug/1997:18:51:06 -0400]
                "GET /icons/back.gif HTTP/1.0" 200 216
DDD-23.some-isp.com - - [23/Aug/1997:18:51:06 -0400]
                "GET /icons/blank.gif HTTP/1.0" 200 148
DDD-23.some-isp.com - - [23/Aug/1997:18:51:06 -0400]
                "GET /icons/folder.gif HTTP/1.0" 200 225
```

This is called the *Common Log Format* (CLF), and it's in pretty much general use by Web servers, Apache or otherwise (which is one reason it's called common). If this omits something you're interested in, or gives you more information than you want, you can change this with the CustomLog directive; see the "Customizing the Access Log" section later in this chapter.

In versions of Apache prior to 1.3, the server assumes that you want it to log requests and that it should name the logfile: logs/access_log. As of Version 1.3, the server no longer makes this assumption — if you don't explicitly request a transaction logfile with the TransferLog or CustomLog directives, you won't get one.

The server can't log the request until it's completed — otherwise the server has no way to tell the status or the number of bytes — which means that the log is susceptible to lossage if the server (or system) crashes between the time the response was sent and the request was logged. This window of opportunity for problems is tiny, though, and I've never heard of it being a problem. If an interruption is going to affect the logging, it's more likely to occur *before* the request is completed, in which case who cares? (Except the user, of course.) The request wasn't finished, so it will probably just be made again.

The Apache server opens (or creates) the log files before it changes its identity (see Chapter 4). You can — in fact, you should — put the files someplace safe and relatively inaccessible to the general public. You certainly don't want to allow your server logs to be modifiable by anyone other than the server itself.

Log Analysis Tools

As you can see from the previous section, the log files can get pretty hairy-looking. If you want to be able to actually do something with the information, you either need a tool to do it for you — or glasses. Several utilities exist for doing this, and many of them are available as freeware out on the Net. I include a couple of them on the CD-ROM that accompanies this book.

Analog

The `analog` utility analyzes a CLF or ECLF transaction log file and produces very aesthetic HTML (web browser readable) reports about what it finds. Figure 5-1 shows an excerpt from such a report.

For more information about the CLF and ECLF log formats, see the "Who's That Knocking on My Door?" and "Customizing the Access Log" sections in this chapter.

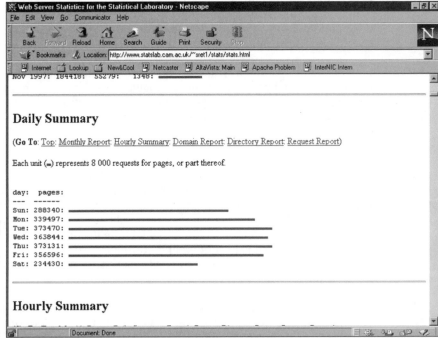

Figure 5-1: Excerpt from analog Log Analysis.

The different sections within the report are cross-linked for easy navigation. You can extensively customize `analog` to control the format of the reports.

See the "About the CD" appendix to find out how to install the `analog` tool on your system.

GetStats

The `getstats` analysis package (included on this book's accompanying CD-ROM) does a pretty good job of analyzing transaction logs and producing a report that you can view with a Web browser. (See Figure 5-2.)

Unfortunately, `getstats` doesn't handle large logfiles very well; the bigger they are, the harder it falls. But it is very good if you don't want to spend a lot of time figuring out how to customize the reports — just edit the program to refer to your system's particulars, compile it, and it's ready to go.

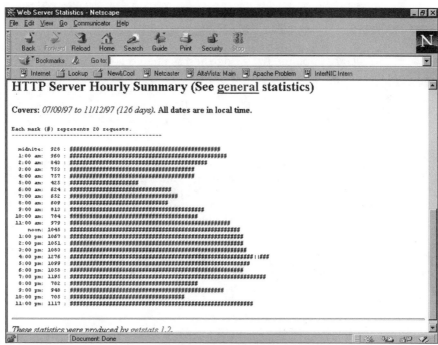

Figure 5-2: Excerpt from `getstats` Log Analysis.

Customizing the Access Log

You say the Common Log Format doesn't give you the information you want? Fine! Go ahead, be that way! But take a look at the `CustomLog` directive.

While the `TransferLog` directive takes only a file name, the `CustomLog` directive takes a file name *and* a format:

```
CustomLog logs/access_log "%h %l %u %t \"%r\" %s %b"
```

The previous statement is equivalent to

```
TransferLog logs/access_log
```

because the CustomLog format in the first example is actually the CLF format syntax. If you want to expand your logging to the ECLF (*Extended CLF*) format, you can use the following:

```
CustomLog logs/access_log "%h %l %u %t \"%r\" %s %b \%{Referer}i\" \"%{User-
          agent}i\""
```

This is the same as the common format with two additions: the URL of the page that pointed to this one and the name of the software the client is using (such as Netscape Navigator).

Custom logs are very handy and flexible; see the description of the syntax in the directive documentation for the usual nitty-gritty details.

Don't forget that each logfile you define uses up a file slot from the fixed number available (see Chapter 2). If you define a lot of virtual hosts (see Chapter 14) and give each of them multiple logfiles, you're likely to run into problems when the server can't open any files because the logfiles use up all the slots.

Tracking Usage with Cookies

"Cookies?" you say. "Cookies?" Yup, cookies. And no, I haven't lost it.

Cookie is a Hackish term for information fed to something to make it perform a particular way. For example, in the UNIX world, the value of various bytes in various locations in a file constitute a cookie that lets the system figure out what the file actually contains. If the first two bytes are the characters #!, for example, UNIX knows that the file is some sort of script, and the remainder of the first line says what kind of script it is.

In the world of the Web, a cookie is a chunk of information the server gives to the client, kind of like a gift certificate with the client's name on it. Whenever the client talks to that server, it presents the gift certificate . . . er, cookie.

This exchange allows clients and servers to remember things about each other, and cookies actually can be used like gift certificates. Suppose the first time you connect to a Web site, it gives you a cookie called Credits that has a value of 100. Every time you use a service the site provides, some amount is subtracted from the cookie value. When the value drops to or below zero, any attempt to use the services gives you a, "Sorry, you gotta pay *real* money to use this now — the free ride is over."

You can use cookies for various other things, but their main purpose in (virtual) life is to maintain some sort of state between the client and the server — for example, the client can come back from a holiday (or maybe a power failure) and pick up where it left off.

Remember the video cameras? One way you can use cookies is to assign a unique identity tag to each client that comes into the site. The cameras (the log files) can keep track of where each client goes in the site, and by analyzing traffic patterns, you can restructure your pages so your clients can easily get to the pages they want.

Don't restructure your pages too often, or the effect may be like those automatic operators who answer the telephone and say, "Our menu has changed! Please listen carefully to all the options . . . ," annoying everyone who calls. If you do restructure your site, set up aliases (see Chapter 4) so people trying to reach pages by their old URLs are redirected to the new ones.

The Apache software includes a module that can assign each client a unique cookie identity, and in combination with the CustomLog directive, the module can record the various locations the holder of the cookie visits — including the order of visitation and where the client last came from.

This module is called mod_usertrack, and the directives it provides are CookieTracking and CookieExpires. The former directive enables the server to assign a tracking cookie to each client, and the latter tells the client how long it should keep the cookie before it becomes stale and should be thrown away.

```
CookieTracking off
CookieExpires interval
```

You can specify the interval in terms of years, months, days, hours, minutes, or seconds (see the specific directive documentation for details). By default, cookie assignment is disabled, and if it's enabled, the cookies go stale as soon as the client exits.

To actually use the cookie for tracking purposes, you need to log it:

```
CustomLog logs/cookie_log "%{cookie}n %r \"%{Referer}i\" %t"
```

This statement records the client's unique ID tag, the request that was made, the page the client was on when it made the request, and the time.

Most client applications that support cookies allow the end user to control the cookie jar. Some simply limit it to "accept cookies, yes or no?" and others actually allow you to grind it much finer and let you see each cookie as it is presented so you can decide if you want it in your cookie jar.

Logging and Advertising

After the commercial sector discovered the market of Internet users and the power and ease of using the Web, the number of electronic storefronts started rocketing upward. Unfortunately, while many people viewed the Web as a gateway to riches, the key that would unlock it wasn't easy to find. Many heads have been scratched as people try to figure out how to use the Web to enhance their business (and, incidentally, make money).

The two methods that seem to be working are

- ✓ **Browse-and-buy or try-and-buy storefronts**: These stores allow you to browse through the merchant's stock, access excerpts (for example, from books or music CDs), search for merchandise based on topics or brand names, and finally select the items you want to buy through an electronic order form.
- ✓ **Advertising**: Merchants use the Web like a set of billboards.

These methods frequently work hand-in-hand; what's the point of having a whizzy browse-and-buy Web site if no one knows about it? Here's where the billboard aspect comes in: Merchants buy space on the pages of high-traffic sites — particularly search engines.

Because the ebb and flow of web interest is so unpredictable, advertisers frequently pay fees based on the effectiveness of the ad — that is, the more people that come to their site as a result of a particular ad on your site, the more they pay you for displaying it. This arrangement can have the effect of giving your advertisers an incentive to try and make your ad more effective, so everybody can win — except possibly the end user. But more about that in a moment.

So how do you figure out how effective your various marketing strategies are? Do you hand each client a survey, including a "How did you find out about us?" question? Not at all. Not only would that approach probably not work — people are generally not interested in filling out surveys — but the information is already available . . . in the web server's transaction log.

One method growing in popularity is the *banner ad* — a rectangular space on a Web page containing some sort of advertising copy, possibly related to the rest of the page's content but also possibly not.

Banner ads are usually graphical in nature, often with animated action to draw attention to themselves. They also usually provide a live link to a web site where you can find more information about whatever-it-is they sell. Because a web site can usually detect where a visitor came from, the merchant with the advertised product usually pays the one with the banner advert something for each "click-through," as it's called.

Those moving banner ads with the cute hopping bunnies, racing snails, and exploding fireworks are fun to watch — the first few times. After that, they get annoying — in at least direct proportion to the amount of motion. Little wiggling things in your peripheral vision are distracting, and people trying to read your content may have their irritation level increased by the distracter factor of your advertiser's ads. You also need to deal with the issue of time and space: Those fancy images and animations take up a lot of space, which means they take a long time to download and they consume space on your clients' disks.

Because web ads are usually graphically oriented, customers can often avoid them by turning off the browser feature for loading or displaying images. Unfortunately, the side effect may be turning off *all* image loading, not just for the sites with the annoying advertisements. More and more of them (the adverts, not the customers) are taking advantage of features of the advancing technology wave front — like Java, JavaScript, and ActiveX — and browsers capable of handling those features usually have an on/off switch for them. But again, it's an all-or-nothing proposition.

As a Webmaster, you should keep customer satisfaction in mind. Think about the things that bother you when you visit other sites and try to avoid repeating them for your visitors. *There are many pet peeves; any discussion of the Web almost automatically includes a Speaker's Corner, complete with people eager to bend your ear about what bothers them. Pay attention, because they're probably representative of some segment of your Web audience.* Alienating people electronically is easier, probably much easier, than in person because the Web creates a sense of distance and anonymity, without any body language to soften the effect.

Social aspects and the privacy issue

One of the big controversies of the day revolves around the potential abuse of web server records. If the server can uniquely identify you out of a crowd of people surging to and from a web site, someone may be able to spot patterns and draw tentative conclusions about your interests. Somewhere in the heart of this debate are Web cookies.

For example, if you visit a virtual shopping mall frequently, but only actually buy things during the first week of every month, someone may come to the conclusion that that week is when you have money to spend and start targeting your mailbox with advertisements during that time. Less intrusive but possibly more obnoxious are the so-called *banner ads,* which take up a chunk of the page like a billboard. If the web server recognizes you and someone notices a pattern in the virtual stores you visit, the content of the banner ads that *you* see may be tailored specifically to you.

Curiously enough, not many people seem to care about the paper mailing lists they get on after buying something with a credit card. They may grumble, but it's accepted as a fact of life. On the other hand, if users buy toys and children's videos and their electronic mailbox and browser page start filling up with the Cyberspace equivalent — targeted advertisements for diapers, deals on baby photographs, and books about saving for college tuition — suddenly they feel like the ad is an invasion of privacy: "They have no right to spy on me!"

Worse yet is the electronic version of selling customer lists: web sites that share visitor activity patterns. Many people get more upset when they start receiving junk e-mails and find out a merchant with whom they've been dealing — in good faith — has made some money from selling their list of customer addresses to someone else. One of the attributes of a web request is usually "where I came from" (called the `referer` [yes, I know it's misspelled, but that's how the Web standards spell it]), so companies that cooperate can actually track you as you surf across the Web.

If you've been on the Web long, you're probably familiar with these topics. If you're becoming a Webmaster, though, you may find yourself growing a brand-new feeling of self-righteousness: "It's my site, and I have a right to know what people are doing there." And merchants will start trying to use *your* web site as a way to reach *their* audience.

It's a very gray area.

Some people rarely click banner ad, and some never at all. Consider adding a way for these people to turn *off* the ad for 30 days at a time — that is, when they visit your site, they won't see the ad, but others will. You're not losing anything, because you won't be getting any revenue from them clicking through, and you will be gaining something: their gratitude.

"Gosh, Ken, how come you got up on a soap-box suddenly? And what does this discussion have to do with logging, anyway?" The answers are:

✔ If you're going to be a Webmaster, I want you to be a successful one. Success in web terms is frequently measured in terms of the popularity of your site — and if you're annoying people, it'll probably limit your success.

✔ This discussion has everything to do with logging, because the temptation is always present (either from yourself or from someone else) to use your web server's tracking abilities to target audiences. That phrase says it in a nutshell — who likes being a target?

Now, if you read through this entire section, give yourself 10 Apache Guru Points. If it made you thoughtful and contemplative about social responsibilities and ethics, give yourself another 20.

Recording Server Errors

Unless you do something silly like let your disks get full or put

```
ErrorLog /dev/null
```

into your configuration files, Apache faithfully records server events and service problems in the error log. You don't need to do anything special to make it happen; in fact, you have to go out of your way to *prevent* it. (If you manage to send your error log into the bit bucket, subtract 15 Apache Guru Points.)

Here's a sample of what the error log contains:

```
[Wed Jul 23 10:04:32 1997] httpd: caught SIGSEGV, attempting to dump core in /
          usr/local/web/apache_1.3.0
[Wed Jul 23 10:08:48 1997] httpd: caught SIGTERM, shutting down
[Wed Jul 23 10:08:48 1997] Server configured — resuming normal operations
[Thu Aug 14 08:26:53 1997] SIGHUP received.  Attempting to restart
[Thu Aug 14 08:28:52 1997] vhash: total hashed = 1, avg chain = 0, #default =
          0, #name-vhost = 13, chain lengths (count x len): 1x1 255x0
[Thu Aug 14 08:28:52 1997] Server configured — resuming normal operations
[Fri Aug 15 10:43:03 1997] httpd: caught SIGTERM, shutting down
[Fri Aug 15 10:47:48 1997] vhash: total hashed = 1, avg chain = 0, #default =
          0, #name-vhost = 13, chain lengths (count x len): 1x1 255x0
[Fri Aug 15 10:47:48 1997] Server configured — resuming normal operations
```

Some error log entries are only informational, others contain real nuggets of information, and some should set the alarm bells ringing. Any line that contains the text, "caught SIGSEGV, attempting to dump core," definitely falls into the last category, because it means that the software blew a gasket. See the "Troubleshooting" appendix for more information.

Apache 1.3 uses a more consistent format across all messages and defines levels of logging as donamed or syslog.

Errors from invoked scripts

Scripts are a way to have some external program, application, or other procedure do things under the Apache server's supervision. Their output stream is used to gather the content the server will send to the client. But what do you do if a script goes bump in the night?

Fear not, Apache handles it (with instructions from you). The ScriptLog directive tells Apache where to put any diagnostic output from scripts; it all gets appended to the specified file. The ScriptLog can be relative to the ServerRoot, but *no* ScriptLog exists by default — you must turn it on if you want it.

```
ScriptLog logs/script_log
```

In the ScriptLog files, the server records anything that the script blithers on about on either the standard output or standard diagnostic streams (stdout and stderr), along with stuff about what was passed to the script and caused its indigestion.

Apache records this information only if the script exits with an error status (that is with an exit status other than zero). If you have a script that's pounding out errors to beat that band, but it exits with a status of 0, Apache will think all the rubbish is normal and will discard it.

Related directives include ScriptLogLength, which sets the maximum size to which the ScriptLog file can grow (note that this is a limit on the entire file, and not a per-script limit), and ScriptLogBuffer, which restricts the amount of request information (for example, URL) that the server includes in the ScriptLog. These directives have the following default values:

```
ScriptLogLength 10385760
ScriptLogBuffer 1024
```

Chapter 12 describes scripts and scriptlike operations in riveting detail. Don't miss it!

Roll Over, Apache

The Apache software keeps the log files open so it can write to them without having to go through a lot of hooey each time (which is important for sites that get hundreds of requests per minute). The log files keep on growing and growing.

Many Webmasters like to keep disk consumption under control by archiving old log files and shrinking the current ones again. The simplest and most reliable way to do this is to

1. **Shut down the Apache server** (`kill -TERM `cat logs/httpd.pid``).

2. **Rename, move, truncate, or otherwise deal with the current log files.**

3. **Restart Apache.**

This has the disadvantages of interrupting any transactions in progress and taking your web server completely off the air for the duration. You may find it an acceptable price for your environment, but many web sites can't afford to pay it.

So what do you do? You use the graceful restart feature (described in Chapter 4) to allow the server to complete current activity cleanly and re-open the log files (that is, accessing or opening new ones). The previous sequence then changes to

1. **Rename the current log files (do not try to move them to another filesystem!).**

2. **Tell Apache to execute a graceful restart** (`kill -USR1 `cat logs/ httpd.pid``).

3. **Wait for all the server children to start using the new logs before doing anything with the old ones.**

Aye, there's the rub — how do you know when it's safe to meddle with the old files? Well, you can use the `lsof` tool to do this:

```
# cd /usr/local/web/apache_1.3.0/logs
# mv access_log access_log.old
# lsof /usr/local/www/server/Apache/logs/access_log.old
```

Repeat the last line at intervals until it doesn't print anything — then you know that the file isn't open by any lingering Apache processes.

You can find the `lsof` tool on the CD-ROM that accompanies this book. See the "About the CD" appendix for more information.

Chapter 6

Authorization and Authentication

● ●

In This Chapter

▶ Authorization, authentication, and the difference between them

▶ The generic ways of proving identity

▶ The specific methods used by the Web

▶ Protection based upon network location and/or user identity

▶ Types of web-user databases supported by Apache

▶ Security-conscious things to do — and not do

● ●

The Web is a very big place, and it's getting bigger all the time as more people start using it for more things. People find the Web so convenient, in fact, that they use it for things they didn't really intend to have a world-wide audience. So, how do you limit access to only those special few? *Authorization* and *authentication* are the answer. They are the equivalent of the peephole in the door, the bouncer asking you "What's the password?" at the door of your favorite club, and locks and bolts on the door of your home. They are *not* the equivalent of the police, vigilantes, Mrs. Grundy down the hall, or your own collection of knives, hand grenades, and pointed sticks.

Both authorization and authentication are long words to say (and write), so I occasionally abbreviate them to just "auth." Which one I mean should be clear from the context. And I refer to the whole process as "auth/auth," meaning "authorization and authentication." Okay?

Do I Know You?

This question is the first thing the server asks a client who is trying to access a protected resource. Down near the bottom of things, where the computers are slinging bits at each other, the server says something like, "I've got a list of who can see this. Who are you, so I can check the list?" (Remember, it's very dark in Cyberspace.) You can rephrase that question as, "May I see your credentials, please?" and do well, because that's what the client's response is called.

Collections of authorization information are commonly used to protect multiple resources (such as an entire directory tree instead of just a single file). The things that a particular authorization database protects are said to be in its *realm*. The server includes the name of the realm in the question it asks the client, so the client can tell which set of credentials to present in case it's been accessing a bunch of different protected areas.

The client usually checks to see if it has accessed things in this realm before, and if it has, it sends the server whatever credentials worked last time. If the client *hasn't* been there before or if the authorization information doesn't work, the client turns to the end user and asks for instructions. (See the next section for more details.)

The first part of this is the *authorization* process: checking to see if the client is authorized to access the resource. If the client isn't on the list, bzzzzt! It doesn't get in. If the client *is* on the list, the server isn't done because all it has checked is that, "You claim to be Neatnik? Okay, Neatnik's on my list." It's time to move on to the second part of the process.

Prove It!

Assuming that the client has provided an identity that the server's records say is valid for the realm, the server needs to take one more step. How does it know the client is who it claims to be? This part of the process is called *authentication*.

The basic types of authentication (proving you're who you claim to be) fall into these categories:

- ✔ What you know
- ✔ What you have
- ✔ What you are

For example, a password falls into the first category: *something* trusts that you are who you claim to be because you know that *person*'s (or *thing*'s) password. Using a key to unlock a door falls into the second group — anyone with that key can open the door. The last group is often considered the most reliable single method, but it's also the most difficult to implement — it requires special procedures like retina scanners, fingerprint verification, DNA analysis, and so on.

Web servers often use a combination of these methods. For example, a *cryptokey* (a device that uses a secret known only to it and the protection system) typically combines the first two methods: You can't use the cryptokey without knowing the password to activate it, and you can't access the resource without using the cryptokey to answer the security system's questions.

Regardless of these fascinating details, the primary authentication mechanism on the web is the userID/password pair. When the server demands credentials before it allows access, the client checks to see if it has any for that realm. If it doesn't, the client pops up a little window on the user's screen that says, "Hey, this server wants a username and password before it will let me in! What should I tell it?" The client then passes along your answer as the credential, and if it works, it stores the credential for future use when accessing that realm.

Authentication credentials aren't supposed to be retained across client sessions, so if you shut down your browser and later try to access a protected resource, you have to go through the "what's the password?" routine all over again. This is good, because it (hopefully) prevents someone from using your system to access stuff as a *virtual* you while the *real* you is actually at lunch.

Basic Authentication

The most common kind of authentication in use on the web is called "basic authentication." Any browser that supports authentication at all should be able to support basic authentication, if nothing else. (Other forms of authentication exist, such as *digest authentication,* but are not commonly used yet.)

Basic authentication works by taking the password you supply, mangling it by following a well-known formula, and sending it along with the username. The security system at the far end compares the mangled value with the value stored with the username in the database, and says "Pass, friend!" only if both match.

The main disadvantage of this is common to all "what you know" implementations: Anyone else who knows the username and password can pretend to be you and get access to the information. Because the username and password are sent across the network as is, anyone who manages to intercept the message can effectively pretend to be you to access that particular realm. Although the probability of anyone intercepting your message, much less caring about it, is incredibly small, you need to be aware of it.

Security-Related Directives

As you may expect for such an important facet of web server operation, a bunch of directives are available for instructing Apache in the particulars of how *you* want things done. The sections that follow cover the more generic security-related directives; each module that adds functionality to Apache adds some directives specific to itself.

The access-control directives apply to the scope in which they occur; if the server finds them outside of any <VirtualHost>, <Directory>, or <Location> container, it considers them the outermost level for all resources on the server.

The Allow, Deny, Order, Require, and Satisfy directives don't directly involve basic authentication; they either use a different authentication method or apply to all auth/auth operations equally.

As of Apache 1.3, the Allow and Deny directives can accept CIDR-based network addresses as well as the more traditional class-based network masks. See the Apache documentation for details — you can find it on the mod_access page.

Allow — *Conditions for entrance*

The syntax of the Allow directive is very simple:

```
Allow from host/network [host/network...]
Allow from env=envariable
```

The first form of this directive works on the "what you are" method — it allows you to restrict access based on the client's hostname or IP address. If the client's hostname or IP address matches any of the values in the list, the server permits access. Using this directive, you can limit access to a set of resources to only people from your own company or department, for example.

If you use the word all for your host/network value, the server treats it specially and interprets it to mean, "Let anyone access this resource."

The second form of the directive is a little more complicated. Many Apache directives can set what are known as *environment variables* (*envariables* for short) according to different conditions. The env=envariable format allows you to use these directives to set (or not set) an envariable according to whatever conditions you like, and then the server allows access by this particular statement if and only if the envariable has been given a value (any value will do).

Don't forget that Apache processes all the directives that apply to a particular location and that aren't disabled because of a missing override. This process means that an unexpected interaction may occur between access directives in different scopes. If you seem to be getting access (or forbidden) when you think you shouldn't, check the directives in all the scopes that apply.

Deny — *"Don't let them in, Sam"*

Like the Allow directive (described in the preceding section), the Apache Deny directive has a simple syntax. In fact, it's identical except for the directive name:

```
Deny from host/network [host/network...]
Deny from env=envariable
```

If the "what you are" test of the client against the hostname or IP address list succeeds (that is, the client's hostname or IP address matches one or more of those same items in the list), the server forbids access to the resource. The way Deny treats envariables is exactly the same as that of Allow; see the previous section for details.

The value all is special, and it means "don't allow anyone to access this stuff."

Remember that the scoping rules may result in a Deny result being overridden!

Order — *Who's on first?*

Apache lets you control who does and who doesn't have access based on network attributes (hostname and IP address). What if you make a mistake and come up with something that meets *both* conditions, like this:

```
Deny from idg.golux.com
Allow from idg.golux.com
```

Would the server allow or forbid the request? (If you can guess the answer, give yourself 20 Apache Guru Points.)

You have control over this, too, with the Order directive, which takes one of the following forms:

```
Order deny,allow
Order allow,deny
Order mutual-failure
```

Hmmm! This directive is an interesting one. If you use the first format, the server processes the Deny directives first and then interprets the Allow directives. The server grants access by default; if the client doesn't match any of the Deny values, the server allows it in.

If you use the second format, the order is reversed: The server checks the Allow directives first and then the Deny ones. If the client doesn't match one of the Allow values, the server locks it out — so, the default condition is no access.

The third format can be construed as being the most specific and restrictive. If you use it, the only way a client is going to get access is if it satisfies both of the following conditions:

✔ It matches a value in at least one Allow list.

✔ It does *not* match any value in any Deny list.

In this case, no default access exists — everything is spelled out.

AuthType — *Authorization method to use*

You use the AuthType directive when you intend to perform access checking based on user-supplied credentials. The format is

```
AuthType type
```

where type is the authentication method. In Apache 1.3, the only supported type is Basic (see the "Basic Authentication," section, earlier in this chapter).

In order to control access by way of user credentials, you must declare an authentication method (AuthType), authorization realm (AuthName), credential requirements (Require), and some set of authorization database directives (that is, AuthUserFile and AuthGroupFile).

AuthName — *Name of the realm*

User credential-based access control on the Web requires labeling the regions to which the credentials apply. To put it another way, if you're gonna use usernames and passwords, you've gotta give a name to the thing they're good for. That way, when the server asks for a password, the client knows which password to send.

You do this with the AuthName directive, which quite simply looks like this:

```
AuthName realmname
```

The client often presents the realmname to the end user when *it* asks for the username and password, so it's a good idea to make this name something informative (like "BusinessPlan" or "PayrollRecords" or "ToonTownBallots").

Require — *Minimum requirements*

The Require directive comes into play when you're using something more than the client's host or network of origin to determine authorization. The server processes it after authentication, so it knows that its information is valid. The Require directive has three formats:

```
Require user username [username...]
Require group groupname [groupname...]
Require valid-user
```

The first format won't allow the client to access resources within the scope unless the authenticated username is in the list.

The second format is slightly more tricky to understand, because it adds another dimension to the check. The authenticated username must be a member of one or more of the groups in the list in order to gain access. (See the "mod_auth — text-based authorization" section in this chapter for more information about groups.)

The third format is the simplest; it means "if the user is authenticated, let him/her in."

If more than one Require directive appears at a particular scope level, the server interprets the situation as requiring *all* of them.

Satisfy — *Mix and match*

If you end up having a scope protected by both Allow/Deny directives *and* Require clauses, the Satisfy directive tells Apache how to interpret the combination. The statement

```
Satisfy All
```

means that the Allow/Deny checks must permit the client in, and the username/password/group rules must also be met. The alternative is

```
Satisfy Any
```

which means that either the network identity-based checks must succeed, or the user identity-based checks need to be okay, or both.

Limiting Access by Method

When a client makes a request of a web server, a number of options exist about how *it* can pass information. (Which options actually work for a particular resource depends on how it's set up.) This is called the *request method*. A number of methods are available, but the most common are called the GET and the POST methods.

The GET method basically tells the resource that it can learn everything it needs to know — any optional arguments or the like — from the URL string. When you type a URL into your browser's location box (or the equivalent), the request will be made using the GET method. Some limitations exist, including a limit to how much information can be passed in the URL.

The POST method is more flexible, but it's also more complicated. When the POST method is used, any additional information is passed separately from the URL. Lots more information can be sent this way, but making something understand POST can be a bit of a chore.

Just because a request is made using the POST method doesn't mean that additional information can't be included in the URL — it can. But a POST request has access to both means of passing stuff to the server, while a GET request has only the URL available for that purpose.

The Apache Web server allows you to impose limits on what methods can be used to access different resources. This is done with a container directive called <Limit> (what a surprise, eh?). The <Limit> directive takes a space-separated list of methods to which the enclosed directives apply:

```
<Directory /usr/local/web/apache_1.3.0>
    <Limit POST>
        Order allow,deny
        Deny from all
    </Limit>
    <Limit GET >
        Order allow,deny
        Allow from all
    </Limit>
</Directory>
<Directory /usr/local/web/apache_1.3.0/cgi-bin>
    <Limit GET POST>
        Order allow,deny
        Allow from all
    </Limit>
</Directory>
```

This prevents the POST method from being used to access any resource except the ones in the /usr/local/web/apache_1.3.0/cgi-bin directory.

It is very common to lose track of what methods are being restricted, and frequently plaintive questions about "why aren't my scripts being restricted?" arise. In many cases the problem is that the scripts now use the POST method, and the server configuration still has a <Limit GET> statement.

The Security Modules

Throughout the history of Apache, users have often wanted functionality that wasn't built into the server. Fortunately, the Apache design readily permits enhancements. Some features that people have wanted to add have been in the area of access control and have been popular enough that The Apache Group has added them to the list of standard modules it ships with the software. The modules described in the following sections fall into this category.

mod_access — *Allow/deny access by origin host*

The mod_access module was stealth-described in the sections about the Allow, Deny, and Order directives. Its sole purpose in cyberlife is to allow you to control access according to the section of the network from which the request came or by checking environment variables you may have set through your own private checks. For more information about this module, see the descriptions of those directives (`Allow`, `Deny`, and `Order`), which appear earlier in this chapter.

mod_auth — *Text-based authorization*

The `mod_auth` module provides for simple and short Basic-style authentication textual databases. Essentially, you declare the name of the file containing the usernames and passwords, and possibly a group file as well.

You *must* specify a full path to the files; you cannot use the ServerRoot-relative shortcut by omitting the leading `/`.

The directives for doing this are

```
AuthUserFile filename
AuthGroupFile filename
AuthAuthoritative Boolean
```

The user file is simply a text file containing usernames and encrypted passwords (mangled with the trap-door function mentioned earlier in "Basic Authentication"), separated by a colon, with one user per line.

Apache looks at only the first two fields of each line, ignoring anything following a second colon (inclusive). This means you can put comments or other information into the same file as the authorization information.

The group file is another text file, with each line consisting of a group name, a colon, and a space-separated list of usernames that are members.

Note that the usernames and groups in this case are solely for purposes of web authentication and don't need to bear any relationship whatsoever to the users in your system's `/etc/passwd` or `/etc/group` files.

The `AuthAuthoritative` directive takes either an `on` or `off` value. If it's set to `off`, it tells Apache that, if the credentials aren't found in the AuthUserfile and AuthGroupFile, other auth/auth modules should be allowed to check *their* databases. If it's set to `on`, the client attempting access must be approved using the values in the AuthUserFile and AuthGroupFile; if the credentials aren't found there, Apache denies access.

Most of the auth/auth modules have a form of the `AuthAuthoritative` directive, although the name is slightly different for each one to keep clear which module is being labeled as having Absolute Power.

mod_auth_anon — *Authorization anonymous FTP-style*

Have you ever used the thing called anonymous FTP? No? Then here's a quick run-down. (If you have, skip ahead a bit or snooze until I catch up to you.)

Anonymous FTP allows you to access files across the network without first having an account set up for you on the system where the files live. A few special usernames are always allowed, and logging into the system's FTP environment puts you into a special directory tree. These accounts don't have specific passwords, but you're supposed to use your e-mail address as the password out of politeness. (Some systems actually check this for validity before they let you in.)

Okay, wake up back there! The mod_auth_anon module lets you set up a similar arrangement to control access to areas of your web server. You specify the list of special usernames and some other attributes, and then you don't have to worry about the additional effort of setting up accounts, dealing with people who have forgotten their passwords, and so on.

Anonymous *username [username...]*

You use this directive to list the usernames that the server recognizes as not needing a specific password. Common ones are anonymous and ftp. You may specify as many usernames as you like on the directive.

Usernames used in authentication are case-sensitive!

Anonymous_Authoritative *Boolean*

This directive mirrors the function of the AuthAuthoritative directive described in the preceding section; if the user credentials supplied don't match any of the usernames listed in the Anonymous directive, the server either returns an error immediately (Anonymous_Authoritative On) or continues checking other auth/auth modules to see if one of *them* recognizes the user.

Anonymous_LogEmail *Boolean*

If this directive is active in the scope of the protected document with a value of on, the password supplied (which is hopefully an e-mail address) will be included in the transaction log.

Anonymous_MustGiveEmail *Boolean*

This directive controls whether the end user has to specify a password at all, or can leave the username blank. A value of `on` means they have to supply something.

```
Anonymous_NoUserID Boolean
```

Like the `Anonymous_MustGiveEmail` directive (only backward), this directive indicates whether the client can leave the username blank. A value of `on` means yes; `off` means the client has to provide some sort of username.

Note that using `Anonymous_NoUserID On` means that not even the usernames you specified in the `Anonymous` directive have to be used.

```
Anonymous_VerifyEmail Boolean
```

The name of this directive is slightly misleading; you may think it actually goes out to the network to make sure the password specified is a real e-mail address. Nope, sorry — it just makes sure that the syntax of the password resembles a valid e-mail address. If the password contains at least one @ character and at least one . (period) character, the server considers it valid.

mod_auth_db *and* mod_auth_dbm — *Database lookup*

The `mod_auth_db` and `mod_auth_dbm` modules allow you to store your authentication information in DBM and Berkeley DB database files. These simple databases are much more efficient than text files (see the "mod_auth — text-based authorization" section, earlier in this chapter), particularly for large numbers of users or groups.

To find out which database library you have available, issue the following commands. If either (or both) command displays a list of topics, you've got that library:

```
% man -k dbopen
% man -k dbm_open
```

The directives for these modules mirror those for the `mod_auth` module, with a slight change to each name:

```
AuthDBUserFile filename
AuthDBMUserFile filename
AuthDBGroupFile filename
AuthDBMGroupFile filename
AuthDBAuthoritative Boolean
AuthDBMAuthoritative Boolean
```

Like the mod_auth directives *(q.v.)*, the filenames you give as arguments to these directives must be specified with absolute paths; they may *not* be specified relative to the ServerRoot.

You can combine the function of the user and group files into a single database by pointing both directives at the same file and making sure the records in the database use the username as the key, the encrypted password as the first colon-delimited field in the value, and the comma-separated list of groups as the second field in the value. For more detailed information, see the online documentation for these modules.

See the "mod_auth — text-based authorization" section for more information about the user and group files used for authentication.

Handling Large User Groups with Databases

The name of this section kinda says it all. If you have lots and lots of users (or lots and lots of groups, or lots and lots of both), using the text-based auth/auth modules is extremely inefficient. The server is going to search through the entire list of entries, one by one, until it either finds a match or runs out of entries. No human would put up with it! (About extra-terrestrials I don't know. . . .)

The answer is to use something better. The database auth/auth modules are much more efficient for medium to large numbers of users or groups, because they can go directly to the entry for a particular set of credentials or tell the server right away if one doesn't exist.

These modules are actually *less* efficient when used with small numbers of entries, because the amount of effort it takes to set up the database routines in order to use them can be more than what is involved in just checking a few lines of text.

One of the drawbacks to using databases is that they can be a little more complicated to manage. You can handle text files with a text editor, but you need some sort of tool to use databases.

You can use the src/support/dbmmanage script to create and manage DB, DBM, NDBM, and GDBM databases (depending on what's installed on your system). It's a Perl script, so you need to have Perl installed on your system. And despite the name of the directory, the dbmmanage script is an unsupported tool.

Security Do's and Don'ts

Some of the following pearls of wisdom come right out of questions and problems reported to The Apache Group and some are just good security sense. Read 'em all and give yourself 5 Apache Guru Points for each one you follow faithfully. (Subtract 2 points when you forget to use one of the rules you said you were going to.)

Do check and prune your databases regularly

Huh? Prune? What is this, a bush? All right, substitute the word of your choice:

- Clean
- Tidy
- Hoover
- Zap

The point is, go through your authentication databases (text or otherwise) at regular intervals to make sure that

- No unauthorized changes have been made.
- No *stale* accounts (that is, for people who don't need them any more) are still present.
- Any accounts that should be there have been added.

Checking and pruning your databases is just good sense and should be part of your regular routine any time someone leaves your organization.

Do enable DNS if using host-based access checking

If you're using `Allow` and `Deny` directives with hostnames instead of IP addresses, you should make sure that Apache is double-checking the names. When Apache gets a request, it should look up the address to turn it into a name — and then look up the name to get one or more addresses. This is needed because name-to-address and address-to-name translations may return different results. Apache already knows the IP address (remember, these are computers talking to each other, so they used the numbers), but it needs to double-check that the number matches the name you used in your server configuration file.

The negative side is that all that research costs resources: time, network bandwidth, and CPU cycles on your web server and the DNS name servers. But better safe than sorry. . . .

You can do this by including the -DMAXIMUM_DNS definition in the EXTRA_CFLAGS line in your src/Configuration file.

Prior to Apache 1.3, you needed to manually enable this with the build-time definition. With Apache 1.3, you can make this behavior the default with a HostNameLookups Double directive. But if all you're concerned about is the matching in your Allow and Deny hostname-based directives, don't worry — Apache 1.3 automatically turns on double-lookups (temporarily) when processing these directives.

Of course, if you use IP addresses in your Allow and Deny directives, this doesn't matter, because it makes the computer happy right away — the computer is comparing numbers (which it prefers) rather than names.

Do protect your log files and back them up

Protecting your log files and backing them up is another example of common sense security. Sooner or later you're probably going to realize that *something* happened a few months ago that you want to look at it. The situation may be as serious as you wanting to check whether someone broke into your system as they claim, or as innocuous as wanting to see just what that error message was and what you did to fix it.

You want to protect your active logs so that nasty people (or computers, or aliens from the Crab Nebula, or even just accidents) don't damage your records. The only account that should be able to modify the log files is the one that the server starts as, and the only accounts that need to be able to read them are the ones that need to perform analysis. No others need apply.

Don't put security files in Webspace

This advice may not be obvious at first blush. What it means is, "Don't put your security-related files anywhere that a URL can be used to reach them." As an example, don't put your user database under your DocumentRoot or in a user's web directory.

If a URL can be constructed that can access a user database, you're asking for trouble. Make sure that all your AuthUserFile and related directives point to locations *away* from the DocumentRoot.

Don't allow local users to access security files

Don't allow people who aren't responsible for managing your web server or its content to fiddle around with the files that control access to it.

Don't use your system `passwd` file for web security

The `mod_auth` module (described earlier in this chapter) allows you to use any text-based authorization file with records that start with `username:password` and follow with a colon and more stuff. This quite accurately describes the default `/etc/passwd` file on many UNIX systems. Therefore, the temptation to use the system auth file for the web auth database is likely to crop up.

Resist temptation, I urge you! This is technically referred to as a Bad Thing, because the controls on the web are nowhere near as stringent as those on your operating system (one hopes, anyway).

`/etc/passwd` **and** `AuthUserfile`:
Not a match made in Heaven

From the Apache FAQ (Frequently Asked Questions) list:

23. Can I use my /etc/passwd file for Web page authentication?

Yes, you can — but it's a very bad idea. Here are some of the reasons why:

✔ The Web technology provides no governors on how often or how rapidly password (authentication failure) retries can be made. Someone can hammer away at your system's root password using the Web, using a dictionary or a similar mass attack, just as fast as the wire and your server can handle the requests. Most operating systems these days include attack detection (such as _n_ failed passwords for the same account within _m_ seconds) and evasion (breaking the connection, disabling the account under attack, disabling all logins from that source, and so on), but the Web does not.

✔ An account under attack isn't notified (unless the server is heavily modified); when the legitimate owner logs in, he/she doesn't receive any messages like "You have 19483 login failures."

✔ Without an exhaustive and error-prone examination of the server logs, you can't tell whether an account has been compromised.

Detecting that an attack has occurred, or is in progress, is fairly obvious, though — if you look at the logs.

✔ Web authentication passwords (at least for `Basic` authentication) generally fly across the wire, and through intermediate proxy systems, in what amounts to plain text. "O'er the net we go/Caching all the way;/O what fun it is to surf/Giving my password away!"

✔ Because HTTP is stateless, information about the authentication is transmitted every time a request is made to the server. Essentially, the client caches it after the first successful access and transmits it without asking for all subsequent requests to the same server.

✔ It's relatively trivial for someone on your system to put up a page that will steal the cached password from a client's cache without them knowing. Can you say "password grabber"?

If you still want to do this in light of these disadvantages, the method is left as an exercise for the reader. It would void your Apache warranty, though, and you would lose all accumulated Apache Guru Points.

Part III
Nuts and Bolts

The 5th Wave®   By Rich Tennant

"GENTLEMEN, I SAY RATHER THAN FIX THE 'BUGS', WE CHANGE THE DOCUMENTATION AND CALL THEM 'FEATURES'."

In this part . . .

Even though it's not strictly necessary for you to understand *how* the Apache Web server works in detail (and it would take another entire book to describe it anyway), sometimes being familiar with at least the basic overview can be useful — such as when you have to consult a guru. Having a basic understanding of how things work can also help you begin diagnosis when you encounter problems.

The chapters in this part are intended to provide just such an overview — or satisfy your need for details if you're morbidly curious. They describe the way new and different pieces can be added to the basic server, and how they all play together when the time comes for them to actually do what they're there for.

Chapter 7

The Modular Approach

In This Chapter

▶ What is a module?

▶ How modules interact with the main server package

▶ The different phases of request processing

▶ Descriptions of the modules included with the Apache kit

▶ Where to find more information about add-on module-based functionality

*O*ne of the most powerful aspects of the Apache Web server software is its extensibility — that is, being able to add features to it. You add functionality to Apache using things called *modules* — which are what this chapter is all about.

Because modules are bits of a program, a lot of the stuff in this chapter may seem unbearably arcane. That's okay; those bits are intended for the programmers who may consider taking on the task of writing a module themselves. If I seem to start babbling in tongues, just blip over the nasty parts — I try to keep them to a minimum.

Callbacks, Handlers, and Hooks

Modules interact with the main part of the Apache server (called the *core*) by asking the server to invoke them at various stages of operation (called *phases*), which is kind of like requesting a bunch of wake-up calls.

When the server enters a phase, it checks the list of modules to see which ones have raised their hands. The server calls each module in turn until it either encounters the end of the list or one of the modules says, "I've got it! I've got it! Don't call anybody else!"

In actual point of fact, the way the server processes each phase is unique to that phase. Some phases keep calling all interested modules regardless of the answers of the ones that have already been called, and some stop the search at the slightest excuse.

A module sets up a schedule of "wake-up calls" by filling in slots in a table. When the server is built, these tables are collected from all the modules, and when the server is running, it scans them and makes the calls accordingly.

Some slots in the table are "ring me when you're doing thus-and-so," and some are pointers to other lists of things (like per-module directives and so on).

The different opportunities that the table provides for module involvement are called *hooks*. The functions (that is, the program stuff) that the server calls in the module to actually involve it are called *handlers*. So if a module takes advantage of the directive hook, the server ends up calling the directive handlers if and when it runs into the directives in the configuration files.

Modules can also declare named "content handlers," which the server invokes when the configuration files instruct it to. The content handlers can do anything from massaging a file corresponding to the URL (that's what `mod_include` does for handling server-side includes) to faking a file and generating the content on the fly (the way the `mod_info` and `mod_status` modules do). Regardless of whence it comes, a content handler is responsible for sending the document contents to the client.

As of Apache 1.3 (and earlier versions, as well), no way exists to pass document content from handler to handler the way UNIX handles piped output. After a content handler has been invoked, that's it. (Enhancing this is on the to-do list for The Apache Group.)

Configuration versus request context

Situations when the server would permit modules to participate in a function fall into two categories:

- ✔ Request context
- ✔ Not request context

Request context means that the server is processing a request from the client *and is ringing the module's doorbell because things have progressed to a point where the module said it wanted to be involved.* The alternative is . . . well, there *isn't* a request active. This is the environment when the server asks the module to parse its directives, set up its configuration for directory and server situations, child-process start-up and shutdown, and so on.

If you intend to write any modules of your own (you mad thing, you!), you need to keep these two environments in mind.

If you're not going to get into writing Apache modules and are just curious, it's simplest to say that some of the module's pieces are called on almost every request, some are called only once, and some are called somewhere in between (though more on the latter side).

Saying that a particular phase executes in "request context" or "not in request context" sounds pretty stupid, so I'm going to call the latter "environment context." Environment context is an arbitrary name, but module functions called under those circumstances are being asked to modify the environment (such as processing directives or setting up per-location information); so, the term is reasonable. Sort of.

With a couple of exceptions, the server calls the "environment context" callbacks every time it is configured — or reconfigured if it was already running. For this latter reason, these callbacks need to be careful so that they don't leave their own feet lying around for themselves to step on later. The exceptions to this are the `child_init` and `child_exit` callbacks, which the server calls exactly once per module per process.

Modules usually keep track of where they are by creating one or more housekeeping records and handing them to the server to store. When a hook is invoked, it asks the server for the housekeeping information it stored earlier and thus keeps from having to say "Huh?" This information is quite handy, because it allows the server to attach the per-request bookkeeping stuff to the request and throw it all away when the request is finished. This is so integral to module operation, in fact, that the first few slots in the table have to do with creating the housekeeping stuff and dealing with inheritance issues from progressively narrower scopes. Basically two different conditions exist in which modules may want to squirrel away private information like this: when dealing with global Web server environments (for example, the server named `WWW.Widgets.Com` and the server named `Internal .Widgets.Com`) and when dealing with a Web location such as a filesystem subdirectory (for example, `/` versus `/warehouse/inventory`). The software handles these two conditions separately, but no reason exists why a module can't do the same functions under each condition — and some do. (More modules just ignore one or the other of the conditions by not putting an entry in the appropriate table slot in the `module` structure.)

The 18 hooks to modular bliss

The main way a module registers itself to the server is at build-time through a table called the `module` structure. (Where *do* they get these names?) The different slots in the table have names, and the following list describes the slots. If they are hooks for module callbacks, I also note the context (request or environment) in which the server calls them. I list these hooks in the order in which they appear in the `module` table.

If you're going to get into writing your own modules (or modifying existing ones), remember this: the server completely processes each phase before it advances to the next one. The server invokes *all* modules that hook into a particular phase, which means that a module handler that gets called *after* yours may modify what yours did. Be warned!

- ✔ `init` — **Module initialization**
  Environment context
  This hook points to a routine in the module that is called when the server is started and is being configured. It gives the module a chance to do any one-time setup necessary. It gets called after the default server invokes the `create_dir_config` and `create_server_config` hooks.

- ✔ `create_dir_config` — **Per-directory setup**
  Environment context
  The server invokes this hook whenever it is traversing a directory to which one or more of the module's directives apply. That is, if the server config files or an `.htaccess` file in the directory contain any of the module's directives, the server calls this hook so the module can do any directory-specific configuration it needs. This hook also gets called during the initial server setup to process the main server's default directory configuration. This hook is invoked before the directive-processing phase so it can set up any data structures that phase needs. The hook gives the created structure to the server, which saves it for later.

- ✔ `merge_dir_config` — **Per-directory inheritance management**
  Environment context
  A subdirectory's `.htaccess` file may contain directives that conflict with the ones in parent directories or the server config files. The module decides how a module's directives should interact with ancestral versions of themselves. When the server encounters this type of situation, it calls this hook with the configurations for both the ancestor and the subdirectory and expects the module's `merge_dir_config` routine to create a combination that does the right thing and to give it back to the server. The resulting configuration is available to subsequent hooks invoked in request context.

- ✔ `create_server_config` — **Per-server setup**
  Environment context
  The server calls this hook (if defined) when it sets up the environment for the default server or a virtual-host server (see Chapter 14 for more information about virtual hosts). This hook is pretty much the same as the `create_dir_config` hook described before, except that it sets up server-wide information rather than directory-specific stuff.

✔ merge_server_config — **Per-server inheritance management**
Environment context
This hook is just like the merge_dir_config hook, except it's given
two module-specific server housekeeping records to merge.

✔ cmds — **Pointer to table of module-specific directives**
Environment context
This pointer doesn't point to a function but rather to a list of directives
the module is declaring (such as IndexOptions and IndexFileName).
The definitions include the number of arguments, where the directive is
allowed to appear, the function that the server calls when it sees the
directive in a configuration file, and (if allowed in .htaccess files) the
override that must be enabled for it to be processed. The server scans
all these tables when processing configuration files and makes the per-
module callbacks as appropriate. Beyond that, don't worry about the
details unless you're going to get into module writing yourself.

✔ handlers — **Pointer to table of content-generating routines**
Environment context
This slot holds a pointer to a list of content handlers. Each handler in
the list has a name and a function; for example, when the server sees
that a resource is supposed to be dealt with by the handler named foo,
it looks through all the handlers until it finds foo and then calls the
associated function.

✔ translate_handler — **URL parsing/translating**
Request context
If a module puts the address of a handler in this slot, the server ends
up calling the routine when it's time to try and map a Web name into a
file name. The module must figure out if it should and actually do it.
Because the translation phase hasn't been completed yet (we're doing
it!), the server hasn't been able to determine an appropriate directory
tree to check for .htaccess files, so no scoped per-dir configuration is
available to this callback. Many modules declare this hook but actually
do work only under certain limited circumstances (such as translating
an ASCII Web name into EBCDIC. Just kidding!)

✔ check_user_id — **Check user authentication**
Request context
This hook checks that any credentials supplied by the client are
actually valid. It doesn't pass judgment on whether the client is allowed
to access the resource, just whether the username and password are in
the authorization database and are valid.

✔ auth_checker — **Check user authorization**
Request context
Here's where the module gets a chance to see if the client is allowed to
access the resource it requested. Any credentials available at this point
have been double-checked and are valid (or else the server wouldn't
have gotten here), so this callback looks at whether the user is on "The
List" of users who are allowed to access the document.

✔ `access_checker` — **"Who You Are" authorization checking**
Request context
The server invokes this callback fairly early in the request processing. This callback's job is to check to see if the client making the request is permitted to access the resource. Because the checks are based on the characteristics of the client (such as its IP address), the server doesn't need to check any user credentials.

✔ `type_checker` — **Determine resource type**
Request context
When the server invokes this callback, all the "is the client allowed" decisions have already been made. This callback's job is to actually look at the resource and figure out what it is. Is it an image? Is it text? What language is it written in? Is it stored in a "funny" way? After the callback has asked (and answered) any of these questions that are appropriate, it lets the server know the results.

Most modules won't need to declare this hook, because a very comprehensive handling of these issues is already available through standard modules included with Apache.

✔ `fixer_upper` — **Final fixes to request**
Request context
Here's where a module gets a chance to do any last-minute things to the request before the server sends the document back to the client. When the server invokes this callback, everything else involved in getting the resource ready to ship has been done.

✔ `logger` — **Module-specific request logging**
Request context
This hook gives modules the chance to do any per-request logging they may fancy. Mostly they don't, because the standard logging modules are quite comprehensive; but the hook is available just in case. When the server invokes this callback, the request is all done — the document has been sent to the client.

✔ `header_parser` — **Request header field processing**
Request context
The server invokes the `header_parser` callbacks quite early in the request processing sequence (after the `post_read_request` and `translate_handler` callbacks). These callbacks have the job of doing anything appropriate for this stage of the game, such as checking the request header fields for specific values (whence this phase got its name).

✔ `child_init` — **Process initialization**
Environment context
If a module declares this callback, the server calls it exactly once, as far as the module is concerned. The server invokes these callbacks when it creates a new child process; the callbacks are responsible for doing any one-time procedures that need that kind of context (such as opening files, linking to a database, or allocating other resources).

✔ child_exit — **Process rundown**
Environment context
Companion to the child_init callback, the server invokes this
callback when a child process is preparing to retire or die (either of old
age or because of a server shutdown or restart). This callback gives the
module a chance to undo anything it may have done during other
callbacks.

✔ post_read_request — **Request pre-processing**
Request context
This callback is the very first one the server activates as soon it
receives a request and reads the headers. This callback gives the
module a chance to make decisions based on the raw request before
any modifications have been made.

Did you notice anything odd about these? No? How about the order in which
I list them? That's right, they seem to start out in a logical order (environment, setup, request) and then begin losing the thread. This is because as
new phases are added, you need to add them at the end of the structure so
you don't have to edit existing modules to make them work.

The child_init, child_exit and post_read_request slots and phases
are new for Apache 1.3. They didn't exist in earlier versions.

Standard Modules Included with Apache

The Apache project takes advantage of the extensible nature of the software
package. The package ships with over 30 modules that provide various bits
of functionality — which you don't have to include in your server if you
don't want to. Many of these modules have made their way into the standard distribution just by being extremely popular, having started life as
home-grown modules developed by Apache users.

The list of standard modules, with brief descriptions, follows. Most of these
modules are built into the server by default, but you can change that setup
if you rebuild the software (see Chapter 9). In all cases, you should refer to
the online documentation for each module to get the details.

Miscellaneous modules

I tried to group the various standard Apache modules into different categories based on what they do, but some unique modules would have been in a
group by themselves. Rather than do that, I put them all here so they can
have some company.

mod_example

The source kit includes this module as a sort of template or demonstration of module operations and the phase interactions. This module isn't built into the server by default (you need to manually edit your Configuration file to get it) because it doesn't really add any value to a web server — it's just in the kit for people who want to look at a simple module to see how to write one themselves.

The example module provides a hook for every single phase of module operation. Probably the most useful hook is the *example-handler* content handler, which (when activated) displays information about the actual calling sequence. If the example module is linked into your server, you can give it a try by adding something like the following statement to your server config files:

```
<Location /example>
    SetHandler example-handler
</Location>
```

You can try the following URL to see a demonstration of this, provided the system it references is up and running:

```
http://Apache.Golux.Com/example
```

Because the example module implements stubs for *all* the phases and hooks, you shouldn't just copy it to another file and start changing it. In particular, it includes some auth/auth stubs that can interfere with normal server operation. If you use mod_example.c as a basis for your own module, one of the first things you should do is comment out each entry in the module structure and insert a NULL, and only insert each hook as you're ready. For example:

```
    :
NULL /*example_init*/,       /* module initializer */
NULL /*example_dir_create*/, /* per-dir config creater */
    :
```

mod_unique_id

The mod_unique_id module has a very simple role in life. The server calls it during the post_read_request phase of request processing, and the module uses the time and client information to generate a text string that uniquely identifies the request. This unique identification string is available to other modules and to the resource itself through the environment variable name UNIQUE_ID.

This unique identification string can be useful for correlating information, such as requests that get logged in multiple server log files.

This module is new with Apache 1.3 and has no counterparts in earlier versions or the Module Registry.

Real-time processing modules

All the following modules enable the Apache Web server to react to requests in real-time somehow, based on what's happening at the time of the request, rather than just passing back a static file that's always the same.

mod_actions

Sometimes you can make a sweeping decision about how the server should handle files, such as "All Macintosh StuffIt archives must be sent in BinHex format," or maybe "All files of MIME type `text/biff` will be converted to uppercase before being sent."

If you want to make these types of decisions, you can do so with the `mod_actions` module. This module allows you to associate a CGI script (for more on CGI scripts see the "`mod_cgi`" section in this chapter and also Chapter 12) with a particular MIME type. When the server determines that a particular file is of that MIME type, it invokes the script and sends the client whatever output the script produces (which must be communicated to the server using the CGI mechanism). The following example would result in the server calling the script `/cgi-bin/upcase` to process any file ending in `.biff`:

```
AddType text/biff .biff
Action text/biff /cgi-bin/upcase
```

mod_autoindex

This module allows the Apache server to generate and provide directory listings to clients. Because the server generates the listing at the time of the request, the listing reflects the actual state of the directory. You can control how complicated the display is (such as whether file sizes should be displayed or descriptions). Figure 7-1 shows the fanciest display available.

The functionality provided by `mod_autoindex` in Apache 1.3 was bundled together with other features in the `mod_dir` module in earlier versions.

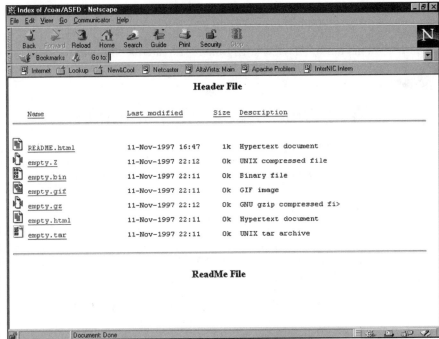

Figure 7-1:
Sample
page
generated
by mod_
autoindex.

mod_cgi

This module arguably gives you the most flexibility and control over document content, because it allows you to use whatever methods you like (shell scripts, C programs, Perl scripts, and so on) to generate the content yourself.

The mod_cgi module implements the server side of the Common Gateway Interface (CGI) specification. It creates the environment variables that are used to pass the script information about the request and the client making it, and the module verifies that the responses from the script comply with its side of the specification.

Although CGI is extremely flexible and supported on many other servers than just Apache, it does have the disadvantage of requiring a lot of overhead, making it slow as well as a resource hog. Although other more efficient methods are available (mod_perl, PHP, FastCGI), they don't have the same transportability as CGI scripts.

mod_imap

One whizzy feature of the early days of the graphical web was the ability to click on a picture and have your browser take you to some other web location. Where you clicked on in the picture controlled where you went.

This feature is called *image mapping,* and the web pictures that you set up to do it are called *active maps.* When image mapping first came out, you needed a separate program to do the translation. To avoid some of the overhead, the Apache server itself includes the same functionality in the form of this module, `mod_imap`.

This is actually called *server-side* image mapping, because the server does the translation from the click on point in the image to the web location. This means that the client and the server have to exchange a couple more messages. The alternative is something called *client-side* image mapping. In client-side image mapping, the web page that contains the picture also includes information about how the browser can translate coordinates to web locations. This feature is a fairly recent addition, though, and not all web browsers can handle the hidden instructions.

mod_include

The `mod_include` module allows you to include documents within other documents, which can include other documents, which can . . . well, you get the idea.

"Why?" you may ask. Consider a web site that has a sort of common "look and feel," with the same color scheme, border, pictures across the top, and so on. That setup starts getting more and more expensive to maintain as you add more and more pages — and what if you want to change it later? Egads!

By putting your common elements into a single file or set of files and having all the other web pages include them, you essentially solve the problem. Want to add a page? Fine — just make sure you include the common files. Want to change your site's presentation? Great! Just edit the included files.

(If you didn't wonder why someone would want to do this, give yourself 5 Apache Guru Points. If your eyes positively lit up at the idea, give yourself another 10.)

The `mod_include` module even lets you (under circumstances controlled by you, the Webmaster) include the output from CGI scripts (see the "`mod_cgi`" section in this chapter), which can make your pages really neat.

Security modules

"The needs of the many are great and varied." (No, I'm not quoting anyone — I just made it up.) With tens of millions of people accessing the Web and over a million web servers providing them with information, inevitably some circumstances exist under which not all people should have access to all the pages.

How do you control this? If you're using the Apache Web server software, you use one or more of the available access control modules. The following sections describe the modules that the server kit provides; other modules are available from the Apache Module Registry (see the "Apache Module Registry" section, later in this chapter). For more information about controlling access to your site, check out Chapter 6.

mod_access

This module allows you to control who can get to see your pages according to the "who you are" identification model (that is, you can limit *who* gets to see *what* based on where they're coming from in the network).

This module handles those `Allow from...` configuration directives you see elsewhere in this book.

mod_auth

The `mod_auth` module allows you to validate client credentials against usernames and passwords stored in a text file, by using a format similar to the UNIX system's `/etc/passwd` file. Note that this module performs authentication based on the "what you know" model — namely, does the user know the password for the account he/she is trying to use?

mod_auth_anon

This module is used in the process of verifying user credentials on a per-request basis, and it uses the "what you know" model. The username that the client supplies must be one that the Webmaster has declared is available, but unlike the case with other auth/auth modules, the server doesn't check the password. Rather, almost *any* password is valid — very much like anonymous FTP systems, which allow you to log in using special usernames such as `ftp` or `anonymous`.

Due to the lack of detail control and authentication, I recommend that you not use this mechanism to protect really sensitive stuff.

mod_auth_db *and* mod_auth_dbm

These modules are identical in function and virtually identical in implementation. Like the `mod_auth module`, these modules check the username and password supplied (as part of the user credentials) against a list of usernames and passwords defined by you (the Webmaster). The only functional difference is that these modules look up the username in a DB or DBM database (hence the module names) rather than searching a text file.

mod_auth_msql

If you like simplicity, I recommend the mod_auth_db and mod_auth_dbm modules. They're simple, easy to use, and easy to maintain. Of course, they aren't good for much besides looking up usernames and passwords, so. . . .

If you want to store your authorization information in a database with other information (such as an address for each individual), you may want to consider using this module. It allows you to use the freeware mSQL database system to manage your access control. (You can find out more about this module, and the mSQL package, from the online Apache documentation that comes with the server kit. Check out htdocs/manual/modmod_auth_msql. html.)

mod_digest

This module provides a different kind of authentication defined by the web standards: *Digest authentication.* However, no one in the web marketplace seems to be supporting this authentication type yet; all authentication is being done using Basic authentication. (See Chapter 6 for more information about authentication.)

Translators

While most web addresses (URLs) actually refer to files, directory structures and file-naming conventions are subject to change, particularly as staffs turn over, product and project lines change, and companies are bought or spun off from one another. How is a conscientious Webmaster supposed to keep the URLs the same if the underlying environment is continually going through upheaval?

I suppose you could use symbolic links in the filesystem . . . except that after a while your web-document directories would be stitched together like Frankenstein's monster, and pulling a single stitch could make the whole thing unravel. (Yuck. I'll try to find better analogies.)

Because the Web is a virtual thing, why not make the relationships between web names and file names virtual things too? What a concept. So elegant. So far reaching. So implemented in Apache.

The modules that I describe in the following sections specialize and delight in translating web addresses into filesystem names — or other things.

mod_alias

The mod_alias module allows you to set up a simple translation, or *alias,* between a web name and a filesystem location. Through the judicious use of Alias directives, you can keep the web name space looking untroubled and serene, even though files and directories are shuffling around on your system. For example,

```
Alias /marketing /usr/users/depts/mktg
```

would cause Apache to turn a web request for

```
http://yourhost/marketing/forecast/july-chart.jpg
```

into a reference to the file

```
/usr/users/depts/mktg/forecast/july-chart.jpg
```

If your organization decides to rename the marketing department, you can keep the URL working by changing the directive to

```
Alias /marketing /usr/users/rad/WildBlueSky-proposals
```

The mod_alias module also provides the ScriptAlias directive, which labels an entire directory of files as CGI scripts — and incidentally aliases them into the web name space.

mod_dir

This module allows you to designate what file names the server should look for if a request specifies a directory but not an individual file. In other words, this module lets you tell the server what to send if the user doesn't ask for a resource by name.

This is a common feature of web servers; default filenames are often set to names like index.html, welcome.html, or default.html. This module allows you, as Webmaster, to set this default. In fact, you can even specify a list of file names, and the server looks for the file names in order until it finds one or the list runs out.

This module translates the URL

```
http://yourhost/somedir/
```

into a request for the file

```
DocumentRoot/somedir/index.html
```

In Apache 1.2 and earlier, this module also included the functionality of what is now mod_autoindex. As of Apache 1.3, these two have been separated. See the "mod_autoindex" section in this chapter for more information.

mod_mime

The mod_mime module is one of the most important modules in the Apache repertoire. I highly recommend that you not try to disable it or build your server without it.

"Why is mod_mime so important?" Well, I'll tell ya. One key ingredient of how the various pieces of the Web work together is the concept of *content types*. When your browser receives a file, content types are what tells it to start a PostScript viewer, or start a word processor, or just display the text on the screen. Content types are how the server knows which script to run for mod_actions. The mod_mime module is intimately involved in helping the server figure out what a file's content type is.

The mod_mime module is also involved in dealing with language issues, such as defining how the server can recognize a document written in Slovakian, so it can tell the client.

And finally, mod_mime tells the server when to use content handlers, like the ones provided by mod_info and mod_status.

mod_mime_magic

The mod_mime_magic module is based on the UNIX file command, which can take a look at the first few characters of a file and tell what kind of file it is (such as a text file, a script, an application, an image file, and so on). By using this module, you can help your server automatically sense what sort of content type it should use for any particular file.

While this module can make your life easier, it does come at a cost: The server has to open all the files and examine them, a process it would not do otherwise. This can have an appreciable performance impact on a busy server.

The mod_mime_magic module is new for Apache 1.3. No version of it is available for earlier versions.

mod_negotiation

Webmasters may find this module very useful when they have to provide content in the increasingly multilingual web. This module can determine the preferred languages of the client, look through the documents available with names matching the request, and select the version that best fits the client's preferences.

When done properly, this is called *content negotiation,* hence the module's name. The mod_negotiation module can also have the server respond with the only file matching the request under certain circumstances. That is, if the DocumentRoot directory contains only the file index.html, the following request would result in it being returned — even though the .html wasn't specified:

```
http://yourhost/index
```

Properly speaking, this isn't negotiation — but the mod_negotiation module takes care of this case anyway.

In order for this module to work, the MultiViews option must be enabled for the directory in which the file exists.

mod_rewrite

The mod_rewrite module is the master of name translation. You can use it to translate almost *anything into almost anything else* — including translating requests into *redirects* to other web servers (that is, telling the client, "I don't have it — but that other system does!").

The mod_rewrite module is incredibly powerful, and it's easy to make mistakes that can lead to baffling problems. Most of the other translation features of the standard Apache modules can be done with some form or another of mod_rewrite directives, but it's like the cockpit of a fighter jet: The documentation is 15 pages long, which is significant when you realize that most modules only require two or three pages.

mod_userdir

When people first started publishing web documents out of their own directories, they couldn't do it directly unless their directory was under the DocumentRoot.

In UNIX-land, you can use a shorthand way to express "joe's home directory": ~joe. Apache and other web servers allow the Webmaster (you) to define a similar shorthand form meaning "joe's Web directory." This module, mod_userdir, lets you do this.

Using directives, you can tell the Apache server to turn URL references like /~joe/foo into a reference to the actual file /usr/users/joe/public_html/foo. Or you can disable user directory translation altogether, which results in clients getting a "resource not found" error. By enabling userdir translation, you're essentially adding your users' directories (or subdirectories thereof) to your server's DocumentRoot web-name space.

As of Apache 1.3, you can selectively disable specific usernames, making them ineligible for directory translation. I highly recommend that you take advantage of this feature to disable the superuser account, `root`.

Decision-makers

Due to the bewildering number of phases involved in processing a request, some information determined at the early stages may be used to control what happens during the later stages. That's exactly what the modules in this section do.

mod_setenvif

Most of the inter-module communication between early and later phases of processing is done by either modifying the request itself (such as translating the URL name into a file name) or by fiddling with environment variables. Some modules allow you to modify their behavior with envariables, and `mod_setenvif` is one of the ways you can fiddle with them.

This module allows you to set (or unset) environment variables according to different aspects of the request. For example, you can set an envariable to one value if the client is running Netscape Navigator and to another value if it's using Microsoft Internet Explorer. (This is determined from the `User-agent` request header field.) Similarly, you can set an envariable depending on whether the request was made through a referral or by the user typing in the URL (or using a bookmark).

Later in the processing, other modules can make decisions based on the envariable settings (if they support it). For example, the following statement would deny access to anyone using the SpamMaster browser:

```
SetEnvIfNoCase User-Agent "SpamMaster" spammer
Order deny,allow
Deny from env=spammer
```

In Apache 1.3, the `mod_setenvif` module replaces `mod_browser`. The `BrowserMatch*` directives from `mod_browser` have been absorbed into `mod_setenvif`, which provides other, and still more powerful, functionality.

Protocol assists

Remember that the *protocol* — the language — that Web servers and clients use to speak to each other is called HTTP: the *HyperText Transfer Protocol*. HTTP has a lot of features; some are in widespread use and others are not. Although the Apache Web server software is in full compliance with the HTTP/1.1 standard, it doesn't implement all the features (the standard notes that many of them are optional). Several modules, written by various people, help the core Apache server take advantage of some of these features. In the following sections, I briefly discuss the modules that are part of the standard package.

mod_asis

This module allows you to label certain files as containing the complete response to a client's request — including those portions normally managed directly by the server. A file processed by this module needs to include the HTTP response header fields as part of it.

mod_cern_meta

The mod_cern_meta module is so named because it incorporates some of the features of the CERN web server (developed where the Web was born) into Apache. It allows you additional control over what HTTP headers are sent out with certain files.

mod_expires

One important attribute of a web document is its expiration. Servers and clients use this to keep from tying up the network by doing some date arithmetic on this and other date aspects of the resource.

Unfortunately, UNIX doesn't have the concept of an expiration date on files, and it's unclear whether it should be applied to web documents in any case. Here's where mod_expires comes in. This module allows you to specify expiration times for all the files in a scope. You can also set the expiration time for files based on their names (for example, you may never change your images and therefore set the expiration date of everything ending with .gif to be the year 3000). And finally, you can set the expiration to be a time relative to the time of the request — that is, you can ask the server to "tell the client the expiration date of this file is ten minutes after it asked for it." This can help keep user information current.

mod_headers

This module allows you to modify the HTTP response header fields to the content sent back to the client. You can add new headers, add values to ones already in place, or remove them from the response.

This capability can be useful if you have a need to apply special headers to all the documents from a particular directory, as in the following example:

```
Header set "X-Author" "John Q Public, Esq."
```

mod_proxy

The word *proxy* means "acting as a substitute or authorized agent," which is exactly what the proxy module does.

The proxy module gets called into play when your server is set up to act as an intermediary between clients and other servers. Clients make their requests to the proxy server, and the proxy server then passes them along to the actual server with the resource. The proxy passes any responses back to the client. This module makes very good sense when you need to control access to Web resources (either in one direction or the other), because it gives you a single point to manage.

One of the most important jobs the proxy can perform is to *cache* requests. When it receives answers from other servers in response to client requests it passed along, it can record the original requests *and* the answer. When the same client or a different one subsequently hands it a request, the proxy can check to see if

✔ It has handled this request before.

✔ It (still) has a copy of the response stored.

✔ The copy isn't stale (that is, it's at least as new as the version on the server from whence the proxy got the copy).

If all of these conditions are met, the proxy can respond to the client immediately with the local copy, rather than having to make a fresh copy over the network.

The proxy module also allows the Webmaster to impose limits on what systems can be accessed and the like.

While the rest of the Apache server is fully compliant with the HTTP/1.1 specification (and has been since Version 1.2), as of Apache 1.3 the proxy module hasn't caught up. For the time being, Apache is still only an HTTP/1.0 proxy. The Apache Group intends to bring this module into HTTP/1.1 compliance in the future.

Management tools

Some modules have been written to help Apache Webmasters manage their servers. In the following sections, I briefly describe the modules that are supplied as part of the standard server kit.

mod_dld

The "dld" portion of this module's name says it all: "*Dynamic LoaDing.*" This module allows you to control which modules and functionality are part of your server at run-time, rather than having to rebuild the server each time you want to add or remove something.

Unfortunately, this module is one case when Apache's very flexibility works against it. Not all UNIX operating systems are identical (now, *there's* a surprise!), and the degree to which they can — or can't — support the dynamic loading functionality varies from one to the next. Because the tools needed to build a new Apache server image are commonly and freely available, most people just do that when they want to change the functionality rather than worry about doing it at run time.

Although the Apache Web server source kit still supplies it, this module is rarely used and may be removed from future distributions.

mod_env

The mod_env module gives you the ability to unconditionally set or unset environment variables that documents use (especially active variables, like CGI scripts). You can also explicitly export an envariable value from the server's own environment to the document's.

Some of the server's envariables are automatically passed to the document environment, but others are not. The mod_env's PassEnv directive allows you to change this default behavior.

mod_info

This module can be quite handy when you want to know how your server thinks it's been set up (as opposed to how *you* think it's set up). Accessed as a content handler through a web browser, this module tells the viewer information such as:

- ✔ The version of the Apache software being used
- ✔ The user and group the server is running as
- ✔ The ServerRoot

✔ The name of the main configuration file used to start the server

✔ The *complete* contents of the server configuration files (if they're readable by the user the server is running as)

The previous bullets represent only a partial list, but you can probably see how useful this module can be. Figure 7-2 shows part of the output from this module.

Because this module can disclose all sorts of information about your server that you may prefer to keep private, I highly recommend that you enable it only within a restricted context, such as in the following example (assume for the purposes of this example that your desktop system's name is WebMan.WidgetMaster.Com):

```
<Location /server-info>
    SetHandler server-info
    Order allow,deny
    Allow from WebMan.WidgetMaster.Com
</Location>
```

This example would only allow someone using your desktop system to see your server's configuration.

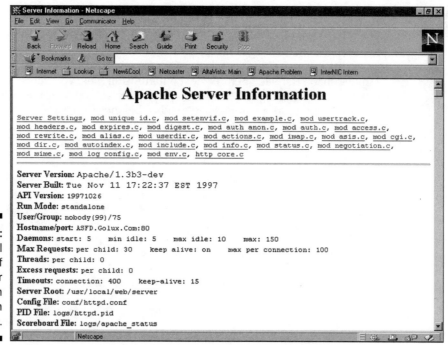

Figure 7-2:
Partial
display of
server
configuration
from
`mod_info`.

mod_log_agent

This module allows you to keep track of the kinds of software that people (or computers) are using to access your web site. One piece of information that's commonly included with the request is a header field called *User-Agent,* which is set to a string intended to identify the source. You can use this module to determine how many people are using your server with Netscape Navigator, Microsoft Internet Explorer, or the terminal-only Lynx browsers, for example.

Because you can trace some access problems to problems in the actual browser making the request, logging this information can be useful to develop workarounds for such bugs. Also, you can estimate from this information how many people use graphics-capable browsers and then increase or decrease your usage of images as a result.

The functionality provided by this module has been largely superseded by the mod_log_config module. I recommend that you use the latter, because I don't know how much longer this one will be included with Apache (although it should always be available from other sources such as the Apache Module Registry).

mod_log_config

The "config" in the mod_log_config module's name refers to it being configurable, not to anything having to do with server configuration. This module pretty much lets you log whatever you want into however many files you want. You define what you want to have logged by using directives in the server configuration files.

Depending on its placement in the configuration files, you can set up the directives to log information only for a specific virtual host (see Chapter 14) or for the server as a whole. Who needs a balanced diet when they have mod_log_config to do everything for them?

mod_log_referer

When a client follows a link from one page to another, the first page is called the *referer.* (Yes, I know it looks like it's misspelled — but that's how it appears in the Internet standards.) The URL of the referring page is one of the bits of information available to the server when it receives a request. The mod_log_referer module allows you to keep a record of which pages were used as jumping-off places to reach yours.

An entry in the mod_log_referer log file looks like this:

```
url -> document
```

where *url* is the page that made the referral, and *document* is the page to which it referred (actually, the local URI of the page). An example of the `mod_referer` log format looks like this:

```
http://Apache.Golux.Com/ -> /pix/apache_pb.gif
```

The functionality provided by this module has been largely superseded by the `mod_log_config` module. I recommend that you use the latter, because I don't know how much longer this one will be included with Apache (although it should always be available from other sources such as the Apache Module Registry).

mod_status

Like the `mod_info` module *(q.v.)*, the `mod_status` module allows you to use a web browser to check on what your server's up to. While `mod_info` displays the server configuration, this module shows what the server is actually doing. Figure 7-3 shows a sample excerpt from its page.

To get the most from this module, you need to build your server with the -DSTATUS definition set in the AUX_CFLAGS line in your Configuration file. (See Chapter 9 for more information.)

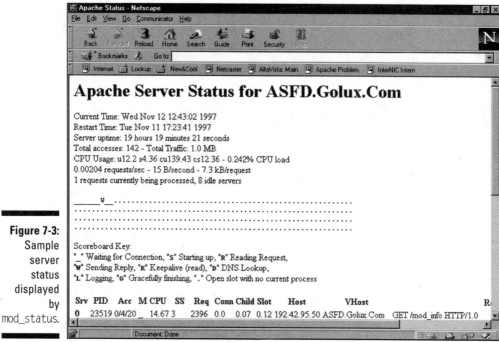

Figure 7-3: Sample server status displayed by mod_status.

The figure shows a Netscape browser window titled "Apache Status - Netscape" displaying:

Apache Server Status for ASFD.Golux.Com

Current Time: Wed Nov 12 12:43:02 1997
Restart Time: Tue Nov 11 17:23:41 1997
Server uptime: 19 hours 19 minutes 21 seconds
Total accesses: 142 - Total Traffic: 1.0 MB
CPU Usage: u12.2 s4.36 cu139.43 cs12.36 - 0.242% CPU load
0.00204 requests/sec - 15 B/second - 7.3 kB/request
1 requests currently being processed, 8 idle servers

Scoreboard Key:
"_" Waiting for Connection, "S" Starting up, "R" Reading Request,
"W" Sending Reply, "K" Keepalive (read), "D" DNS Lookup,
"L" Logging, "G" Gracefully finishing, "." Open slot with no current process

Srv	PID	Acc	M	CPU	SS	Req	Conn	Child	Slot	Host	VHost	R
0	23519	0/4/20	_	14.67	3	2396	0.0	0.07	0.12	192.42.95.50	ASFD.Golux.Com	GET /mod_info HTTP/1.0

Because this module can disclose all sorts of information about your server that you may prefer to keep private, I highly recommend that you enable it only within a restricted context such as in the following example (assume for the purposes of this example that your desktop system's name is WebMan.WidgetMaster.Com):

```
<Location /server-status>
    SetHandler server-status
    Order allow,deny
    Allow from WebMan.WidgetMaster.Com
</Location>
```

This example would only allow someone using your desktop system to see your server's configuration.

mod_usertrack

This module allows you to use cookies to track how clients move around in your web site. By using this module's directives, you can instruct the Apache server to include a Set-Cookie header field in its response to the request; subsequent requests to your server from the same client should present the cookie each time, and you can have the pages logged through the configurable logging capabilities.

Because of the controversy about cookie usage, this module may not be completely reliable — clients may choose not to accept cookies, which means they won't be presented for logging. See Chapter 5 for more information.

The Apache Module Registry

The preceding sections described the modules that are considered stable and common enough to be included with the Apache server kit itself. But they're not the whole story — oh, no! Many of the hundreds of thousands of Apache users on Earth (our polls of other planets are not yet complete) have seen fit to enhance the functionality included in the Apache kit.

The Apache Module Registry was created to be a master list of bits of contributed functionality. It is maintained on the Web (where else?), and you can find it at the following URL:

```
http://www.zyzzyva.com/module_registry/
```

Chapter 8

Life Cycle of a Client Request

. . . .

In This Chapter

▶ The steps the server takes in accepting a client request

▶ How the server determines which directives apply

▶ Details about the different stages of request processing

▶ Which standard modules get called for which phases

. . . .

*W*eb servers are in the business of handling client requests — meaning clients ask for something, and the server is supposed to give it to them. Like a clerk in a store, the server tends to be more familiar with the stock than the client is, giving it the opportunity (if well-trained) to figure out what the customers want — even if the customers don't know themselves.

The Apache server receives its training from the modules compiled into it and the directives in the configuration files. This helps it make educated guesses about what a client really wants when it asks for "the thingamajig with the whatchamacallit."

Chapter 7 describes the idea of Apache modules in terms of what they can do; this chapter describes the order in which they do it.

Pages versus Requests

Right up front I need to make something clear: *Requests and pages are not the same thing.* A page, what the end user sees, may actually be composed of multiple documents (text, pictures, and so on) — and each of these documents needs to be requested from the server as a unique resource. So, a page may result in *several* requests.

The server doesn't know what the client does with all the resources it's requesting, so it can't make any assumptions. From the server's perspective, each and every request is unique and completely unrelated to all other requests — even requests from the same client made within a few milliseconds of each other.

First, the Autopsy! (Huh?)

You perform an autopsy when you want to determine the cause of death. You take the body apart to find out what went wrong with it. In the case of a web server, you need to take the body apart *first*, so you can figure out what to do with the request. (All right, so it's a lame metaphor. C'mon, work with me here.)

When the Apache server receives a request, it knows some information about the request without even looking — a side effect of it saying, "Yes, I'll take this call." These include

- ✔ The IP address of the client
- ✔ The IP address used to contact the server (a single server can handle multiple IP addresses; see Chapter 14)
- ✔ The port number requested

As part of taking the call (that is, accepting the request), Apache can also do the equivalent of caller ID — namely, finding out the username of the person using the client. Like the telephone equivalent, both ends need to cooperate; you need to tell the server to try and collect this information (by turning the IdentityCheck directive on), and the client needs to be able to provide it (by running an RFC1413 identd daemon). Because this requires a lot of extra network activity, and not very many clients implement the daemon, this is usually only worthwhile in small well-known networks.

After taking the call, Apache can derive some additional information from this data — such as the client's hostname (if it can be translated from the address) and possibly the username of the actual user on the client (if the client is running the right software).

Next, the core part of the server reads the request headers. The request header may be just a single text line, or it may be a few lines followed by a blank one. With this information, Apache is ready to start making determinations about what to do with the request.

In order to figure out how to handle the request, the server has to determine which set of server configurations apply to it. Apache takes three available pieces of the information and determines which virtual server configuration matches the request (for a simple single-server environment, this question is answered as soon as it's asked); the data involved are

- ✔ The IP address the request came in on
- ✔ The port the client made the request to
- ✔ The value of the Host request header field (if present)

From knowing these three pieces of information, the server can settle on a server scope to use and start walking the request through the process.

Getting a Second Opinion (And a Third, and a Fourth . . .)

After Apache determines the server scope that applies to the request, it begins involving the modules, phase by phase.

Chapter 7 describes the different request processing phases.

During request processing, each module callback uses its return value to let the server know the results of whatever the callback did. The possible return values are success ("Whatever it was, I did it"), decline ("I don't want to have anything to do with this!"), complete ("I've done all that was needed; don't bother calling anyone else"), or an error ("This request is bogus, and here's why").

Phase processing works in one of two ways, depending on the phase:

- ✔ The server keeps invoking all the modules that declared a callback for the phase until it's done them all.
- ✔ The server stops calling modules as soon as one returns the "I did it" status.

(The server always stops phase processing if a callback returns an error.) For some phases, all modules get a crack at the request — and for other phases, only one module is allowed to fiddle with it.

For example, the phase that lets modules log information falls into the former category — all the modules get a chance to log the activity. On the other hand, the phase that does the translation of the Web name to a file name stops calling modules as soon as one says it can translate the name. This makes sense; otherwise, another translator may try to change the translated name rather than the original one or ignore the first translation altogether.

The post_read_request *phase*

The first stage of processing is the post_read_request phase. The server looks at the list of modules who raised their hands for this and calls them one by one. These modules get a chance to look at the raw request before anything changes it. They're not supposed to actually *touch* it, just examine it and say "hmmm."

When the server is processing the request through this phase, it invokes all module callbacks unless one returns an error.

Modules that hook into this phase are: mod_example, mod_setenvif, and mod_unique_id.

The translate_handler *phase*

After the post_read_request phase comes the translate_handler phase, when the server gives any interested modules the chance to turn the Web name into a file name — or do whatever other type of translation they like. At this point, the modules are allowed to fiddle with the request in order to indicate what the translation should be.

The server stops calling modules for this phase as soon as one says it has handled the task (or returns an error). This prevents subsequent modules from wiping out the changes made by earlier ones; on the other hand, it keeps the later ones (which may have something to contribute) from being called at all.

If all modules decline to take up the gauntlet for this phase, the core server does a simple translation against the DocumentRoot.

After the server knows the translation (if one exists) from the Web name to a file name, it can look through its records and determine the scope — and therefore figure out which directives apply for later phases.

Modules that hook into this phase are: mod_alias, mod_example, mod_proxy, mod_rewrite, and mod_userdir.

The header_parse *phase*

After the translation phase comes the header_parse phase. Module callbacks invoked at this point should do whatever things they need to do based on the request headers and the translated file name.

When the server is processing the request through this phase, it invokes all the module callbacks unless one returns an error.

The module that hooks into this phase is mod_example.

The access_checker *phase*

This processing phase allows modules to determine whether the client should be allowed access based on "who they are" tests made against *the information available at this point*. Note that no user credentials are available, so all the tests need to be made against things like the client's IP address and so on.

When the server is processing the request through this phase, it invokes all the module callbacks unless one returns an error. This phase usually either runs to completion, or else it ends because a module determines that the client should be kicked out and returns an "access forbidden" error.

Modules that hook into this phase are: mod_access and mod_example.

The check_user_id *phase*

This phase comes after the check_access phase, which means that the request passed any access tests based on the client itself. At this point, modules have the opportunity to actually look up the user's credentials in whatever database they use or return "hey, I need some credentials here!" if the client didn't supply any.

The server stops calling modules for this phase as soon as one says it has handled the task (or returns an error). At least one module *must* raise its hand and tell the server it did the work; otherwise the server aborts the request and reports an error to the client.

If no user credentials are available but some are needed, the core server routines abort the request and demand the credentials. The client probably then asks the user for the login information and submits the credentials with a *new* request. If a module gets called during this phase, it's assured of having something to verify.

Each module called at this point has three choices:

- ✔ If the credentials are valid (the password matches, and so on), return the "it's cool, I did it" result back to the main server.
- ✔ If the username is valid but the password isn't, return a "try again" error to the server, which closes this request and starts the process over again.
- ✔ If the username isn't in the module's authorization database, either
  - Return the "login failed" error to the main server if we're the Final Authority, or
  - Return the "I don't want to deal with this" status so the server can give another module a shot at the request.

Modules that hook into this phase are: `mod_auth`, `mod_auth_anon`, `mod_auth_db`, `mod_auth_dbm`, `mod_auth_msql`, `mod_digest`, and `mod_example`.

The `auth_checker` *phase*

After the user credentials have been validated in the `check_user_id` phase, Apache moves on to the next stage: figuring out whether the user — validated or not — has access to the requested resource. Apache does this by comparing the credentials against the settings of the `Require` directives for the scope of the document.

The server stops calling modules for this phase as soon as one says it has handled the task (or returns an error). At least one module *must* accept responsibility for checking out the user, or the server aborts the request and returns an error message to the client.

Modules that hook into this phase are: `mod_auth`, `mod_auth_anon`, `mod_auth_db`, `mod_auth_dbm`, `mod_auth_msql`, `mod_digest`, and `mod_example`.

The Diagnosis: What to Do?

After the patient has been dissected and his/her insurance verified . . . er, that is, the server has concluded that the client has made a valid request and should be given what it wants, Apache goes on to tie everything up with neat little bows. This is done so that the client not only knows that it got what it asked for, but also knows *what* it got.

The `type_checker` *phase*

This phase begins after the server and its modules agree that the client is allowed to access the document in question. Modules that the server calls for this phase have the opportunity to figure out the type of data the document contains, so the server can tell the client, and the client can do something semi-intelligent with the document (like display it or save it to disk).

The server stops calling modules for this phase as soon as one says it has handled the task (or returns an error). Perfectly sensible; you wouldn't want one module to label the document as a text file, and another one to say, "Naah, it's a picture."

Modules that hook into this phase are: `mod_example`, `mod_mime`, `mod_mime_magic`, `mod_negotiation`, and `mod_rewrite`.

The `fixer_upper` *phase*

As you may expect, this phase is a sort of last-chance opportunity for modules to look at the request and possibly make changes right before we actually start fulfilling it. Because the next thing that happens is that the server starts processing the document, any environmental changes should be made here (such as setting environment variables for scripts, and so on).

When the server is processing the request through this phase, it invokes all the module callbacks unless one returns an error. This gives all the participating modules a chance to fix up their own stuff.

Modules that hook into this phase are: `mod_alias`, `mod_cern_meta`, `mod_env`, `mod_example`, `mod_expires`, `mod_proxy`, `mod_rewrite`, and `mod_usertrack`.

And the Answer Is . . .

If you've read this riveting chapter from the beginning, you know that the server is teetering on the verge of actually sending a response back to the client. Give yourself 10 Apache Guru Points for sticking it out.

If you jumped right to this section because of its name, you need to know that the last several sections describe what the server does from the point it receives a request until it's ready to respond. The following section takes the server over the top.

The content-handler *phase*

This phase is the Big Cheese of the request processing activity. At this point, the client *finally* gets what it's been waiting for.

Somewhere along the way, the server recorded the name of the handler that actually has the burden of shipping the response back to the client. The handler may execute external routines in real-time (such as CGI scripts), or it may manufacture stuff out of whole cloth at run-time (like the status and info modules), or it may perform some sort of transformation on existing files (such as parse them for server-side includes), or it may be the default handler (which just copies the translated file to the client).

Regardless of what the handler does, the server runs exactly one content handler, and that content handler had better do it all — because no one is backing it up.

Modules that hook into this phase are: mod_action, mod_asis, mod_autoindex, mod_cgi, mod_dir, mod_example, mod_imap, mod_includes, mod_info, mod_negotiation, mod_proxy, mod_rewrite, and mod_status.

Making Notes about the Operation

After running the content handler (see the preceding section), the server has basically fulfilled its duty: it served something. The server is happy because it completed the request, and the client is happy because it got what it asked for. (The users may or may not be happy, depending on whether what they asked for is what they actually wanted.)

All that's left for the server to do at this point is housekeeping. . . .

The logger *phase*

After handling the request, the server looks around to see if any modules want to take notes about what happened. It does this even if the request was denied or had some sort of problem, so *that* fact can be recorded if desired.

When the server is processing the request through this phase, it invokes all the module callbacks unless one returns an error. Changes to the request information at this point are meaningless, because it's already been satisfied.

Part IV
Going Further

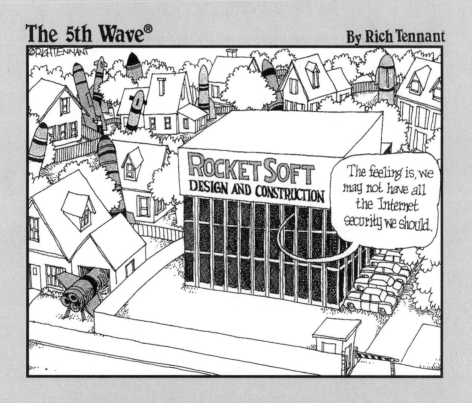

In this part . . .

With over two dozen feature modules and more than a gross of configuration directives, there's an awful lot you can do with your Apache Web server. Lots of those pieces are pretty basic, and take care of themselves automatically if the server is left as it's distributed. If you want to take advantage of more and more of the capabilities, though, they're ready and waiting for you.

The chapters that follow describe how to rebuild your server, including and activating (or *un*-including) the selection of modules *you* want. They describe how to see what your server is doing, and how to make it do what you want. In short, they provide flagstones along the path from a basic configuration to a really sophisticated web site.

Chapter 9
[Re]compiling the Software

● ●

In This Chapter

▶ Creating the `Configuration` file

▶ Setting the build rules and switches

▶ Including modules in your server

▶ Installing your server

▶ Making the Apache Web server build on your system

● ●

*T*he Apache Web server package includes all the source files needed to not only rebuild it, but modify it to your heart's content — which is one of the reasons it's so popular. Users have the freedom to twiddle, tweak, and wrench the software until it does what they want it to do.

You're reading this chapter because you want to know how to rebuild the server, right? Either you lost or damaged a binary, or you never got one, or you want to change how the server behaves, or. . . . Well, *why* doesn't matter. This chapter is here to help you with the *how* part. Read on!

Configuring the Configuration File

The `src/Configuration` file is the key to building the Apache executable. You use it to define what modules you want to include, what build flags to use, and so on.

To get started, you need to actually create your `Configuration` file. Well, you can actually copy it from another file provided for this purpose:

```
% cd /usr/local/web/apache/src
% cp Configuration.tmpl Configuration
```

You only need to do this once! You're going to be modifying this file, so repeatedly copying the template over it would mean remaking all your changes.

To make sure your `Configuration` file results in a server that has the features you want, you need to make changes (or at least verify the current settings) in several places, which I describe in the following sections.

Throughout the `Configuration` file, octothorpes (#) at the beginning of lines indicate comments.

Selecting build-time configuration options

The `Configure` script, which uses the `Configuration` file, takes care of all the things needed to make Apache run properly on your operating system. Making sure Apache builds properly is *your* responsibility, however. You do this by making sure that the right tools are used to make the image.

The first three settings to verify are near the top of the `Configuration` file:

```
#CC=
#OPTIM=-O2
#RANLIB=
```

These settings tell `Configure` what it should use for the C compiler, the compiler optimization flags, and the command used to make program libraries random-access. If you don't set any values for these, the build scripts use the `cc` command, an optimization level of `O2` if the compiler is actually `gcc`, and the `ranlib` command to reformat program libraries.

If these settings don't match your environment, uncomment the lines (remove the # at the beginning) and set the values to the correct ones.

Version 1.3 no longer assumes any optimization setting. If you want your server compiled with any specific level of optimization, you must modify this line.

Extra! Extra!

Near the top of the `Configuration` file are four lines that let you control the compiler and linking flags used during the build of Apache. The `Configure` script comes up with settings that make the default server compile (they don't show up in these lines), but you may need to make some additions — for example, if you're including a module of your own that needs some external libraries or something of the sort.

The four *extra-setting* lines appear in the `Configuration` file as:

```
EXTRA_CFLAGS=
EXTRA_LDFLAGS=
EXTRA_LIBS=
EXTRA_INCLUDES=
```

The names of these lines are probably self-explanatory to a bit-twiddling code-whacker, but here are the details anyway:

✔ EXTRA_CFLAGS

This line is probably the extra-list you modify most, because here you can enable a lot of server double-checking through the use of definitions, such as -DBIG_SECURITY_HOLE. (I describe these in the next section.) You also use this line to add any special keywords or flags that you want your C compiler to use.

✔ EXTRA_LDFLAGS

This line is for including things that should be made known to your system's loader. You probably won't ever have to modify this line; most changes relating to the load phase of image building go into the EXTRA_LIBS line instead (see the next bullet).

✔ EXTRA_LIBS

If your system, or some of the modules you're including, require additional libraries beyond the ones the Configure script selected for you, this line is the place to name them. The documentation for some external modules (that is, modules that aren't included with the Apache kit) may tell you about things you need to add here. You can usually tell you need to put something in this definition when the make fails with errors like that ones that follow:

```
ld:
Unresolved:
frexp
*** Exit 1
Stop.
```

If this happens, consult the Apache problem report database and tell it to search for "ld:" — most of these occurrences are known problems with known solutions.

✔ EXTRA_INCLUDES

If you're using modules that require additional header files to compile correctly, you need to list them here. Use the usual C compilation flag, as in the following example:

```
EXTRA_INCLUDES=-I/usr/local/lib/include
```

If you want to tailor how the build happens, you need to do it through these definitions. In fact, the src/Makefile invokes make in several different subdirectories, and these definitions get passed to each subordinate make to ensure that everything builds with the same set of switches. The Configure script automatically creates the Makefiles in each of the subdirectories, too — which means that any changes you make *outside* of these definitions are probably lost.

But don't worry — these definitions have proven sufficient to build Apache on dozens of different platforms; why should yours be any different?

Compile-time server switches

You can use switches to change some of the default behaviors of the Apache server or work around some operating system shortcomings. To use one of the following switches, precede the switch with -D (for example, -DFD_SETSIZE=12) and add it to the EXTRA_CFLAGS= line in your Configuration file. Make sure a space separates the switch from any other settings on the line.

✔ BIG_SECURITY_HOLE

Ordinarily, the Apache server won't permit you to run it as the root user during normal operation. (You need to be root in order to start it, but only for a moment until the server changes its identity.) If you try, the server displays horrible warnings about the incredibly dangerous thing you're trying to do and won't start. In order to do it anyway, you have to add -DBIG_SECURITY_HOLE to the compilation flags so the server knows you really mean it.

This flag and behavior are new for Apache 1.3. In earlier versions the server didn't complain if you configured it with a User root directive.

✔ DEFAULT_PATH

This switch allows you to define the default setting of the PATH environment variable for things invoked by the server (such as CGI scripts). The default setting is /bin:/usr/bin:/usr/ucb:/usr/bsd:/usr/local/bin, but you can override it by setting it in your EXTRA_CFLAGS line as follows:

```
EXTRA_CFLAGS=-DDEFAULT_PATH=\"/usr/sbin\"
```

✔ FD_SETSIZE

The ability to open files is very important to Apache, and it gets upset when it needs to open a file and can't. Different operating systems have different limits on how many open files they permit at once. Some systems permit you to increase this limit at build-time, which is where the FD_SETSIZE switch comes in. However, this is an area of medium-depth magic, so I suggest not using this switch unless an expert advises you to do so.

✔ HARD_SERVER_LIMIT

The setting of this switch defines the absolute maximum number of server children that are allowed. Under no circumstances would more children be spawned; any incoming requests that would ordinarily cause more to be created just have to wait. This keeps a runaway server from using up all your process slots. The default value is 256, but you can change it with something like the following example:

```
EXTRA_CFLAGS=-DHARD_SERVER_LIMIT=128
```

✔ `HIGH_SLACK_LINE`, `LOW_SLACK_LINE`, `NO_SLACK`
This set of switches that affects Apache and files (see `FD_SETSIZE`) also deals with an external-to-Apache issue. Some routines that Apache uses, either from the operating system or some other application, occasionally require a file descriptor number at the extreme low end. If Apaches uses up all these numbers for its log files, those routines won't work very well. As a result, Apache tries to allocate all of its file descriptors above a certain number. This doesn't work in all environments, but the defaults that the build process determines should be correct for your environment. In other words, don't fiddle with this without expert guidance.

✔ `MINIMAL_DNS`, `MAXIMUM_DNS`
When Apache receives a request, it knows only the client's IP address, not its hostname. In order to translate the number to a name, Apache goes through the normal routine of looking it up, which usually involves sending a question off to a Domain Name System (DNS) server. Because this process adds still more network traffic, you may not want it if your web server is in great demand. However, if you still want detailed records, you may find it more convenient for the logs to contain the name rather than the address. And if you use names rather than addresses in your Apache access-control directives, you want the server to be really sure the name is right before granting access.

In Apache 1.2, the `MINIMAL_DNS` switch told the server to do address-to-name translation only when it had to. `MAXIMUM_DNS` told it to be really paranoid, and the server would translate the address to a name, and then translate that name back to an address, just to make sure the addresses and names were synchronized. (Sorry, but sometimes the forward-and-back translations reveal discrepancies. The world's an imperfect place.) The default behaviour was to do just one translation.

Apache 1.3 no longer uses the `MINIMAL_DNS` and `MAXIMUM_DNS` flags. Instead, it replaces them with the `HostNameLookups Off` and `HostNameLookups Double` directives, respectively. The server still performs an address-to-name-to-address lookup when needed for auth/auth processing, regardless of the setting, so using the `Off` setting can reduce your network overhead and increase your server's response time. Of course a cost is involved — all the logging is done with the IP address, and not the FQDN, of the client system.

✔ `NO_LINGCLOSE`, `USE_SO_LINGER`
These switches affect how the Apache server deals with network connections under certain conditions. These switches are pretty Deep Magic, so you shouldn't even *think* about using them unless a certified Apache Guru tells you to.

✔ SERVER_SUBVERSION

One item that Apache always sends back as part of the response headers is its version number. (You see this string in the error log when the server starts up.) If you made changes to the base package and want to label responses as being specifically from your modified server, you can define this switch. The version information sent to clients would then be the base Apache version followed by a space and then the value of this switch. It's a string, so you need to set it using something like this:

```
EXTRA_CFLAGS=-DSERVER_SUBVERSION=\"WM2000\"
```

✔ SHELL_PATH

This switch allows you to define the path to the shell that should be used instead of /bin/sh for scripts and things executed by the server. Twiddle this switch with care.

✔ SUEXEC_BIN

This switch defines the path to the suexec image, which is used to run scripts as users other than that being used by the server. The online suexec documentation describes how to use this switch.

✔ USE_FLOCK_SERIALIZED_ACCEPT, USE_FCNTL_SERIALIZED_ACCEPT, USE_USLOCK_SERIALIZED_ACCEPT, SAFE_UNSERIALIZED_ACCEPT

These switches instruct Apache to use a different way to coordinate between the children processes. The build procedure normally knows the best selection for your platform, so you shouldn't use any of these switches unless an experts suggest that you do.

✔ XBITHACK

By adding -DXBITHACK to your compiler flags, you make the server act as if an XBitHack Full directive exists in all scopes that don't use the directive at all. (The XBitHack controls whether the server uses the file's last modification date as the value for a Last-Modified response header. For more information, see the mod_includes online documentation.)

The rules of the game

After you chose the compiler, optimization level, and compilation switches, the next section you need to modify in the Configuration file is the rules. Hey, how about that? You get to change the rules!

But seriously. . . . The Configuration file includes a set of rule statements that conceal some much more complex activity. Here are the rules:

```
Rule STATUS=yes
Rule SOCKS4=no
Rule IRIXNIS=no
```

```
Rule IRIXN32=yes (only in Apache 1.3)
Rule PARANOID=no (only in Apache 1.3)
Rule WANTHSREGEX=default
```

The possible settings for these rules are *yes, no,* and *default.* If you set a rule to *yes,* you want the corresponding functionality regardless. If you set it to *no,* you don't want it under any circumstances. And if you set it to *default,* you're telling the build scripts to use the value that they've been pre-programmed to know is best for your environment.

✔ STATUS

The mod_status module (see Chapter 7) can reveal wonderful information about how your server is operating. If you set the STATUS rule to *yes,* it (the module, not the server) unfolds its full capabilities, at the price of an extremely modest performance degradation imposed by the data collection. If you turn on this rule without including mod_status in the configuration, you still incur the performance hit, but you won't be able to see why.

✔ SOCKS4

Set this rule to *yes* if you want to use the proxy module with your SOCKS4 library and environment.

✔ IRIXNIS

You should set this rule to *yes* if you're using SGI's IRIX operating system *and* NIS (Network Information System). If you set it to *yes* and neither of those conditions apply, it doesn't do anything.

✔ IRIXN32

Set this to *yes* if you want Apache built with the SGI IRIX n32 libraries (if it can find them). If your IRIX system doesn't have the libraries, or you don't set this rule to *yes,* Apache is built with the o32 libraries.

✔ PARANOID

When Configure is run to construct all the appropriate pieces for the actual building of the server, it checks each of the modules included in the configuration to see if they have any module-specific commands they want executed. If Configure finds any of these commands, and the PARANOID rule is set to *no,* it merely displays a brief note on your screen that it did something for the module. If the rule is set to *yes,* Configure tells you what it actually did.

This feature of module configuration is new with Apache 1.3.

✔ WANTHSREGEX

This rule controls whether the Apache server is built with your system's regular-expression library or with the H Spencer library included in the Apache kit. The meaning of the value is fairly obvious: *yes* means use Apache's library instead of the system's, *no* means contrariwise, and *default* means that Configure should make a decision based on its built-in rules about what systems have reasonable libraries.

Modulating the Module List

The last part of the `Configuration` file is the list of what modules you want to have built into your server.

The `AddModule` instruction in the `Configure` file is new for Apache 1.3. It is more flexible than the `Module` instruction used in previous versions because you need to specify only the file name, not the file and the (sometimes nonintuitive) module structure name.

Adding or removing any of the standard modules is very simple: You just uncomment or recomment (put a # at the beginning of the line) the `AddModule` lines for the modules you want to affect.

Don't forget — if you alter the `Configuration` file, you need to re-run the `Configure` script before the change takes effect!

If you want to add modules other than the ones that came with the server (the standard module set), read the documentation that comes with them. Bear in mind that the documentation is probably going to be referring to adding the modules to an Apache 1.2 source tree, so don't follow it blindly. Read the next paragraph first, and be sure to read the "Order is important!" section in this chapter before you feel you're done.

Here's the simplest way to add a new module to Apache 1.3:

1. **Put the source files (any** `.c` **and** `.h` **files) into the** `src/modules/extra` **directory. (If you have any** `.h` **files, you may need to add** `-I.` **to your** `EXTRA_CFLAGS` **line so the module can find them.)**

2. **Add an** `AddModule modules/extra/mod_mumble.o` **line to your** `src/Configuration` **file.**

3. **Run** `./Configure` **and** *make* **and see what happens.**

The `Configure` script constructs a `src/modules/extra/Makefile` to build the module, and it's included in the build. That's the theory, anyway.

This is fine if the module consists of only a single `mod_mumble.c` file and some header files. If it's more complicated and comes with its own `Makefile`, you need to do something like this instead:

1. **Create a** `src/modules/mumble` **directory for the module and put all the files (including its** `Makefile`**) in it. (If you have any** `.h` **files, you may need to add** `-I.` **to your** `EXTRA_CFLAGS` **line so the module can find them.)**

2. **Add an** `AddModule modules/mumble/mod_mumble.o` **line to your** `src/Configuration` **file.**

3. **Run** ./Configure **and** make **to verify that the module is built correctly.**

Anything that goes wrong with this process is probably due to some missing elements in the EXTRA_CFLAGS or EXTRA_LIBS definition lines in Configuration.

Order is important!

The order in which you list the AddModule statements in the Configuration file can be very important, because it controls the order in which Apache calls the modules. Apache invokes the modules in a last-in, first-out manner, which means you need to list the most important modules *last*.

This setup is particularly important for those modules that Apache calls during phases that stop after the first "I did it" response, such as the auth/auth processing. If you list the auth/auth modules in the wrong order, and the modules don't follow the rules exactly about when they should pass the torch, Apache unexpectedly ignores some of them.

The comments in the Configuration file give some limited guidance about module placement.

Hidden dependencies

The order of the standard modules in the Configuration.tmpl file (which is what you should be building your Configuration file) has been very carefully determined, with a full awareness of how the different modules interact. Some interactions may not be obvious, but they're included notwithstanding. The moral? Don't change the order of the standard modules!

Of course, if you add you own modules, you need to determine the best placement yourself. No one can give you a precise cookbook for this decision, unfortunately. Be very observant of changes in the server's behavior; these changes can indicate that your module(s) are listed too far down the file and are getting in the way of the operation of one of the standard modules. Contrariwise, if the server doesn't seem to be calling your module properly, the module may be getting blocked, and you may need to make it more important by moving it closer to the bottom of the file.

These interaction problems are not common. Most "the *mumble* module won't run properly" issues are actually due to some sort of configuration problem with the directives.

Doing the Build

After you set up your `Configuration` file the way you want it, you need to put it into action. You feed this file into the `Configure` script and then use the generated scripts to actually build the server as in the following example:

```
% cd /usr/local/web/apache/src
% ./Configure
Using config file: Configuration
 + configured for DEC OSF/1 platform
 + Adding selected modules
    o status_module uses ConfigStart/End:
 + doing sanity check on compiler and options
Creating Makefile in support
Creating Makefile in ap
Creating Makefile in regex
Creating Makefile in main
Creating Makefile in os/unix
Creating Makefile in modules/standard
% make
```

Several dozen lines of output follow as the server image is built. Hopefully it will all come out without any errors, in which case: Congratulations! You've just built the Apache Web server! Give yourself 20 Apache Guru points.

If you get errors, check out the "Troubleshooting" appendix, and then come back.

Installing the New Server

Although some operating systems allow you to copy files on top of others that are in use, it's not a very good idea. In order to start the new server, you're going to need to shut down any existing one anyway, so you may as well do it *before* you copy the image.

1. **Shift into the ServerRoot directory:**

   ```
   # cd /usr/local/web/apache
   ```

2. **Shut down any existing server:**

   ```
   # kill -TERM `cat logs/httpd.pid`
   ```

3. **Wait for the server to completely shut down; repeat the following command every couple of seconds until it doesn't list anything:**

   ```
   # ps -aux | grep httpd | grep -v grep
   ```

You may need to use different flags on your ps command; check your system's documentation. If it's not clear, try different combinations while the server is running until you find one that lists all the server processes — and then adjust the preceding command appropriately.

Possibly, although unlikely, your server may not shut down when you ask it to. If the server processes are showing no signs of going away, you need to kill each one with a `-KILL` signal.

4. **Copy the new server image into place and make it runnable:**

```
# cp src/httpd .
# chmod 755 httpd
```

5. **Start the new server using the new image:**

```
# ./httpd -d `pwd`
```

At this point, your server should be up and running again, using the newly-built image.

Porting to a New Platform

Oh, dear. You're here because the Apache `Configure` script doesn't know about your system, or you're reading this book from cover to cover, or your NQ (nerd quotient) is high and you're 'satiably curious.

Well, whatever. This section describes what you need to do to make Apache recognize your system. If you port Apache to a new platform, you earn 200 Apache Guru Points.

If your compiler chokes, or doesn't understand ANSI C, and you're sure the problem is the compiler and not your system configuration, I recommend obtaining, installing, and retrying the build with GNU C. The GNU C compiler, `gcc`, is free and widely used, and you can download it off the Internet from the GNU FTP site (directory `/pub/gnu` at `prep.ai.mit.edu`). You can privately install GNU C in your account, and you don't need to set it up for the entire system — an important consideration when installing freeware.

The Apache Group tries to make the compilation process as generic as possible, meaning that it *should* work with almost any compiler. However, a couple of compilers may have difficulty.

If you're using the C compiler that comes bundled with the HP-UX operating system, it is *not* ANSI-compliant and you won't be able to build Apache with it. Don't even bother to try. You need to either pay to get the Hewlett-Packard ANSI-compliant compiler or use something like GNU C.

If you try to run `src/Configure` and you get a display similar to Figure 9-1, you *know* you need to do a port — Apache doesn't recognize your system.

```
% ./Configure
Using config file: Configuration
Creating Makefile
./helpers/GuessOS: hostinfo: not found
Sorry, but we cannot grok "system-ident"
uname -m
hardware-platform
uname -r
OS-release
uname -s
OS-name
uname -v
OS-version
uname -X
uname: illegal option -- X
usage: uname [-snrvma]
Ideally, read the file PORTING, do what it says, and send
the resulting patches to The Apache Group by filling out a
report form at http://www.apache.org/bugdb.cgi - or, if
your browser isn't forms-capable, you can send them via
email to apache-bugs@apache.org. If you don't wish to do
the port yourself, please submit this output rather than
the patches.
Thank you
```

Figure 9-1:
Configure
says: "What
kind of
a system
is this,
anyway?"

Porting Apache to a new platform may be simple, or it may be extremely complex. The simplest case occurs when your system is just like a system that Configure already knows about; the most complex case occurs when your system resembles nothing Configure has ever seen on Earth. (Or wherever fine Apache Web servers are sold.)

Seeking help is okay

A major resource — in fact, the *primary* resource — needed for a porting effort is the file src/PORTING, which is included in the Apache source kit. The next most important resource is probably the Apache problem report database:

```
http://bugs.apache.org/
```

(search for one of the keywords displayed after the uname commands in the "can't grok" output from Configure, as shown in Figure 9-1).

If you don't feel up to the task of porting Apache to your platform, other Apache users who inhabit the `comp.infosystems.www.servers.unix` USENET newsgroup may be able to help. Who knows? Maybe another user has already done it for your system!

If all else fails, you can ask The Apache Group for help. Enter a problem report at the previous Web page — include the complete "can't grok" drivel from `Configure` — and ask for help. An Apache Group contact probably will ask you to run various tests to find out the capabilities of your system, and the end result should be (hopefully) a patch to the build scripts that work for your platform. If it works, The Apache Group will probably merge it into the official kit for the next release.

Chapter 10

Examining the Running Server

● ●

In This Chapter

▶ What the info and status modules are

▶ Information divulged by the monitor modules

▶ How to use the info and status modules to investigate server operation

▶ How the server can help you automate performance analysis

● ●

*P*robably the two most common questions a new Apache Webmaster asks after getting the server up and running are:

1. "Why did it do *that?*" and

2. "Just what is it *doing,* anyhow?"

Two of the standard modules that come with the Apache source kit are designed to help answer these specific questions. If they're built into your server, you're on the way to finding out the answers. This chapter serves as your faithful guide to reading these maps of server behavior. Ready? Onward into the unknown!

Under the Microscope

Unfortunately, UNIX systems don't share a universal set of monitoring utilities; each operating system tends to have its own tools and applications. This actually makes some sense, since a lot of the things you'd want to keep an eye on, such as memory usage, I/O activity, and so on, are pretty deeply entangled in the implementation of the system itself.

To work around this issue, the Apache kit includes two modules to help you find out what the server is up to. These are the *information module* (named mod_info) and the *status module* (named, surprisingly enough, mod_status). In a way, these are even better than generic system monitoring tools, since they're geared specifically to Apache and can tell you details other applications couldn't.

Both the info and status modules display intimate details about the operation of your server — information which you may or may not want the Wide World to see. In addition, their displays concern the entire Apache server process tree, and don't display things according to server, directory, or location scope. That means that you'll see information about *all* of your virtual servers, if you're running any, and won't be able to use these to check on the configuration of individual directories. To control who can see this information, protect the locations using auth/auth mechanisms (see Chapter 6), preferably using the IP addresses of clients you want to be able to see this stuff. For example:

```
<Location /server-status>
    SetHandler server-status
    Order allow,deny
    Allow from 127.0.0.1
    Deny from all
</Location>
<Location /server-info>
    SetHandler server-info
    Order allow,deny
    Allow from 127.0.0.1
    Deny from all
</Location>
```

These modules generate their displays using the *content handler* mechanism (see Chapters 7 and 8), so you activate them by associating their handlers with a file, a file extension, or a directory.

It's Alive!

Is the server actually up and running? It needs to be, or else you can't use the methods described in this chapter — because they depend upon the server being able to examine itself and tell you what it found. The info and status modules aren't really intended to be used for troubleshooting problems with the server being uncommunicative, but rather to check configuration issues and performance.

You interact with these modules through a Web browser, so if you can't even access the server from your desktop, you need to go to the *"Troubleshooting"* appendix, not this chapter. On the other hand, if you *can* reach your server, and you want to snoop on it, you're in the right place. Welcome!

Seeing the Directives in Effect

With over a gross of configuration directives available, and several server configuration files in which they may occur, and multiple scopes within those files . . . well, it can sometimes be hard to keep track of everything and all the interactions.

Surging to the rescue comes the *information module,* mod_info. This is one of the standard modules included with the Apache kit. Its whole purpose in life is to help you understand what modules are active in your server, and what directives are being used to control them. As to figuring out the interactions between the directives . . . that's up to you, I'm afraid. Just keep accumulating Apache Guru Points, and all will become clear.

The browser display from the info module frequently runs to several pages, but there are only three basic *kinds* of information divulged. The first kind is clearly shown by Figure 10-1 — the names of the modules built into the active server and some information about the server itself. The list of modules at the very top are actually hot-links to the specific module reports farther down the page.

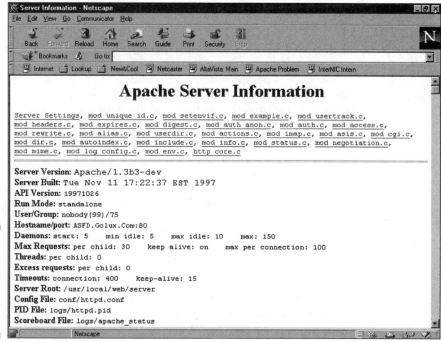

Figure 10-1:
Page One
of the
configuration
information
display.

Figure 10-2 shows the next kind of information: details about a particular module, brief descriptions of the directives used to control its operation, and the actual occurrences of the directives in the configuration files. (The module actually opens the files and reads them to get this information.)

When you ask the info module to show you stuff, it's being run just like any other module — that is, the server is running under the access rights of the user named in the `User` directive. If that user doesn't have access to the files, none of their contents will be displayed. They get processed, though, at server startup because the server reads the files before it changes its identity.

Don't forget that the info module displays the contents of the server configuration files as they exist on the disk. If you have made changes to them but haven't reloaded the server, then the display does *not* reflect the configuration in effect, but what will be used the next time the server is started or reloaded. So don't spend a lot of time pulling your hair because what you see in the info display doesn't explain what the server's doing — there's probably a very good reason for it.

The info page displays the same things about each module currently built into the server:

✔ `Module Name`
Simply enough, this is the name of the module's source file.

In actual point of fact, the value displayed on the *"Module Name"* line is the name of the file that declared the module structure (see Chapter 7). If a module is comprised of several different source files, the one that declares the structure is what will be listed — so hopefully it has a reasonably identifiable name. It's customary for even multi-file modules to have *one* named `mod_mumble.c` which declares the structure.

✔ `Content-types affected`
This is actually a bit of a misnomer. No, its a *big* misnomer. This line isn't actually listing *any* content-types — what it lists is content *handlers* the module has declared, such as "`server-info`" or "`server-parsed`". You can associate these handlers with certain content-types if you like, but no one's forcing you to — and if you don't, don't associate the handler with anything else either, it will never be invoked. If the module being reported on doesn't declare any content handlers, then this line will say "none."

✔ `Module Groups`
This is another misleading name. What this line lists is the phases of request processing in which the module has declared an interest (see Chapters 7 and 8). Every request-related callback slot in the `module` structure that the module filled in is listed here.

✔ Module Configuration Commands

Even though they're called "configuration commands" by mod_info, what's really meant here is "directives." These one-line descriptions of the current module's directives are very similar to what you see if you use the "-h" command-line switch (such as, "./httpd -h"). In fact, they're not only similar — they're identical.

✔ Current Configuration

Ah, now we come to it. Under this header, mod_info will list all of the actual uses of the directives declared by the module. It displays the actual text of the directive line as it appears in the file, and separately lists each file that contains relevant directives.

Actually, there's a bit of weirdness here. Apache allows multiple modules to use the same names for directives; when encountered during configuration, each module that mentioned it is given a chance to figure out if the current config line is for it or not. The info module can't tell by looking at it which module really owns the directive, so it appears under every module in the list.

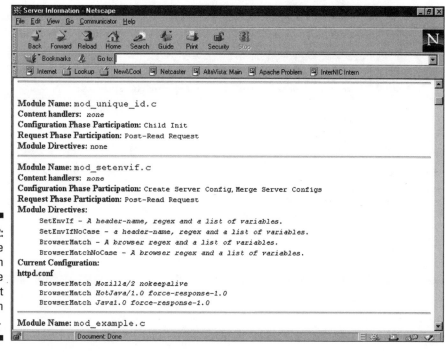

Figure 10-2:
Sample
configuration
directive
excerpt
from
mod_info.

The third kind of information displayed by this module is really only a special case of the previous one. If module directives appear within scope containers such as `<Directory>` or `<Location>`, then `mod_info` will reveal that. Note that it's only going to show you directives relevant to the current module; if other directives appear in the container, they'll be displayed elsewhere as part of the appropriate module report. Figure 10-3 illustrates this behavior.

As a final note about the info module, you can jump directly to a specific module report by naming its source file in the Web URL. For instance,

```
http://yourhost/server-info#mod_mime.c
```

will take your browser directly to the section about the `mod_mime` module.

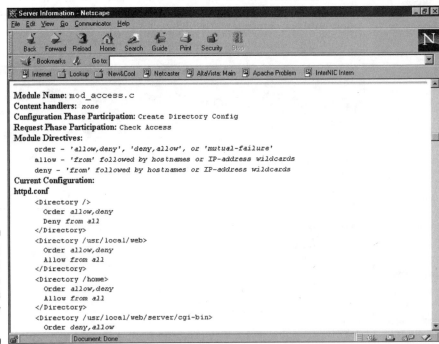

Figure 10-3:
Scoped
directive
display as
shown by
mod_info.

What's the Server Doing, Anyway??

The server status module, mod_status, tells you about the current Apache process tree. Figures 10-4 and 10-5 show you a sample display of its output.

Each position in the funny rectangular bunch-o'-dots shown in Figure 10-4 (called the *scoreboard*) represents a potential child process. If the position contains a dot, than that's all it is — a *potential* process, which means that the server either hasn't had to start up that many children, or else it *did* at some point in the past, but demand fell back and it was able to reap the ones that were no longer needed. Non-dot positions represent actual living child processes.

You control the maximum number of potential children — the size of the scoreboard, in other words — with the value of the HARD_SERVER_LIMIT definition set at server build-time (see Chapter 9). If you continually see most of the scoreboard filled with active processes — and your performance is acceptable — you may want to consider rebuilding the server with a higher limit. As I said, see Chapter 9 for the details. Regardless of the setting of HARD_SERVER_LIMIT, each line in the scoreboard will have a maximum of 64 positions.

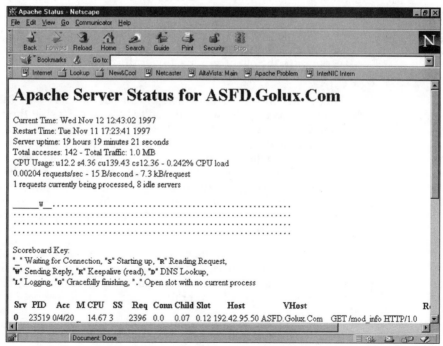

Figure 10-4: First screenful of exciting news from mod_status.

Each position in the scoreboard can contain one of the following characters, which tells you what the corresponding child process is doing. You may note that the different meanings are listed in a more-or-less chronological order, matching what the server does with a request.

✔ **. (period)**
   If the scoreboard position contains a period, it means that there really *isn't* a corresponding process. It's just an unrealized potential; either the server has never needed that many children, or else it did at some point(s) in the past but cut back when the traffic demands fell to a lower level and didn't need as many children I order to keep up.

✔ **_ (underline)**
   This means that the child process exists, but isn't doing anything at the moment. It's waiting to be assigned a request to work on.

✔ **S**
   A child marked as being in this state has been activated by the server and handed some work to do. It's currently in the process of getting itself set up to actually *do* the work.

✔ **R**
   An "R" in the scoreboard means that the corresponding process is busy reading the details of the request from the client. This may be the first time, or the child may be performing a subsequent read on a kept-alive connection (see the "K" state farther on).

✔ **W**
   This means that the child process is occupied sending (writing) the response to the client's request over the connection.

✔ **K**
   Some connections are marked as having the "keepalive" attribute, which means that the server doesn't automatically shut them down as soon as the first request is finished. Instead, it keeps them alive so the client can send *another* request over the same link without having to go through the highly expensive (in terms of network activity) process of opening a new connection. This makes a lot of sense when you think that many web pages actually consists of several documents (like graphics) from the same server; keeping the link open allows better performance for downloading conglomerate documents like that.

✔ **D**
   If the scoreboard position contains a "D" it means that the child is busy trying to translate an IP address to a name, or a name to an IP address. Remember that this is very important for network-identity-based auth/auth operations (see Chapter 6).

If yours is a busy server, and you see a lot of "D" entries in the scoreboard, you're probably doing too *much* looking up of host information. You probably have the HostNameLookups directive set to "Double", don't you? This is probably affecting your performance, so you might want to consider changing that to "Off" and doing the address-to-name translation in your logfiles as part of a separate process that won't interfere with your server's ability to respond to requests. "Double" lookups are done automatically (in Apache 1.3) any time a name or IP address is used in auth/auth processing, anyway.

✔ L

This means that the child process has actually finished servicing the request, and is now just making a record of the fact.

If you see a lot of "L" entries in your scoreboard, double-check to see whether you're doing your logging over some sort of low-throughput or unreliable mechanism (such as to an NFS-mounted file system). Since the request has already been handled, extra time spent here doesn't hurt your response time directly — but it can artificially drive up the number of children processes if too many are too busy logging to handle new requests.

✔ G

The appearance of a "G" in the scoreboard means that the child process received a "graceful restart" signal (see Chapter 4), and is wrapping things up with the current request before dying. (In contrast, a "graceless" restart causes the child to completely blow away any current processing and commit suicide immediately.)

As Figure 10-5 shows, the status module also gives you some statistics about the recent history of the server. The farthest back any of these figures go is the time the server was last started or reloaded.

Each of those positions in the scoreboard is called a *slot*. The server records information about the current occupant of each slot (if any), and some overall totals too, such as the number of megabytes of information that have been served to clients through the slot by the various tenants.

Don't forget that child processes are periodically retired, so if your server has been running a long time the statistics shown by the status module only apply to the children which are *currently* running — any that have shuffled off this virtual coil into the great Process Graveyard in the Matrix will have left not a wrack behind except in the slot totals.

The statistics table includes one line for each currently-occupied slot in the scoreboard. Empty slots (that is, those with no children in them) are not displayed, even though they may have some historical totals available. Here are the details about each of the columns in the statistics table:

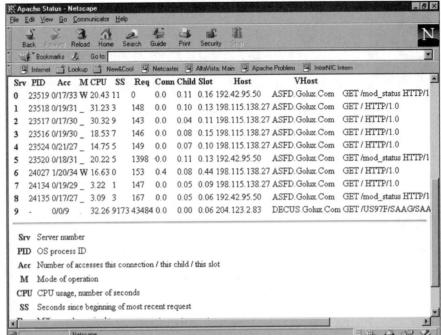

Figure 10-5:
Statistics
from the
status
module.

Srv	PID	Acc	M	CPU	SS	Req	Conn	Child	Slot	Host	VHost	
0	23519	0/17/33	W	20.43	11	0	0.0	0.11	0.16	192.42.95.50	ASFD.Golux.Com	GET /mod_status HTTP/1
1	23518	0/19/31	_	31.23	3	148	0.0	0.10	0.13	198.115.138.27	ASFD.Golux.Com	GET / HTTP/1.0
2	23517	0/17/30	_	30.32	9	143	0.0	0.04	0.11	198.115.138.27	ASFD.Golux.Com	GET / HTTP/1.0
3	23516	0/19/30	_	18.53	7	146	0.0	0.08	0.15	198.115.138.27	ASFD.Golux.Com	GET / HTTP/1.0
4	23524	0/21/27	_	14.75	5	149	0.0	0.07	0.10	198.115.138.27	ASFD.Golux.Com	GET / HTTP/1.0
5	23520	0/18/31	_	20.22	5	1398	0.0	0.11	0.13	192.42.95.50	ASFD.Golux.Com	GET /mod_status HTTP/1
6	24027	1/20/34	W	16.63	0	153	0.4	0.08	0.44	198.115.138.27	ASFD.Golux.Com	GET / HTTP/1.0
7	24134	0/19/29	_	3.22	1	147	0.0	0.05	0.09	198.115.138.27	ASFD.Golux.Com	GET / HTTP/1.0
8	24135	0/17/27	_	3.09	3	167	0.0	0.05	0.06	192.42.95.50	ASFD.Golux.Com	GET /mod_status HTTP/1
9	-	0/0/9	.	32.26	9173	43484	0.0	0.00	0.06	204.123.2.83	DECUS.Golux.Com	GET /US97F/SAAG/SAA

Srv Server number

PID OS process ID

Acc Number of accesses this connection / this child / this slot

M Mode of operation

CPU CPU usage, number of seconds

SS Seconds since beginning of most recent request

✔ Srv
This identifies the child within the scoreboard by number. The first slot in the scoreboard is numbered "1". With an active scoreboard, this doesn't necessarily make it easy to locate the child, though, so try using this number to find the approximate location in the scoreboard (remember, each line has 64 positions), and then use the "M" value (described a little further on) to narrow it down.

✔ PID
This lists the process identification that was assigned to the child. This is of limited usefulness on highly active servers because of child turn-over. However, if your system appears to be getting taken over by one of the server's children, you can make a note of the PID of the runaway process and then look here to see what the server thinks it is doing.

✔ Acc
This column displays the number of requests that have been handled. The value is three numbers separated by slashes ("/"). The first number is the count of requests that have been made over the current connection, which will probably be only zero or one unless a client is taking serious advantage of the keepalive capabilities of Apache and you catch it in the act (while the connection is still open). The second number represents the number of requests that have been handled by the child process currently occupying the slot; this will go back to zero when the

current process retires. The third and final number is the number of requests since the server was (re)started that have been handled by all the children who have occupied the slot.

✔ M

This is the current mode of operation of the child. It's a one-letter field, with the same values as the positions in the scoreboard (described several paragraphs back, near the beginning of this section).

✔ CPU

This is the number of seconds of CPU time that have been used by the current inhabitant of the slot. When the current child retires and a new one is created, it will start over at zero.

✔ SS

This is a crude measure of how active your server really is, because it's a count of the number seconds since the beginning of the most recent request handled by this slot. (The current request, if there is one, doesn't count.) If this number is in the thousands for all your server children, your server really isn't very busy. If it's quite low, however, your clients are keeping the Apache children busy.

✔ Req

The "Req" column displays the number of milliseconds it took for the child to handle the last request. This is a crude way to check on server efficiency, because it gives you an idea how long it takes to turn around and answer client requests. This is measured in wall-clock time rather than CPU time, so if these numbers are consistently high either your server is sending large responses or you and your clients are probably the victims of some sort of network congestion. You might want to investigate in either case.

This column was added for Apache 1.3.

✔ Conn

This and the next two columns measure the amount of information actually flowing. The "Conn" field contains the number of kilobytes (multiples of 1024 bytes) that have been transmitted over the currently-open connection.

✔ Child

The number of megabytes that have been handled by the current child are displayed here. Remember that each child can potentially handle multiple connections (though not all at the same time), so this number should always be as large or larger than the "Conn" value.

✔ Slot

This holds the count of the megabytes transferred for all children who have occupied this slot. Naturally enough, this should be larger than the "Child" value in the previous column.

In order to get the most out of the status module, the server needs to be built with the appropriate instrumentation activated. In other words, you need to set the STATUS rule in your Configuration file to "yes". If you don't, your display will look more like that shown in Figure 10-6. See Chapter 9 for information about configuring options during the server build process.

More tricks with the status module

The status module is designed to let you tailor the display slightly, depending upon your web browser's capabilities and what you want to do with the information. You can control these aspects by including some additional keywords on the URL. If you're going to add keywords, you must separate them from the actual URL with a question mark ("?"); if you want to use multiple keywords, separate them from each other with an ampersand ("&"). Example:

```
http://yourhost/server-status?auto&refresh=10
```

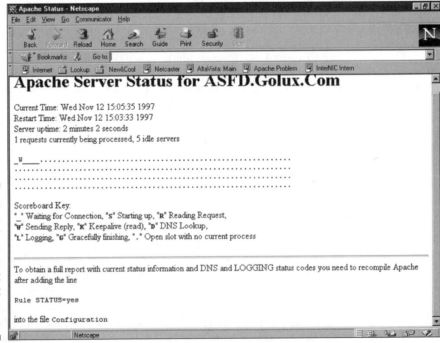

Figure 10-6: Lame status display when server is built without "Rule STATUS=yes".

Here are the keywords that the mod_status module understands. Any others will be ignored.

- ✔ notable

  If you include "notable" in the URL for the status display, the module will not take advantage of the HTML 3.2 <TABLE> tag features, and the display will be changed to resemble that in Figure 10-7. By default, mod_status uses automatic table generation to keep the statistics table display tidy and properly spaced.

- ✔ auto

  If you include the "auto" keyword, the result will be formatted in such a way that it might be useful for automatic processing — for instance, you might have some cron job or other that picks up the status report every hour and makes up charts from it. Or something like that. Figure 10-8 shows what this format looks like.

- ✔ refresh[=n]

  By including the "refresh" keyword, you tell the status module to inform your client that it should repeat the request for the status page at intervals, every *n* seconds. If you don't give the keyword a value, the default is one.

This only works if your browser is capable of understanding the "Refresh" HTTP response header. Most modern browsers are, but don't be surprised if you use an older one and nothing happens when you request a refresh interval.

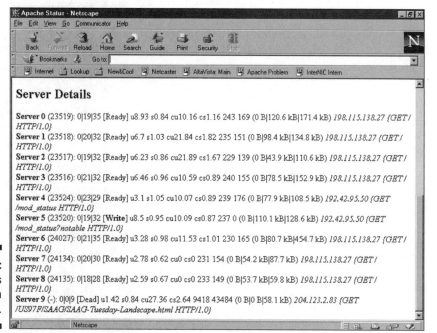

Figure 10-7:
Status
display with
"notable".

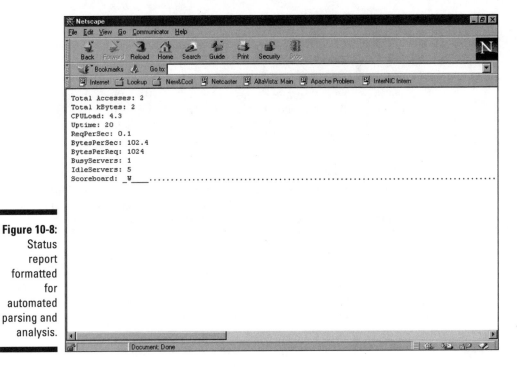

Figure 10-8:
Status
report
formatted
for
automated
parsing and
analysis.

Chapter 11

Document Selection and Content Negotiation

In This Chapter

▶ Using Apache to point visitors to new locations

▶ Understanding the underlying concepts behind content negotiation

▶ Finding out how Apache performs content negotiation

▶ Recognizing the points in the network at which requests may be cached

▶ Exploring how you can affect the caching of your documents

*H*ave you ever made a telephone call to a number that had been changed and received a recorded message like, "The number you have reached has been changed. The new number is . . . ?" Or stood outside a restaurant looking at the menu, wondering what all those exotic dishes mean in your language? These things can happen on the Web, too, and the Apache Web server software can take them one step further: It can actually dial the number for the caller or put up a translated copy of the menu (assuming the restaurant has one in the visitor's language, of course). This chapter explains how it works, and how you can make it so automatic that the visitor doesn't even have to *ask*. Sound like magic? Well, get out your magic wand because you're the wizard!

Advanced Redirection

Before I describe "advanced" redirection, I should probably explain "basic" redirection.

Redirection happens when you ask a server for X and it gives you Y instead. In Apache terms, if the server handles the substitution of Y for X within itself and the client never knows about it, it's called an *internal* redirect; if the client is told to make the substitution, it's called an *external* redirect. However, as far as the user's client is concerned, a redirect is a redirect even though all it ever sees are externals. (Give yourself 5 Apache Guru Points for good behavior. Stay with me, now. . . .)

"Okay, so what's a redirect, and how does it differ from the alias thing described in Chapter 4? And why are you making nouns out of verbs?"

- ✔ An *alias* is a translation made between the URL that the server receives and a location on the disk somewhere. The client sends the right information the first time — that is, the right URL — but the alias translates it into system terms.

- ✔ A *redirect* is an answer the server sends back to the client that says, "Sorry, that URL is stale — here's where that resource lives now," and gives the client a new URL where it can find the resource. Typically the client automatically re-issues the request with the new URL — but the end result is that the client has to use a different URL to reach the document. A redirect does a translation from one URL to another, and the system's details about disks and directories are completely irrelevant.

- ✔ And redirect is used as a noun because . . . well, just because. Modern technological discourse has a habit of warping the language. Maybe it's used as a verb because it's easier to say than "redirection?"

The two basic types of redirect are temporary and permanent. As you can guess, these redirects tell the client how long the requested resource is going to be away from home. (Other types exist, but I get to them a little later.)

A *temporary redirect* tells the client, "The resource you requested isn't *here* right now. You can find it over *there* for the moment, but it should be coming back to live *here* again eventually. You can keep using the old address if you like, and I'll keep giving you this same message until the resource comes home again." In contrast, a *permanent redirect* tells the client, "That resource now lives over *there*. It will never live *here* again, and if it will, nobody told me about it. You should always use the new address."

This allows really smart clients to figure out which URL they should remember. It has an effect on which requests get cached (remembered) and which don't — temporary redirects usually aren't cached and permanent ones typically are. In other words, the next time you ask for the same URL, the client probably goes all the way to the server again (and maybe gets redirected again) if the last response was a temporary redirect, but the client probably goes directly to the *new* location if it was a permanent one. That's the theory, anyway.

So what's all the fuss? Why would you want to use redirects? Well, how about if your friend Chris moves to another system and takes along the (very popular) frog-jumping statistics page? To be nice to people looking for the page in its old location, you'd probably want to automatically deliver them to the new one, wouldn't you? Rather than giving them a "not found" error? That scenario would be a redirect, and Chris would probably remain your friend if you added it.

Consider the case of a poorly chosen URL path, such as

```
http://yourhost/people/eng/jonnie/project_Zed/
```

which Jonnie set up when he started working on his neat little project. But now the project is very popular, and is Officially Sanctioned, and The Powers That Be want that fact known even though Jonnie is going to continue handling it. They want the new URL to be

```
http://yourhost/whizzo/projects/Zed/
```

You can set up an alias, as in the following example, to do this:

```
Alias /eng/projects/Zed/ /usr/users/people/jonnie/project_Zed/
```

This alias allows people to find the project at its new URL. However, anyone can still access the project at the old URL, and people who have saved the old URL won't know (or even find out) about the new one.

By setting up a permanent redirect from the old address to the new one, anyone who looks at the project under the new name is fine, and anyone who uses the old name is told about the new one. Hopefully, users will eventually stop using the old name, making The Powers happy.

All right, so these examples are a little contrived. You get the idea. (And if you don't, subtract 15 Apache Guru Points.)

Apache provides several different ways to set up a redirect. Most of them are implemented in the mod_alias module, the same one that handles (surprise, surprise!) the Alias and ScriptAlias directives (described in Chapter 4).

For a redirect (or an alias) to be processed, the path must match as a series of components. That is, /this/path would match /this/path/ and /this/path/forward, but *not* /this/path-here. Another way of looking at a redirect is that the path must either match the requested resource exactly or be a proper ancestor of it.

In each case in the following example, the *path* is the part of the URL that follows the server portion; that is, in a URL such as <http://yourhost:80/this-is/The/place>, the path is the string /this-is/The/place. You don't need (and in fact can't) specify the part that precedes the path because it's assumed. This is the same behavior that Alias and ScriptAlias use. Apache already knows the server part because, well, because it *is* the server. The *target-URL* argument should be a complete URL string, including the scheme (http: or whatever) and the server/host portion — that is, the same complete string you give someone in a mail message.

```
Redirect path target-URL
Redirect Temporary path target-URL
RedirectTemp path target-URL
```

All the preceding lines tell Apache to send the client a temporary redirect message and the target-URL string as the new location. (You couldn't guess?) The just-plain-Redirect means "temporary," but I suggest using one of the other formats to make this clear.

```
Redirect Permanent path target-URL
RedirectPermanent path target-URL
```

As you may expect, these directives are quite similar to the last bunch of directives, except that they tell the client that whatever-it-is isn't coming back.

Okay, guess what? It's later, and here are the other types of redirects.

```
Redirect SeeOther path target-URL
```

Unlike the preceding types of redirects, which tell the client that the re-source has moved, this one says that the document has been *replaced* with something newer or more appropriate. However, it still doesn't give the client the old document; it tells the client where the replacement is. So the original resource is essentially unavailable. You may use a SeeOther redi-rect when a rough draft at one location gets superseded by the final form at another.

```
Redirect Gone path
```

All right, so this directive doesn't really look like a redirect, because it doesn't specify a target. In a manner of speaking (technical, that is), it *is* a redirect — but to an inaccessible place. Instead of telling the browser, "Nope, I can't find it," the redirect says, "It used to be here, but it has now gone to the Great Bit-Bucket. Don't bother looking for it anymore, here or anywhere else." This information is particularly good because it tells your visitors that you're paying attention to the content of your site and that you removed the document intentionally rather than by accident.

Finally, the incredibly powerful `mod_rewrite` module allows you to do redirects based on really complicated path-name patterns and expressions. For example, if you want to point all requests for Marketing and Sales documents — which used to be in the marketing and sales/docs directories on your server — to the DocumentRoot of the new server that they have, you can do it like this:

```
RewriteEngine On
RewriteRule /marketing/(.*) http://marketing.yourdomain/$1 [R]
RewriteRule /sales/docs(.*) http://marketing.yourdomain/$1 [R]
```

As you can see from the preceding example, the rewriting module can do a lot — and can be very confusing if you're not sure what's going on. Give yourself 20 Apache Guru Points for each of your first five successful attempts to use this module correctly.

Client Preferences

"All browsers are created equal." In a word — *not!* Take the simple issue of graphics: Some browsers can handle them, some can't, and some can handle only certain types. And how do you deal with a truly international audience, with wildly differing language tastes? How do you please as many of your clients as possible? What's a conscientious Webmaster to do? The answer is to let the computer do as much of the work as possible. Aren't computers supposed to be our servants? (Wanna buy a bridge?)

The World Wide Web is becoming increasingly international in content, which is as it should be. The first stages of this involved site offering content in a specific tongue, such as French, and not necessarily the current *lingua franca* of the Web, English. This outlook was still not very global, because only visitors who knew the language could understand the content. For example, consider what the effect would be if the Olympics were held in Dublin, and the Dublin web site that contained the official information was available only in Irish Gaelic.

The next steps beyond that involved offering multilingual content, which web sites typically implemented by providing links labeled "click here for this page in German" (or whatever language) on each page. This format is a little more user friendly, because it allows the visitor to select the translation in the language of his or her choice, rather than the Webmaster's.

The obvious next approach is to let the *computer* figure out the correct

The obvious next approach is to let the *computer* figure out the correct language, according to the preferences of the end user, thus saving the visitor from having to make the choice on a server-by-server or page-by-page basis. The user just needs to tell the browser that he or she prefers documents in Danish if they're available in a Danish translation, then German if that's provided, and finally English if nothing better is around. (Or whatever the individual's preferences are.) After the user instructs the browser, the browser can pass along these preferences to each server it contacts.

This sort of user preference-setting isn't limited only to language; the same feature applies to other attributes, such as content type (for example, a preference of Microsoft Word over WordPerfect when it comes to word-processing documents, or GIF over JPEG when graphics are involved) and encoding (if the document is stored in a not directly usable format, such as compressed).

Modern browsers permit the user to indicate some types of preferences, and the browser dutifully passes this information along to the server. The browser itself may have other preferences of its own (such as one sort of graphics or audio format over another) and can include them as well. And maybe, just maybe, the server knows what to do with all that information.

Apache is one of the servers that actually takes advantage of these tidbits of preferential idiosyncrasy and can do something with the information. Because the server is figuring out what kind of file to send (from what it has available, obviously) based on the client's stated desires, the process is called *content negotiation.*

Although you can set up Apache to automatically perform this negotiation to provide the end user with the document that best fits his or her prefer-ences, the server can choose only from what you make available. Telling it to handle Italian, German, Portuguese, and Japanese won't make it automati-cally translate your documents into those languages — *that* you still have to do yourself!

Variable dimensions

The different versions of a document that are available are called its *variants,* and the ways in which they differ from one another are called *dimensions.* The dimensions along which Apache can negotiate a response are type, encoding, and language.

The *type* dimension refers to the content-type of the resource, such as text/html, text/plain, image/jpeg, application/msword, and so on. For example, a nongraphical browser may tell the server "I can accept text documents, but no images," and Apache would never negotiate a picture to send to it.

If a resource isn't in its final usable format, it's said to be *encoded*. For example, if you have to uncompress the resource before using it, the document on the server is considered to be encoded. To handle things along this dimension, the *encoding* dimension, the client can tell the server what types of encoding it can handle.

The only encodings currently recognized by the web transport standard are compress and gzip, meaning the document has been shrunk using either the UNIX compress(1) method or the GNU gzip method. The Web will probably support other encodings in the future; it can handle encodings now if they're preceded with x- to indicate "eXperimental" (for example, "x-stuffit"). Encoding documents into a compressed form is a Good Thing, because they're transmitted that way — the network prefers that you ship small files rather than large ones.

The *language* dimension applies primarily to text documents, but it doesn't necessarily have to. For example, you can easily have two different pictures, one containing Greek words and one containing Finnish, and arrange for the server to negotiate them appropriately.

This illustrates an important point: Documents can be negotiated along multiple dimensions at once. If you take the example of Finnish versus Greek graphics in the last paragraph, you may have the variants for your "logo" picture as shown in Figure 11-1.

Figure 11-1:
Images with
language
attributes.

```
logo.gif.fi  # Finnish words in GIF picture
logo.gif.gr  # Greek words in GIF picture
logo.jpg.fi  # Finnish words in JPEG picture
logo.jpg.gr  # Greek words in JPEG picture
logo.jpg     # English words in JPEG picture
```

(For the purpose of this example, I'm assuming that your server has been configured to recognize that gr and fi represent languages.) Now if a client indicates that it prefers Greek documents along the language dimension and GIF documents along the content-type dimension, the server negotiates to the logo.gif.gr variant.

You tell the Apache server that certain file extensions indicate a language variant by using the `AddLanguage` directive:

```
AddLanguage language-code [file-extension...]
```

For example, you may decide not to run a truly internationalized server and offer only variations of English; so your config files may contain no more to do with this stuff than

```
AddLanguage en .en
AddLanguage en-gb .en-gb .en-uk
AddLanguage en-us .en-us
```

Alternatively, you may by fiat declare that all versions of English are equivalent with something like

```
AddLanguage en .en
AddLanguage en-gb .en
AddLanguage en-us .en
```

That has the effect of negotiating to the same `.en` variant regardless of whether the client requests a specific dialect.

Nothing says the file suffix needs to match the actual language code, and in some cases it's a good idea to *not* do that. For example, the language code for Polish is `pl` — but it's also a common suffix for Perl scripts (which only look like a foreign language to non-Perl speakers). You can use the `AddLanguage` directive to map the language code to a different suffix as in the following example:

```
AddLanguage pl .po
```

By adding this directive, the server negotiates requests that specify Polish as a preferred language against files containing `.po` in their names — and your Perl scripts continue to function properly, too.

There's no magic associated with the language codes; nothing tells Apache that *it* means *Italian*. All this does is let the server know that it can check these values against the language preferences that come from clients. For example, if you list `ooga-boing` as a language in your Apache server configuration files, and a client includes `ooga-boing` in its list of acceptable languages, negotiation proceeds as though `ooga-boing` is a real language.

Quality time

What if a client says it can handle Greek, English, German, and Dutch — and the server has variants for each of these languages? How does the server determine which one to send?

Because I listed it first, you may expect the server to pick the Greek version and give it to the client — but that assumption is not correct. Computers are very literal-minded, and they obey only the rules that you give them. One rule in the area of content negotiation is that *all* variants have equal priority unless you state otherwise, and the order in which you list them is unimportant.

You indicate the priority of variants through what's called the *quality* of the preference. Quality values range from 0.000 (which means "I *never* want anything of such poor quality") through 1.000, with the higher numbers meaning more preferable.

So if the client wants to indicate that the server should evaluate the language dimension by giving Dutch the most preference, followed by German or French (equally acceptable), English, and finally Greek (only as a last resort), it may tell the server "Dutch (quality 1.000), German (quality 0.9), French (quality 0.9), English (quality 0.5), Greek (quality 0.001)." In fact, for the sake of the discussion that follows, I assume that the client did give these preferences.

The server, too, can set quality values on different variants. These values come into play only when a decision has to be made between different variants that are equally acceptable to the client, and they allow the server to narrow the field the rest of the way. For example, if the server doesn't have a Dutch variant but *does* have both German and French versions available, it uses its own rules to decide which version to send because the client didn't state a preference.

One very good reason for the server to set quality values has to do with, er, well, with quality. Consider a document that was originally written in Icelandic. Say you ask me to translate it into Spanish. Because I know neither language, my translation is probably going to be of poor quality — so you'd have a good reason to assign my Spanish version a low quality value.

In some cases, Apache uses some common-sense rules rather than really strict definitions. For example, if the client can accept content-types of text/html, text/plain, text/*, and */*, and doesn't specify any quality values, the formal rules indicate that Apache should regard all the content-types with equal priority. The client probably didn't intend to not specify quality values, though, so what Apache *actually* does is assign a quality of 0.02 to the text/* value and 0.01 to the */* one. The result is as if the client said "Give me the thing in HTML or plain text if you have it, or any *other* kind of text if that's all you have. I'm desperate enough to take *any* format if you can't give me either of my preferred formats."

Note that this happens only if the client doesn't indicate *any* quality settings. If client does specify settings, Apache assumes the client knows what it's doing (not necessarily a safe assumption, but . . .) and treats the preferences exactly as it receives them.

Another way in which Apache tries to do the right thing for the end user has to do with variants with no language attribute. Take another peek at Figure 11-1. Got it memorized? Good. Now "play computer" for a moment and see what happens if the client requests different combinations of variants.

In the following examples, all the lines except the Object: lines are valid HTTP header fields. Give yourself 10 Apache Guru Points if you didn't know that.

```
Object: logo
Accept: image/gif, image/*
Accept-language: fi
```

In this specific case, the server has an exact match and sends the client the file logo.gif.fi. But what if I change things a little; what happens in the following example?

```
Object: logo
Accept: text/html, text/plain, image/*
Accept-language: fi, gr
```

Because no text representations of the logo object exist, the Apache server is going to try to find something that matches the image/* content-type. Aha! It finds some! Now, which ones are preferable? Either the GIF or JPEG versions are acceptable, and both the Greek and the Finnish variants are likewise within the client's preferences, so Apache gets to use its own rules to choose the right variant from among those four files.

Let's try again; the following example illustrates the point that I mentioned a few paragraphs ago about the way Apache fiddles with language preferences. (Remember that?)

```
Object: logo
Accept: text/html, text/plain, image/*
Accept-language: ru
```

This example is the same as the last one, except that Russian is the only acceptable language. No Russian variants exist, so what should Apache do?

Ta-daaaah! Here's that "do the right thing" option Apache takes: *Give variants with no language attribute a quality of 0.001.* So Apache lists them as a last-resort possibility for *any* request. In the previous example, that's what would happen — the server would send the logo.jpg file to the client.

Apache allows the Webmaster to cast a tie-breaking vote in cases where multiple language variants appear to have equal quality settings. You do this with the LanguagePriority directive:

```
LanguagePriority language-code [language-code...]
```

You list the languages in decreasing order of preference. For example, if your server provides content mostly to U.K. readers, you may want the U.K. language variants to have a slight edge:

```
LanguagePriority en-gb en en-us
```

This allows Apache to give preference to a British translation of a document (if available) if the client says "any old English will do."

One final way that the Apache Web server software tries to make the right thing happen has to do with scripts. (A script is recognized by its content-type, which is defined by its extension.) If a client makes a request for foo, and a foo.cgi script is available as one of the possible variants, the server gives it a very low quality. This is based on the assumption that hand-prepared documents are likely to better suit the request. However, if the client makes the request with query arguments, the server gives the script a very *high* quality, under the assumption that you want the server to negotiate the request to the variant that can actually make use of such arguments.

Query arguments in this context mean that the request was made either using the POST method or a GET request with arguments following the actual resource name in the URL (such as after a ? character).

You have two options for persuading the Apache Web server to perform content negotiation: by using *type maps* and by enabling *multiviews*. I cover these features in the next two sections.

Data-driven content typing

You can pre-arrange what file a server supplies in response to a negotiated request by using a *type-map file*. You can create and maintain this text file with any editor, and it contains a list of the different files and their attributes. Clients use a type-map file by requesting the map file itself; the Apache server processes the content of the file, negotiates the correct variant, and performs an internal redirect to have that variant delivered to the client.

One advantage of this approach is that it gives you total control over what variants are available; if a file gets accidentally dropped in the directory, it won't interfere until your type-map is modified.

You activate type-maps by enabling the `type-map` content handler. (I'm glad the rest of this stuff isn't so obvious, or you'd never have bought this book!) The canonical way to do this is with a declaration, such as the following example, somewhere in the server config files:

```
AddHandler type-map .var
```

The server now regards all the files ending in `.var` (within the appropriate scope, of course) as containing negotiation instructions.

Another advantage of using a type-map is that it can be better for performance. The number of requests it needs to make of the file system to find out the negotiation details is typically a *lot* smaller than if multiviews are being used (see the next section for more on multiviews).

Unfortunately, this method does have some drawbacks:

- ✔ You need to keep the map file up to date. You can conceivably write a `cron` script that would do this automatically, based on the files in the directory, though.

- ✔ *All* requests go to the map file and not to the actual resource (for example, the requests go to `<http://yourhost/some/dir/resource.var>`).

- ✔ You need to maintain a separate map file for each resource that you want the server to negotiate this way.

These can make things complicated when you want to have different contents with the same name (such as `foo.html` and `foo.gif`).

Probably the most important reason to use this method rather than the multiviews method is the performance — if you have directories with lots of files in them, the names don't change very often, and your server is really busy, you may want to whip up a few type-maps to avoid the overhead of repeatedly accessing the file system.

Find out more about type maps by browsing to these Apache documentation pages:

```
http://www.apache.org/docs/content-negotiation.html
http://www.apache.org/docs/mod/mod_negotiation.html
```

Multiviews

Multiviews is an option of the Apache Web server that allows it (well, actually *instructs* it) to try and find the document that's the best match for the client's preferences. For example, if multiviews are enabled, the client requests foo, and the only files are foo.gif and foo.jpg, Apache sends the one that most closely matches what the client says it likes best. If multiviews *aren't* enabled, the server complains with a "not found" error — because no just-plain-foo file exists.

Multiviews differs from the type-mapping method described in the previous section because the server is automatically determining what variants are available. If no file exactly matches the request and the multiviews option is enabled in the scope of the document requested, Apache does multiview-based content negotiation.

Enable (and disable) multiviews with the Options directive, like this:

```
Options MultiViews
```

That turns multiviews on and makes sure that they're the *only* option enabled in the current scope. To enable multiviews in *addition* to any other options already active, you use

```
Options +MultiViews
```

And to turn multiviews off, you either specify an Options directive that doesn't list the Multiviews keyword or turn off *only* the multiviews option with a statement like this:

```
Options -MultiViews
```

Multiviews is the only option that isn't automatically enabled by an "Options All" directive. You always need to turn it on explicitly, as with "Options All Multiviews".

The server examines the variants along the different dimensions for which the client has specified a preference. For example, if the client doesn't express a preference for one language over another, the server won't check for .fr *versus* .en *versus* .de *versus* whatever unless it absolutely has to do so — because those are all along the language dimension and the client didn't say anything about that.

If the only variants that exist *are* along one dimension or another that the client doesn't specify, the server still tries to find a variant that matches. For example, assume that a client requests foo.html and doesn't list any language preferences. Now assume that versions of foo.html exist in French, Italian, German, and Russian, but no just-plain-foo.html file exists. Apache *still* tries to pick one to send by negotiating the language variants according to its own rules. In this case, it attempts to break the tie between the different language variants by looking at the settings for the LanguagePriority directive (described at the end of the previous section):

```
LanguagePriority en-us en-gb en it
```

All *right!* Italian appears in the priority list, and it's one of the variants available, so the server sends it. (None of the other variants appear in the priority list, so their priorities are all automatically lower than anything that *is* on the list.)

But what if an Italian variant didn't exist? Oops! None of the language variants available appear in the priority list, so Apache has to make a decision. To be network-friendly, if it can't find any other way to choose the "best" variant from its subset, it selects the smallest one.

The major advantage of multiview negotiation is that it's automatic. The major disadvantage is that it tends to be hard on disk I/O activity, because it scans the directory involved for variants on each request (one reason it isn't included when you specify Options All).

When negotiations break down

What happens if none of the variants available on the Apache Web server match the requirements of the client? In that case, the server puts together a page listing what's available so the client (or the end user driving the client) can make a manual choice. This page looks something like Figure 11-2, although the actual variants listed would be different.

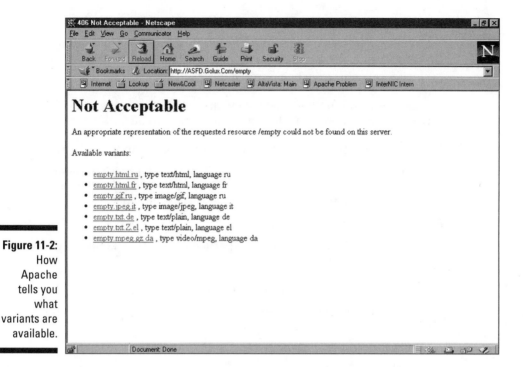

If a type-map is being used for the negotiation, the list of variants are limited to what's in the map file. If multiviews are being used for the negotiation, the variants shown are all the ones that the server finds in the directory.

Controlling Cache Eligibility

Many people have come to think that WWW really stands for World Wide *Wait* because of the network congestion. This is indisputably a problem. (Go ahead — dispute it. I dare you.) One way to cope with the network traffic jams is through what's called *caching*.

Caching consists of remembering the results of a request so it doesn't have to be completely fetched again in the future. As I reveal in a nanosecond's thought, a lot of issues exist with caching. These issues include

✔ How do you know when the original document gets updated so you can get a fresh copy (called "freshening the cache")?

✔ How does a user keep the cache from consuming all the space on the hard drive, and the one next door too?

✔ How do you keep some things (like business transactions or credit information) from being stored in a cache?

Caches exist at multiple points along the path between the client and server. Two main points exist at which a cache is likely to be used:

✔ Most clients maintain their own private cache on the client system.

✔ Many companies connected to the Internet allow web access only through systems called *proxy servers,* which usually cache the stuff going through them. ISPs (Internet Service Providers) typically provide this for their turnkey customers, as well.

So having at least three copies of a particular web transaction is not uncommon. The three copies include

✔ The master copy on the source web server

✔ The copy made by the proxy server as the document passes through on its way to the client

✔ The copy on the client system itself

These copies usually get accessed in the following order:

1. When the user asks for a document, the client checks to see if it already has a copy of it and displays it if does. If not, the client makes the request to the owning server.

2. If the client request has to go through a proxy server, the proxy checks to see if it has a copy of the document. If it does, it sends the copy back to the client. If not, it passes the request along to the owning server.

Each proxy server can, of course, refer to yet *another* proxy; so the chain may actually be even longer.

This can be very efficient if it's set up correctly, because the proxy server supplies its cached copy to any and all of its clients that ask it to, not just the client that requested it first. Consider an immensely popular event, such as the unmanned landing on Mars in 1997. The web servers that provided the source pages about the event got *millions* of requests *per day*. Think what would have happened if lots of those requests weren't coming from service providers that cached the copies on behalf of their customers!

Mostly, caching is a Good Thing because it reduces the traffic on the network. However, sometimes it isn't. The already-stated case of caching sensitive information is an obvious example; a less immediately clear one has to do with negotiated documents (see the preceding sections). If two users of a particular cache have different preferences (say one wants documents in Portuguese and the other wants them in Arabic), one user (the one that made the request that got the document into the cache in the first place) will be happy with the cache and the other won't. So you may want to mark negotiated documents as being uncacheable even though it would mean more load on the network.

As Webmaster of the server that owns the document, you can control some of the instructions about how long the document should live in a cache — or whether it should even be cached at all. You can't control others, though, such as the total size of the cache. Nor can you enforce that your instructions will be followed, unfortunately.

The two things over which you have some influence are:

✔ Whether the document should get cached at all

✔ How long it should stay in the cache before being thrown out

Figuring out whether a cached copy is fresh or stale is a pretty complicated process, with lots of rules based on the header fields associated with the requests. But you don't need to worry about that; all you need to be concerned with is how *you* affect the rules.

The primary header fields that affect caching (and that you can control) are

✔ Expires

✔ Last-Modified

✔ Pragma (specifically, Pragma: no-cache)

Setting arbitrary header fields

The mod_headers module allows you to modify the headers in the response that your server sends back to the client. You can insert your own headers, replace existing ones, add to existing ones, or remove them altogether. This flexibility is one way to affect the cacheability of the response.

For example, you can mark the response as "don't ever store in a cache" with a directive like this:

```
Header Append Pragma "no-cache"
```

The Append keyword tells the server to add the no-cache option to the Pragma header field if it exists or create the field with that value if it doesn't.

Similarly, you can set the document's expiration time to an arbitrary value with

```
Header Set Expires "Fri, 11 Jul 1997 11:52:57 GMT"
```

If you use the preceding approach, you need to be very careful about the syntax that you use for the date. The format is strict, but if you follow this example, you should be in good shape. Just don't make any assumptions or take any liberties.

The caching software uses the expiration date to tell whether the document is still worth keeping or even storing in the cache to begin with. The decision about whether the document is healthy enough to even display to the end user is one that browser needs to be make itself.

Rather than using this method to set the expiration date for a document, you can use the mod_expires module, which is probably better suited. (See the "Calculating the Expires date" section for more information about mod_expires.)

You can also use this method to set a value for the Last-Modified header field, but this is usually handled automatically for most documents. The common exceptions are the output from CGI scripts and files that are parsed for special directives (Server-Side Includes, or SSIs). CGI scripts need to generate this header themselves, and parsed documents can be handled by the *x-bit hack,* described later in this chapter.

Calculating the Expires *date*

While the mod_headers solution described in the preceding section is good for tweaking arbitrary headers, a better way exists to handle the setting of the Expires response header field. In other words, why drive in a screw with a hammer when you've got a screwdriver handy?

This "better way" is the `mod_expires` module, which deals exclusively with this header field. With it, you can do things like say

- ✔ All images expire in 30 days from the time the client asks for them.
- ✔ All HTML files expire a fortnight after their modification date.
- ✔ All documents in a particular directory and its descendants expire a year after they're requested.

(That last one is probably a little unrealistic; I doubt very many caches retain things for a couple of *months,* much less an entire year. But you can if you want to.)

The effects of this module can be scoped all the way down to the directory level (if the `Indexes` override is active), and it's *not* turned on by default.

Currently, the `mod_expires` module can set expiration dates only for documents that come from real files. Server-generated content, such as from `mod_status` or `mod_info`, won't be affected by this module's directives. It *is* valid within `<Location>` containers, though.

The `mod_expires` directives are:

```
ExpiresActive On-or-Off
ExpiresDefault <code>seconds
ExpiresByType content-type <code>seconds
```

The first directive is pretty straightforward; it indicates whether the module should apply the `Expires` header to requests at the current scope and below it. You can actually use this directive to turn off the effect for lower subdirectories.

The `ExpiresDefault` directive needs a little more explanation. The `<code>` is either the letter *A* or the letter *M,* meaning that the expiration time is relative to the request's access time or the file's modification time respectively. The `<code>` is followed immediately (no spaces!) by a numeric value indicating the number of seconds to be added to the appropriate value. For example, the following directive sets the default expiration time for all documents within the current scope to one week after the client requests them:

```
ExpiresDefault A604800
```

This default expiration calculation can be overridden by the `ExpiresByType` directive.

The `ExpiresByType` directive is very similar to `ExpiresDefault`, except for the small detail of an additional argument. That argument is a content-type value, such as `image/gif` or `text/html`.

You cannot specify wildcard types, such as `text/*`, in an `ExpiresByType` directive. Well, you can specify them, but they won't do any good — the server doesn't give the wildcard its normal special treatment, and the directive applies only to documents that actually *have* a content-type of `text/*`, which is illegal.

The judicious use of these directives can make your server very cache-friendly. For example, if you have a lot of documents that change regularly or frequently, and they all refer to the same collection of images, you may want to give the images a long expiration time and the volatile stuff a shorter one — or let their `Last-Modified` times drive the caching rules.

Caching negotiated resources

Sometimes allowing negotiated documents to be stored in a cache is a Bad Thing. As a result, Apache marks such negotiated responses as noncacheable by default.

On the other hand, sometimes you may *want* a proxy server to cache responses that were the result of content negotiation. In such cases, you can override the Apache default behavior with the `CacheNegotiatedDocs` directive, which looks like

```
CacheNegotiatedDocs
```

Note that this directive doesn't take any parameters or arguments at all; if you specify it, it's on — if you don't, it isn't.

This directive can appear only in a global scope, affecting the default server or a virtual host. And in any event, it applies only to requests made using version 1.0 or earlier of the HTTP protocol; requests using Version 1.1 or later have much more control over caching attributes.

In versions of Apache before 1.3, the server automatically marked *all* multiviews-negotiated documents as noncacheable, even if only a single variant was available. With Apache 1.3, such a singleton response *is* marked as cacheable as long as the original request is HTTP/1.0 or earlier. (The semantics of HTTP/1.1 and later requests shouldn't — and don't — have this "helper" change applied.) In other words, a request in a multiviews scope for a document that has only one variant is treated as though `CacheNegotiatedDocs` is present. In cases where actual negotiation occurs (two or more variants from which one must be selected), the behavior is as described in the preceding paragraphs.

The x-bit hack

The *x-bit hack* feature of the Apache Web server is a way of getting the server to know it needs to parse documents without having to rename them or parse all documents.

Remember what *parsing* a document means? If you do, give yourself 5 Apache Guru Points and skip the next couple sentences. Parsing an HTML document means the server scans it for instructions that the server needs to perform before handing the result back to the client. (If you thought you remembered the definition but were wrong, you don't get an Apache Guru Points penalty. It's okay to be mistaken.)

This feature is called the x-bit hack because you give the server this hint by marking the file as being executable or not. The file attribute on UNIX that does this is called the *X* (for eXecutable) *bit*. Marking a nonapplication file as executable doesn't do any harm, so it's a pretty low-impact way to let the server know you want the file parsed.

Many people consider the x-bit hack to be inelegant, and other ways of accomplishing its main purpose do exist. One of the disadvantages is that by using the x-bit hack you're storing some of the server's configuration information someplace else; another is that files often have their protections changed in ways that make sense by someone who's not the Webmaster and therefore not aware that the web server is interpreting the protection a certain way.

A second feature of the x-bit hack is that you can use it to have the Apache server set the `Last-Modified` header field for parsed documents. Usually, Apache *doesn't* set this field, because it may not be telling the truth — pieces of the document may be modified by the parsing, in which case it *wasn't* modified a while ago, but right during the request processing itself! Nevertheless, if your configuration contains a

```
XBitHack Full
```

directive, requests for parsed documents within that scope tell the server to set the `Last-Modified` header field to the actual last modification time of the document on disk.

Chapter 12

Reacting in Real-Time

. . . .

In This Chapter

▶ Finding out about CGI scripts

▶ Discovering how the Apache server works with CGI scripts

▶ Researching for CGI scriptwriting

▶ Exploring Server-Side Includes (SSIs)

▶ Uncovering what you can do with SSIs

. . . .

*A*lthough static pages — pages that just contain text or a picture or something else that doesn't change — are still the most common documents on the Web, they are not the limit of what the Web technology can do. Oh, no! Whereas static pages are the sort of thing that most web servers specialize in, you can either *subcontract* the processing of a request at run-time or tweak the content of a page between the time it leaves the disk and the time that the server sends it to the client.

Both have their own strengths and weaknesses, but one positive aspect that they share is that they can enhance your web site and make it a more interesting and exciting place to visit. If you want to know more, find yourself a comfy chair, put a tall glass of something refreshing within reach (because some of this stuff is fairly technical), and read on!

Scripts and CGI

CGI is an acronym for Common Gateway Interface, and it describes a manner in which web servers can communicate with other programs on the same system. These CGI scripts, as they're called, run under the supervision of the web server, and their entire lives consist of taking information that the server gives them about web requests and providing responses that the server can send back to the client.

Because CGI scripts aren't built into the server itself, you have tremendous freedom within them as long as you follow the rules. Kind of like a *haiku* poem, the rules that you have to follow are pretty strict, but you can say whatever you like within their parameters.

The Apache Web server can run as a script almost anything that's executable. You can write yours in shell commands, C, Perl, Ada, or whatever else you feel most comfortable with. The server just passes a command line to the operating system, and the system needs to figure out how to make it actually run.

If you're just getting into writing your own scripts, you may want to give serious consideration to using a language that lots of other web script authors use — that way you have a large pool of talent to consult when you have questions or problems. For example, Perl is a very popular scripting language because of its incredibly powerful text manipulation features.

You can find the current version of the CGI specification at

```
http://hoohoo.ncsa.uiuc.edu/cgi/
```

As of this book's publication, there is no authoritative CGI specification. A number of contributors are working on an RFC, but the RFC is in its infancy.

However, you may want to keep an eye on the following URL from time to time; if the project to formalize the specification ever gets off the ground, it will be noted here:

```
http://www.apache.org/related_projects.html
```

The CGI environment

After the Apache Web server figures out that it needs to run a script, it starts up a new child process to do it. This child process inherits much, but not all, of the environment that the server itself is running. One of the most important aspects of this operating environment is access rights.

Unless you're using an intermediate wrapper or control program, such as `suEXEC` or `cgiwrapper` (which I don't cover in this book at all, so don't bother rushing off to the index), the child processes running the script are using the user and group identifications of the parent server. So whatever the server can access, the script can access too.

After the Apache Web server starts a script in a child process, most of the information about the request — which the script is supposed to handle — is made available to the script through the use of *environment variables,* or *envariables* as they're sometimes called. Several standard envariables exist that are defined and described by the CGI specification, and additional ones may be available as well depending on the circumstances.

Scripts, security, and sanity

Your server may face tremendous security implications if it allows arbitrary scripts to run. The Apache Web server tries to short-circuit most of them by taking care of sensitive things before shifting to the non-superuser identity. However, a moment of inattention on the part of you, the Webmaster, can leave your system open to an attack by a malicious script.

For example, the Apache server opens all the logfiles before it does its identify change. Because the files are already open, the server can keep writing to them regardless of their protection. However, if the files allow access by the new identity, such as being owned by the server user or group, an arbitrary script can easily modify the activity logs.

Taking this one step further, if the logfile directory is even writable by the server user, a script possibly can fiddle with things in order to break into the system and get superuser access. (Excuse me if I don't provide details!)

The most important thing to remember is that scripts can do anything — they aren't limited to just displaying the time or sending mail. So think carefully before enabling them widely, such as by putting a

```
AddHandler cgi-script .cgi
```

in a server-wide or other very wide scope, or allowing an `Override FileInfo` (which allows the `AddHandler` directive to be used in `.htaccess` files) to be inherited in user directories.

Just consider the effect of giving your server's username and password to your worst enemy. If you feel comfortable that your system, and particularly your web environment, would be safe from that person — and would stay safe — go ahead and enable scripts globally.

Another aspect of this is the directories that are marked as containing only scripts by virtue of being listed in a `ScriptAlias` directive. Those scripts, too, are run with the server's access rights, but most servers need to have them around. The `ScriptAlias` directive can't appear in `.htaccess` files, so you don't have to worry about just anyone setting up such a directory — only those with access to your server config files. However, because they *are* implicitly trusted in a way, you should take particular care to see that they and the directories in which they live are secure from malicious damage — including the server user.

Scripts can be a double-edged sword: They can provide marvelous capabilities and slice through boring and mundane Web pages like the proverbial hot knife through butter, but they also can cut you to the bone if you're not aware of their potential dangers.

These envariables need to be considered *read-only* — that is, the server uses them to get the information to the script, but the script can't use them to send data back to the server.

Aside from envariables, the other means of sending information between the server and the script is through the standard input and output streams. The server passes any appropriate additional data to the script in a way that allows the script to read it as normal input, and the script sends information back to the server by writing it to the output stream in an entirely normal fashion.

Envariables passed to scripts

The Apache Web server passes a standard set of environment variables (or envariables) to scripts that it starts. In addition, other variables may get set depending on whether extra header fields were present in the request, authorization had to be performed, and so on.

Some standard Apache envariables are actually supplied over and above what the CGI specification calls for, so be careful if you intend to use your scripts elsewhere under non-Apache Web servers.

Here is a comprehensive list of the environment variables that the Apache server makes available to CGI scripts. I note the cases in which the envariable's existence is situational. Several of them refer to different portions of the URL that was requested; to illustrate these, I use the URL shown in Figure 12-1.

Figure 12-1:
A URL cadaver for dissection into envariables.

```
http://your.host.com:8080/cgi/foo.cgi/path-before?queryval
```

✔ AUTH_TYPE: This envariable is present only if the request has to path (successfully) through some sort of auth/auth process to get to this point (see Chapter 6 for more information about authentication and authorization). If this envariable does exist, its value is the type of authentication that was used — which almost always is Basic. If you check the value of this, beware of case sensitivity! If you actually use this envariable successfully in any of your scripts, give yourself 10 Apache Guru Points — not because it's difficult, but because it's neat.

- ✔ DOCUMENT_ROOT: As a moment's careful figuring reveals, the value of this envariable is the setting of the DocumentRoot directive in your server's configuration files. This can be useful if your script needs to locate files in your server's web space, but you should be careful not to display it to the end user because it gives away some details about your system's layout.

- ✔ GATEWAY_INTERFACE: This envariable indicates the version of the CGI specification to which your server is adhering (and to which your script should be adhering, as well). In practice this is almost always CGI/1.1, but your scripts should check it just to be on the safe side.

- ✔ HTTP_*: The HTTP_* envariable is actually a set of envariables. The Apache web server creates an envariable named like this for each header field in the request that isn't already represented by another envariable. Typical examples of this include the HTTP_HOST, HTTP_ACCEPT, HTTP_ACCEPT_LANGUAGE, and HTTP_USER_AGENT header fields. The rule is: If you remove the HTTP_ prefix and change all the underscores (_) to hyphens (-), the result is the name of the corresponding header field from the client request. This lets your script be really smart (if it wants to be) and take full advantage of the capabilities of the HTTP web protocol.

- ✔ PATH: This envariable is the normal UNIX path variable, which tells the shell the names of the directories in which it can find executable files. This can be useful because either the CGI script is itself a shell script or it may create a child process using a shell script. However, the CGI script is always free to override its own path, so this envariable is just a starting point.

- ✔ PATH_INFO: This envariable is not always present; the server creates it if and only if the requested URL includes what's called a (wait for it . . .) *path info* element. If the URL does include a path info element, the server sets the value of this envariable to it. A path info element is one way that the client can communicate additional information to the resource (which is the script in this case).

  To understand what path info really is, say you have a script named foo.cgi in your server's DocumentRoot. In the example URL shown in Figure 12-1, the server would set the PATH_INFO envariable to the value /path-before. In other words, the path info is the portion of the URL that follows the filename and precedes the query string (if any).

- ✔ QUERY_STRING: This envariable always exists in the script's environment, even if its value is an empty string. The server sets it to any portion of the request URL that follows a question mark (?). For example, in the case of a script invoked by the URL shown in Figure 12-1, the server would set the QUERY_STRING envariable to queryval. Note that the value doesn't include the delimiting character, the ? — unlike the PATH_INFO value.

✔ PATH_TRANSLATED: The server creates this environment variable is only if the request contains a path info element. This envariable is of limited usefulness, because the server essentially sets it to {DocumentRoot}{PATH_INFO}. For example, in the case of the URL shown in Figure 12-1, and assuming the DocumentRoot setting that I've been using all along, the server would set this envariable to /usr/local/web/apache/htdocs/path-before.

✔ REMOTE_ADDR: This envariable is always available to CGI scripts, and it is the IP address of the system from which the server received the request. Because this envariable is based on a numeric value, the server always defines it. Remember, computers *like* numbers.

In the case of a request that comes through a proxy, this envariable is the address of the proxy system itself rather than the original client that started the whole thing.

✔ REMOTE_HOST: This envariable is a companion to REMOTE_ADDR, but it's available to the invoked script only if the parent Apache server process is able to translate the IP address into an FQDN (Fully Qualified Domain Name). If the main server either has translation disabled (which is possible because doing so can improve performance noticeably on busy servers) or tries and is unable to do the translation, the server doesn't set the envariable at all.

✔ REMOTE_PORT: Like the REMOTE_ADDR envariable, this one is numeric in nature, and the server therefore always defines it for CGI scripts. This envariable is the port number, at the far end, of the system with which the server is communicating. If you're not sure how to use it, don't worry — it's really only there "just in case."

✔ REMOTE_USER: Like the AUTH_TYPE envariable, the server creates and passes this one to the script only if the request successfully passes through some auth/auth process. If this envariable does exist, its value is the username that was used to gain access.

The password used is not available to CGI scripts; it is just too easy to capture it and use it against you. And sometimes the REMOTE_USER envariable may exist but actually be a null string. In some cases a null username is allowed, and this is how it would be represented to the script.

✔ REQUEST_METHOD: The server always defines this envariable for CGI scripts and sets it to the HTTP method that was used to make the request. This HTTP method is usually (but not always!) one of the following:

- GET: This HTTP method is far and away the most common method in use on the Web today. It means what it says: It's a request to *get* a resource of some sort. Your script can be sure that any extra information coming from the client is available in the QUERY_STRING and PATH_INFO envariables.

- **HEAD:** This access method is very similar to the GET method that I just described, except that it means "don't actually give me the document itself; give me the response header fields that you would give me if I asked for the whole thing." Lots of things use HEAD requests to find out stuff about resources without actually having to pull over the items themselves. For example, some browsers use the HEAD method to check to see if they need to freshen their caches; they send a HEAD request for the document and then compare the response header fields against the ones that were stored with the cached copy. This is considered Network Friendly.

- **POST:** The POST method is the most complicated of the Big Three request methods. It's a sort of super GET, because the client can use all the GET ways of sending additional information (the query string and the path info), and it also can send an arbitrary amount of additional information. This is very useful when you want to keep the URL simple, but you have to process a lot of Web form fields, for example, or you don't want visitors to actually see what additional information is being passed around. This method is quite powerful, and it's commonly used to pass huge chunks of information from one page to another as a visitor moves around a site. The negative aspects of this method include the fact that it's more difficult to program for, and that all that additional information is being downloaded to the client and then uploaded to the server again. (That's only if you're using this method to maintain information as the visitor wanders around your site.)

HTTP access methods are *case-sensitive,* so a GET is as different from a Get as it is from a POST. If your scripts check the method that the server used to invoke them (and they should!), don't fall into the trap of thinking the scripts are all the same.

- ✔ **REQUEST_URI:** The Apache server always sets this environment variable when it invokes a CGI script. It sets this envariable to the portion of the URL that is specific to the server in question; in other words, the scheme (usually http:), server name, and server port are all removed, and what's left is stored in REQUEST_URI for the script to use. If you look back at Figure 12-1, the server would set the REQUEST_URI envariable to /cgi/foo.cgi/path-before?queryval.

- ✔ **SCRIPT_FILENAME:** The server always sets this envariable to the name of the file that it invokes as the script. It should be the full filesystem path to the script that's actually running.

- ✔ **SCRIPT_NAME:** Unlike the SCRIPT_FILENAME envariable, which is the operating system path to the script file, the SCRIPT_NAME environment variable is a *web* path to the script. In the example URL shown in Figure 12-1, the server would set the SCRIPT_NAME to /cgi/foo.cgi. The server always sets this variable.

✔ SERVER_ADMIN: This envariable is, quite simply, the value given to the ServerAdmin directive in the configuration files for the current server. The script is free to use this in error pages that it generates.

✔ SERVER_NAME: This variable is set to the name of the server that is handling the request, and it's always defined for CGI scripts. This envariable is not always the same as the server name specified in the original URL; in the case of a system with multiple virtual hosts, the requested server and the one that actually gets chosen to respond may be different. (See Chapter 14 for more information about virtual hosts.)

✔ SERVER_PORT: Like the REMOTE_PORT environment variable, this one is always available (it's a number). It is set to the port number on the server's end over which the request came. It's usually 80 (or 443 if you're running SSL), but it reflects the actual port.

✔ SERVER_PROTOCOL: The Apache server uses this environment variable to tell the script the version of the HTTP protocol that the client used to make the request. The value is in the form HTTP/m.n, where m.n is the major and minor version of the protocol that the client used. Common values are HTTP/1.0, HTTP/0.9, and HTTP/1.1. The Apache server always makes this envariable available to CGI scripts.

✔ SERVER_SOFTWARE: The server always sets this envariable, which indicates the actual version of the Apache server software itself. The format is Apache/version, where version may be something like 1.3.0, 1.2.4, or 2.0b1 (which indicates a beta-test release — and *no*, that version doesn't exist yet! It may exist by the time you read this book, in which case: What took you so long to buy this book?)

✔ UNIQUE_ID: The server gives every request that comes in to it a unique identification string that the Webmaster can use however he or she wants to use it. The server sets this environment variable to an encoded version of this unique identifier value, and always defines it for CGI scripts if the server was built with the mod_unique_id module and the module is active (which it is unless you perform some fairly Deep Magic — in which case, why aren't you writing your own book?). Scripts can use it as database keys, logging identifiers, or whatever else they like.

The UNIQUE_ID environment variable is new for Apache 1.3. The standard-with-1.3 mod_unique_id module generates the envariable, and no corresponding module is available for older versions of Apache.

Command-line arguments

In some cases, such as requests made using the GET method with a query string (see the preceding section for more on the GET method), the Apache server starts up a script and passes it some information on the command line. The command line is never the only place the information is available (it's always accessible through one or another of the environment variables), but simple scripts can find the command line more convenient to use than checking the envariables.

The stuff that the server passes along on the command line is the same as is in the QUERY_STRING environment variable (see the preceding section), with any appropriate shell meta-characters (such as &, ?, and *) escaped with a preceding backslash. What shows up in the QUERY_STRING as a&*bc?d shows up in the command line as a\&*bc\?d.

The following rule defines when you can use the command line arguments and when you have to use the QUERY_STRING:

Look at the value of the QUERY_STRING environment variable. If it doesn't contain an equal sign (=), you can use the command line arguments. If it does contain an equal sign, you *must* use the QUERY_STRING value instead.

Take a look at a couple of sample URLs and apply the previous rule. For example, in the URL back in Figure 12-1, the QUERY_STRING value would be queryval. Because the URL doesn't contain an equal sign, the script would be able to use the stuff passed on the command line. Now take a look at the URL in Figure 12-2 — whoops, the QUERY_STRING is ka=a&kb=b. It definitely includes some equal signs, so any script that URL invokes has to regard the command line as off limits.

Figure 12-2:
Another
URL
cadaver.

```
http://your.host.com:8080/cgi/foo.cgi/path-before?ka=a&kb=b
```

Communicating with the server

Any web server that uses the CGI specification to communicate with a script has several different ways of passing the script information:

- ✔ Environment variables
- ✔ The script's command line
- ✔ The script's input stream

The server uses the last one, the input stream, only when the request method says to use it. (In the common environment, that means, "when the method is POST".)

On the flip side, to communicate information back to the server and through the server to the requesting client, the script has exactly one option: Its output stream. Yes, friend, CGI scripts provide the results of their labors by just printing them normally on the standard output. You have to follow some rules to do this, though. Read on!

The head and the body are separated

Throughout this book, I blather on about request header fields and response header fields until you probably get sick of the phrases. Well, if you're going to get into the business of using the CGI interface and writing scripts, you need to know something about these fields. Go refill your glass, and I'll begin when you get back.

Okay. Each web message (such as a request or a response) consists of two parts: the header and the body (or "bodyer" if you want it to sound similar and don't mind people giving you strange looks and psychiatric advice).

The *header* is full of information about the message, such as what it's trying to do, how many bytes are in it, what kind of information it contains, and so on. The *body* contains the stuff (if anything) that the header is talking about. For example in a response to a page request, the body contains the actual text of the page. A blank line separates the header and the body. Not a line containing blanks, but a really blank line, like you get if you hit the Enter key twice. Blank lines are how the computers know where the header is done and the body is beginning.

The header portion isn't really meant to be seen by anyone except the computers — the client and the server — but if you're writing a CGI script, your script is part of the server, and you get to play. In fact, you *have* to play, or the server kicks you off the field and tells the client you're a bozo.

The header portion of a web message consists of a series of lines of text. Each line is called a *header field* and starts with a phrase that describes what's on the line. These phrases are called the *field names,* and they look kinda funny — just letters, numbers, and the odd bit of punctuation, no spaces at all. (What do you expect from a computer's reading material?) A bunch of field names exist, and you must use them — you can't just make up your own file names and expect everything to work properly.

Figure 12-3 shows a sample request as the server sees it, and Figure 12-4 shows the response — header and all. The <> characters mark the blank lines.

Figure 12-3:
The nitty-gritty details of a simple client request.

```
GET /foo.txt HTTP/1.1
Connection: close
Host: www.somewhere.net
Accept-language: en
Accept: text/html, text/plain, image/gif, */*
<>
```

Figure 12-4:
The equally nitty-gritty details of a server response.

```
HTTP/1.1 200 OK
Date: Wed, 17 Sep 1997 02:10:14 GMT
Server: Apache/1.3b1-dev
Cache-Control: max-age=1000000
Expires: Sun, 28 Sep 1997 15:56:54 GMT
Last-Modified: Wed, 10 Sep 1997 02:21:09 GMT
ETag: "13227-c-34160415"
Content-Length: 40
Content-MD5: B7ovTFKhzuo163ATMqQMsA==
Accept-Ranges: bytes
Connection: close
Content-Type: text/plain
<>
This is the body of a very
boring file.
```

If you look closely at the dates in Figure 12-4, you see that the value of the `Expires` header field is one million seconds later than the time in the `Date` header field. This was done with the `mod_expires` module.

That response is the part in which your CGI script gets involved. Looks pretty grim, doesn't it? Well, don't worry — the server itself supplies most of those response header fields.

Actually, most CGI scripts can get away with sending only one header field: the `Content-Type` one. However, a variety of CGI scripts exist with which you should have at least a nodding acquaintance, and I describe them in the next section.

The second most common single header field is the `Location` field, which is how you can cause a redirect from within a script (a very common operation).

Response header fields that I've known — and you should too

You should be marginally familiar with five different header fields. You probably won't use more than a couple of these fields for most of your scripts, but if you're aware of the capabilities of the other fields, you can keep them fermenting in the back of your mind.

All CGI script responses *must* include at least one header field. Sending the actual document without first sending the header is illegal, and if you do, the server ignores the document and tells the client that your script is a bozo. This makes a weird sort of sense, for what use is a body without a head?

All of the following header fields are valid for both `HTTP/1.0` (which, at the time of writing this book, is the most common protocol used on the Internet) and for `HTTP/1.1` (which is the next version that the Internet is migrating to):

✔ `Status:` *code description:* You probably won't use this special header field very often, which is rather a pity because it's extremely powerful. It's special because it's not a *real* header field that gets sent all the way back to the client. Rather, the script uses it to tell the server how things went so that the server can take whatever action is appropriate (such as setting the status value in the first line of the response — see Figure 12-4). With this header field, you can tailor the status of the request (as reported to the client) using any of the three dozen or so formal HTTP status codes. If you don't include a `Status` header field in your script's output, the Apache server assumes `200 OK`, which means everything is hunky-dory, the request was processed smoothly, and the response content is forthcoming in the script's response body.

✔ `Content-Type:` *type/subtype:* This header field is by far the most common header field that you use and is frequently the only one that you need to supply. The general rule is that either `Content-Type` or `Location` is required. The types `text/html` and `text/plain` pretty much do what you'd think, and if you want to get fancier than those types, you need to research into the additional MIME types yourself.

If you want to transmit binary stuff in the body, such as a GIF image, go right ahead. The web transport technology accepts binary stuff without any problem, unlike many electronic mail systems that require you to encode the binary data into some sort of textual form first.

✔ Location: *full-URL:* This header field is how CGI scripts signal redirects (see Chapter 11 for more on redirects) to the client, indicating that the real resource is located elsewhere. The field value must be a complete URL; you cannot use a partial one or one that is relative to the original request's URL. You should supply a value for either this field or a Content-Type field in your response to the server.

✔ Last-Modified: *HTTP-date:* This field is optional, but your CGI scripts can include it to help ease network congestion by helping documents get cached. Use your judgment; if you're sure the output of your script actually has a lifetime, you can include this header field with a value of the effective natal date of whatever you based the output on.

The Last-Modified field value cannot be in the future. You can set it to the current time or any time in the past, but a future date is forbidden.

✔ Expires: *HTTP-date:* Like the Last-Modified header field, having your CGI script send an Expires header field may be inappropriate; script output often differs slightly between invocations even with the same URL, or may be based on external data that changes frequently. So you may want to either set this field to a very short time in the future, or omit it altogether.

Don't forget that the format of the date is pretty strict; you may get unexpected results if you don't follow the format correctly. See Figure 12-4 for an example of a valid date string.

✔ Content-Length: *byte-count:* This header field is a nice one to include if you can, because it helps the client on the other end verify that it received the entire body. Unfortunately, CGI scripts may have trouble predicting just how many bytes they're going to send, and because this header needs to be set before the body is actually transmitted, you may get stuck in a catch-22. However, calculating the size is the neighborly thing to do, if you can.

Don't forget to follow your header fields with a blank line! If you don't, the server doesn't know where the header ends and the body begins, and it complains bitterly.

Server buffering of CGI output

To be friendly to the network and not fill it up with lots of teeny-tiny packets containing only a few characters, most web servers do what's called buffering, particularly buffering of CGI script output.

In general, *buffering* refers to collecting as much of something that you can before acting on it. Buffering of a script's output means that the server fills a bucket with whatever the script has to say, and then after the bucket is full or the script is finished, the server empties the bucket onto the network for transmission to the client.

Other things do buffering, too. For example, the output routines of most programming languages (Perl and C included) don't immediately send what the program tells them to send. Instead, they let it build up in a buffer, and then they do something with it after the buffer gets near full. The process of sending the buffer's contents and marking the buffer as empty and reusable is called *flushing the buffer.*

This buffering behavior can cause problems in two places in the process of getting a script's output to the client. One has to do with any buffering that stands between the script and the server, and the other involves the server itself.

The Apache Web server insists that any CGI scripts (that Apache starts) deliver at least the header portion of the response within a specific interval. Then Apache can be sure that the scripts are actually working and not consuming resources without accomplishing anything. The default interval is 300 seconds (5 minutes), but you can change this setting with the Timeout directive.

If your script is written in a language that buffers its output, your headers may not make it to Apache before the timeout expires. After all, script header fields commonly don't consist of more than a few bytes, and they may easily languish in the output buffer until you start filling it up with the actual body content.

To work around this, you should take advantage of any buffer-flushing abilities that your language has. Print all the header fields that you need as quickly as you can, print the empty line that follows them, and then flush the buffer to make sure that they reach the server. After you send the header and the blank line that follows the buffer, you can go back to generating your output as usual.

For example, if your script is written in C, you can call the fflush() routine to make sure that your header fields get sent to the server; if your favorite scripting language is Perl, you can set the $| (dollar-vbar) variable for the STDOUT filehandle to a non-zero value, and all subsequent output operations force a flush of the Perl output buffer.

The Apache Web server, too, buffers the output from scripts, collecting as much output as possible before bundling it up and sending it to the client. In versions of Apache before 1.3, you had only one way to work around this: using what's called an NPH script (for more on NPH scripts see "Do-it-(all)-yourself scripts," later in this chapter).

Apache 1.3 adds another condition to the decision about when to send the buffer contents to the client: If the buffer is full, or the script has exited, or the server ever ends up waiting for information from the script, the server passes along anything that it has already received before it starts waiting. Therefore, the scripts can provide periodic status reports when they're working on something time-consuming, and the server can then send the reports along to the client. Of course, for this scenario to work, the script has to flush its output buffer to make sure the information reaches the server. In other words, the server listens to the script until either its buffer fills up, or the script dies, or the script pauses for breath — then the server sends whatever it has and goes back to listening.

Do-it-(all)-yourself scripts

One special form of CGI script that the Apache Web server supports is called an *NPH* script — for *Non-Parsed Headers*. The name is kinda misleading, because there's more to it than that.

Apache knows which scripts are NPH scripts from their file names: If the file name begins with `nph-`, the script is an NPH script.

When Apache invokes an NPH script, it basically hooks up the script's output to the client's input and then gets out of the way. The script talks directly to the client, and the client gets the script's output as soon as the script flushes its own buffers.

This is where the name comes from — the Apache server isn't checking (or *parsing*) the headers from the script to see if they're valid or bogus.

NPH scripts are generally for people who are well-versed in the Deep Magic of the HTTP protocol and network performance — people who let terms like RST, Transfer-Encoding, RTT, If-Modified-Since, and FIN_WAIT_2 fall trippingly from their tongues without thinking twice about it. The only rational reason that anyone else would want to use an NPH script is to take advantage of the instant-gratification nature of the communication between the script and the client. And, as I note in the last section, changes to the Apache Web server software in Version 1.3 address this.

Give yourself 20 Apache Guru Points if you can figure out a justifiable reason to use NPH scripts and write a script that implements it flawlessly. Writing an NPH script is not particularly difficult, but you have to be very, very cautious and abide by the HTTP rules.

Dynamic Content with Server-Side Includes

A *Server-Side Include,* or SSI, is an instruction that's embedded in an HTML document that tells the server to do something when sending the document to a client. SSIs get their name from the fact that the web server, rather than the end user's application, is handling them.

You can use SSIs to:

- ✔ Include other files (even the output from scripts!)
- ✔ Display server and document information
- ✔ Conditionalize your HTML with if-then-else-endif blocks

SSIs are a very powerful feature of the Apache Web server, but as with most potent abilities, a correspondingly great potential for disaster always exists. SSIs have a definite impact on performance because the server isn't just picking up the file and tossing it to the client; the server reads the file first and maybe makes notes in the margin. And, because SSIs cause the server to do things at run time, you should read the sidebar "Scripts, security, and sanity," earlier in this chapter.

Other web servers besides Apache provide SSI functionality, and most of them follow the same format and provide (mostly) the same capabilities. Your mileage may vary, though — don't be surprised if you move an SSIful document to another system and it doesn't work quite right.

The process of scanning HTML files and processing SSI directives inside is called *parsing* the file. HTML files that are configured to be handled like this are called *parsed HTML* (even though the parsing hasn't happened yet).

One interesting side effect of using SSIs is that the end user can't be sure what you did. The results of an SSI directive are inserted into the document in its place, so the final document that reaches the client includes only what the SSI(s) *did,* not what they *were.*

Would you like to read about how you configure Apache to parse files, or about the details of what you can do with SSI directives? Check out the next two sections to find out.

A-parsing we will go. . . .

Here are the two ways to tell the Apache server that it needs to parse an HTML file:

✔ Label the file as food for the `server-parsed` content handler

✔ Set the user x-bit on the file, and make sure it's located in a scope covered by an `XBitHack On` or `XBitHack Full` directive (for more on x-bits, see "The x-bit hack again," later in this chapter)

The first method generally is considered to be better, primarily because it keeps web server configuration information inside the web server's configuration files, and not lying around in the file system where it's also used for something else and may get changed. Also, the second method is, well, a hack.

The usual way to mark files as eligible for server parsing is with these types of directives:

```
AddType text/html .shtml
AddHandler server-parsed .shtml
```

The first line tells the Apache server that it should mark any file that ends in .shtml as containing HTML. Without this line, the server doesn't know what type to give the file and uses the default (which is usually text/plain, but you can change it with the `DefaultType` directive). The server needs to know what type to give the file so it can tell the client, which makes the decisions about what to do with the file when it arrives.

The second line tells Apache to parse any file ending in .shtml for SSI directives before transmitting it.

If you want to have *all* the HTML documents on your web server parsed before delivery, you can add the following line to your server configuration files:

```
AddHandler server-parsed .html .htm .htp .shtml
```

(This directive includes common suffixes for HTML files.)

The `AddType` and `AddHandler` directives can appear in any scope. If they're in an .htaccess file, the `FileInfo` override must be active (that is, some parent scope must include `FileInfo` in an `AllowOverrides` statement).

The x-bit hack again

In Chapter 11, I describe the x-bit hack in terms of how you can use it to affect document caching. That function is actually only a side effect — the real reason that the x-bit hack exists is to tell the server that it needs to parse the file. (Check out Chapter 11 for more on the x-bit hack.)

Here's the rule the Apache server uses to determine if the file should be parsed because of its x-bit-ness:

If the current document is in a scope covered by an `XBitHack On` or `XBitHack Full` directive, and the x (execute) permission bit is set for the owner of the file, the Apache server parses the file.

The Apache Group discourages the use of the x-bit hack but doesn't officially deprecate it. File permissions can too easily be changed by accident, without any awareness of the (potentially huge) impact on the web site.

The who-what-huh of SSI directives

Because of the way Apache implements SSIs, putting them into an HTML document doesn't break it at all. In HTML-speak, a *comment* (something that shouldn't be displayed to the end user) looks like this:

```
<!-- this is a comment, and the user won't see it -->
```

SSI directives take advantage of this by appearing *inside* the comment:

```
<!--#ssi-directive arguments -->
```

That way, when the Apache server examines a document for SSI processing, it has to scan only for `<!--#`. Because `<!--#` is inside a comment, you won't have a problem if SSIs are disabled or unavailable.

Be sure to insert a space between the end of your directive and the `-->` marking the end of the enclosing comment — otherwise something may not `recognize` it as the end of the comment.

Although I don't display the entire lexicon of SSI directives in this chapter (see Appendix C for that), Figure 12-5 shows some of the things that you can do with them.

As of Version 1.3, the Apache server can parse only static files. It cannot scan the output from a script, for example, and parse directives that it finds there.

✔ The `config` directive allows you to control the format of values displayed by other directives. For example, the following `echo` directive

```
<!--#config timefmt="%Y-%m-%d %H:%M" -->
<!--#echo var="LAST_MODIFIED" -->
```

would cause something like the following to appear in the final display:

```
1997-09-17 02:17
```

✔ The `exec` directive includes the output from the given shell command or CGI script. Some restrictions exist about when you can use this directive and what commands you can specify; see the `mod_include` online documentation page for details.

```
<!--#exec cgi="myscript.cgi" -->
<!--#exec cmd="/bin/date" -->
```

✔ The `include` directive is one of the most powerful directives. You can use it to insert static files (such as a common header or footer for all your pages) or the output from a script (this method is preferred over `exec cgi`). If the item that you're including is a static file, it is subject to further parsing according to the usual rules.

```
<!--#include file="footer.html" -->
<!--#include virtual="/cgi-bin/myscript" -->
<!--#include virtual="/header.html" -->
```

✔ Another extremely powerful capability is *conditional HTML* — that is, using SSIs to control which portions of the file are included. The following fragment displays different things depending on whether the `AUTH_TYPE` environment variable is set.

```
<!--#if expr="$AUTH_TYPE = /..*/" -->
Welcome, O Authorized One! How may I serve
your noble self?
<!--#else -->
Hi! You're not from around here, are you?
<!--#endif -->
```

Figure 12-5:
See the
power of
the SSI.

Chapter 13

Actions, Handlers, and Types

• •

In This Chapter

▶ Understanding how Apache can tell what's in a file by looking at the name

▶ Finding out how *you* can tell Apache what's in a file

▶ Defining a content handler

▶ Telling Apache to treat certain files in a particular way

▶ Tailoring web error messages to look the way you want them to

• •

*B*ecause most of what a web server serves comes from actual files living on disk, you need some way to determine what kind of stuff is stored in any particular file. The client is going to want to know this info so it can display a picture, play a sound, or format text for reading. In addition, the Apache server bases an awful lot of its decisions on this content-type aspect.

The easiest way to figure out what's in a file is to have the file convey this information to the server. This has been rather taken for granted so far in this book; sorry about that! But I explain everything in this chapter — hopefully you forgive me.

This technique of using the file name to tell about what the file contains is central to the operation of many web servers, and the Apache server is no exception. The way that it's done is to have some sort of configuration file that tells the server, "when you see a file with a name ending in `.html`, it's content-type is `text/html`; files ending with `.gif` are content-type `image/gif`" and so on.

The canonical (remember "canonical"?) file that the Apache Web server uses for this purpose is named `{ServerRoot}/conf/mime.types`. It's a normal text file that you can modify with any editor, and each line contains the content-type and the file suffixes that indicate a file is of that type, as in this example:

```
text/html                    html htm
image/gif                    gif GIF
image/jpeg                   jpeg jpg JPG
application/mac-binhex40 hqx
```

Even though the `conf/mime.types` file is editable, actually *editing* it is not recommended. The file is part of the standard distribution of the Apache Web server package, and it gets updated from time to time. So a future upgrade of the package may incidentally wipe out any changes that you make. The preferred method is to use the `AddType` directive in the server configuration files instead. I describe this directive shortly.

You may notice that the suffixes on each line *don't* include any periods. You can include them if you like, but they aren't necessary — they're assumed to be there.

Apache handles file typing by looking for suffixes in a right-to-left manner. First, Apache removes encoding and language extensions from a copy of the file name (for example, Apache would pare down `foo.en.html.gz` to `foo.html`, assuming that `en` was declared as a language with the `AddLanguage` directive (see Chapter 11) and `gz` was declared to be an encoding suffix with the `AddEncoding` directive) and then looks at the last suffix on the file. If Apache finds the suffix somewhere in its list, it marks the file as being of the appropriate content-type. If it doesn't find the suffix, it marks the file as being of the type set by the `DefaultType` directive.

Now that you have an overview, here are the details:

✔ By using the `TypesConfig` directive, you can tell Apache to look elsewhere for the `mime.types` file with the `TypesConfig` directive. You can even change the name to something else. The `TypesConfig` directive looks like this:

```
TypesConfig types-file
```

This new file name can be relative to the ServerRoot directory; you indicate that by not starting the file name with a slash (/). For example, the default value for this new file can be represented by `conf/mime.types`, which means it's in the `{ServerRoot}/conf` directory.

✔ To enhance the canned list of content-types or declare specific (possibly additional) suffixes as being of a particular content-type, you use the `AddType` directive:

```
AddType content-type suffix [suffix...]
```

If the Apache Web server doesn't already know about the content-type (possibly because it isn't in the `TypesConfig` file, or maybe you made it up), this directive *makes* the server know about it. Then the directive tells the server to make a note that files ending with the listed suffix are of that type.

✔ You tell the Apache server that a particular extension indicates that the file is encoded somehow with the `AddEncoding` directive, which looks like this:

```
AddEncoding encoding extension [extension...]
```

When the server tries to serve such a file in response to a request, it tells the client that the file is encoded according to `encoding` — for example, `gzip` or `compress`. This directive also alerts the Apache server to the fact that it can ignore these extensions when trying to determine the content-type of a file — the extensions indicate how the file is encoded, not what it contains.

✔ The `AddLanguage` directive lets you declare an extension as indicating a particular language bias in the file. I describe this directive in more detail in Chapter 11, but the main effect you're interested in here is that language extensions aren't used to determine content-type.

✔ By using the `DefaultType` directive, you can tell the Apache Web server what content-type to use when it can't figure it out automatically:

```
DefaultType content-type
```

The usual value for this is `text/plain` because most web servers contain primarily text documents of one form or another. If your server specializes in binary files or images, you may want to us something like this instead:

```
DefaultType application/octet-stream
```

which means that when Apache can't figure out the content-type of a particular file, it tells the client, "This is a binary file of some sort — *you* figure it out."

There! Now you have a good handle on how file names are meaningful to the Apache Web server, and you can make a highly educated guess about what the server may think about and do with any particular file.

Declaring an extension as meaning multiple things is not a good idea, for obvious reasons. For example, if you declare `zot` as a content-type suffix *and* a language extension *and* an encoding, what would Apache going to tell the client about a document named `foo.zot`?

Content Handlers

The basic idea of content handlers has been broached in a sideways sort of way in previous chapters, but I see no reason not to drag them, kicking and screaming, back into the text at this point.

A content handler produces the output that gets sent to the client. All successful requests were processed by a content handler. A content handler even takes care of those simple requests that result in a file being copied to the client without any special bells or whistles — in this case, the handler is the default (sort of a "last-chance") content handler, which does exactly that and no more.

A content handler can generate its results completely out of whole cloth (making it up as it goes along, so to speak), or it can twiddle with data coming from a file or somewhere else. The mod_status and mod_info modules (see Chapter 10) fall into the former category: They don't give you a translated or converted file, but rather they generate their display pages on the fly. Contrariwise, the mod_include module (see Chapter 12) does the latter sort of thing: It takes a file on the disk, translates it by processing any embedded SSI directives, and then sends the (possibly) modified result onward. Even the script processing mod_cgi module (also described in Chapter 12) uses a content handler, although it's somewhere between the two extremes that I just mentioned.

The current implementation of the Apache Web server permits only a single content handler to act on any particular request — which is why script output can't be parsed for server-side include directives. Allowing content handlers to feed their output to one another *is* on the design wish list, however.

Data Massage from Outside the Server

So far in this book I've described different content handlers that are part of the Apache Web server itself. Things like a module that says, "It's a script — let's run it!" or, "Let's check this file for SSI directives!" One thing that different content handlers have in common is that they're part of the core server, and you can't easily change what they do if it doesn't exactly match what you want. But what if you want to be able to define your own special processing, such as "Send me a mail message any time someone accesses this document." Apache won't do that automatically and would require some code modifications to make it happen.

But wait! Put away your software scalpel and your debugging dialysis machine, because you can do it within the framework of normal Apache configuration and operation, through what are called *actions*.

The Action directive (part of the mod_action module, for a wonder) allows you to tell Apache, "Run *this* CGI script whenever someone requests a file of *that* type." Naturally this directive is subject to the usual scoping rules, so it doesn't have to affect your entire server.

You need to remember a bit of indirection. File names are used to determine content-types, and content-types are used to determine which content handler (such as Action scripts) should be invoked. You can't base an action directly on the file name.

Suppose that you *do* want to get some mail whenever someone accesses a particular text file. If you put the following lines into the .htaccess file in the appropriate directory (where the files live)

```
<Files letmeknow.txt>
    AddType private/x-mail-notify .txt
</Files>
Action private/x-mail-notify /~chris/cgi/notifier
```

then whenever a client asks for the letmeknow.txt file, the Apache Web server should invoke the notifier CGI script in the cgi directory under Chris's home directory. Because of the scope that the <Files> container imposes, no other .txt files in the directory are affected — they are handled normally.

The FileInfo override controls the AddType directive , which means the scope within which the previous .htaccess file falls must have an Overrides FileInfo directive (or the equivalent) active or it won't work.

Here's an idea of what that script may look like:

```
#!/bin/sh
echo "Status: 200 OK"
echo "Content-type: text/plain"
echo ""
/usr/lib/sendmail - t<<EOF
From: fromuser@yourdomain
To: root
Subject: "Web request for $REQUEST_URI"


EOF
cat < $PATH_TRANSLATED
```

Notice anything odd about this sequence? I told the server to process that file in a special way, and I tied an Action script to it by marking it as being of a special content-type. And then when the Action script runs, the server changes the content-type back to what it *really* should be before processing it. (If you noticed that, give yourself 20 Apache Guru Points.) Because the server runs only one content handler run *per* document, this is a trick that you can do only once per request — you can't fool Apache into running multiple content handlers by changing the document's content-type and handing it off to the next handler in the chain.

The preceding example is extremely simplistic; I made it up just to demonstrate how you can use Action scripts to supplement the built-in processing that Apache can do. (I *did* test it, though. It works.) It's not very bullet proof, nor secure. And in the case of the previous script, the mail would come to you from the username that the server is running as.

Because Action scripts are true CGI scripts, they're subject to the same rules, restrictions, and concerns as their brethren.

If you haven't read it yet, please go back to Chapter 12 and take a look at "Scripts, security, and sanity."

Isn't this neat? Now you know how to tell Apache to treat documents with a certain kind of content in a particular way — and you *don't* have to write your own Apache module in order to do it! You can still do it that way if you like and gain a lot of Apache Guru Points, but you would need to invest a significant amount of time to figure out how to write an Apache module.

Error Handlers

Okay, content handlers *massage* (or produce) the actual document content that gets sent to the client. Well, what if what the client sees is an error message? Where does that message come from?

It comes from another kind of content handler, of course. The status of the request that gets sent back to the client isn't the usual 200 OK code (that I discuss in Chapter 12), rather it is the real error code. For some types of errors, an actual body of text may accompany the error; for others, only the error code is sent.

Error codes in this context refer to HTTP error codes, not UNIX errno values or anything like that. The HTTP status codes and their values are defined in the HTTP specification documents.

The Apache Web server has a default content handler for dealing with errors, too, just as it does for dealing with unremarkable file requests. And like other aspects of the server, Apache allows you to say "Webmaster knows best" and override the default behavior. You can override it by declaring an *error handler* with the `ErrorDocument` directive:

```
ErrorDocument code handler
```

The `ErrorDocument` directive can appear in any scope, but the `FileInfo` override must be active for it to work within `.htaccess` files.

The `code` is quite simply the three-digit HTTP error code, and the `handler` tells the Apache web server what to do when it encounters that error while trying to access a document. Common error codes are `301` ("moved temporarily"), `302` ("moved permanently"), `403` ("forbidden"), `404` ("not found"), and `500` ("internal server error").

That's the simple part. The `handler` portion of the directive is a little more complicated, because you can actually tell the server to do several different *kinds* of things, from changing the default error message associated with the HTTP error code to actually redirecting to a different URL.

Error handlers that are actual URLs can be CGI scripts or normal web documents of any sort. If they're CGI scripts, they have the usual environment available to them (see Chapter 12).

The simplest ErrorDocument `handler` type that you can set up is to have the server send just a one-line explanatory text message. You do this by putting the text of that message in the directive, starting with a quotation mark (`"`).

```
ErrorDocument 404 "Sorry, couldn't find it
```

The quotation mark is *not* part of the message, so you don't need to (and shouldn't) put one at the end of the string. It simply tells the server that the text that follows is just text, not a URL or anything special.

The next thing that you can use for the `handler` argument is a local URI (that is, the portion of a URL that follows the scheme and server portion):

```
ErrorDocument 403 /cgi-bin/not-permitted
```

If a client tries to access a document within a scope covered by the previous directive, and something (access rules, file permissions, or whatever) denies the client access to it, the server invokes the previous CGI script to deal with the situation. This is done as an internal redirect, so the client doesn't see that the display came from a different URL than the one that it originally requested.

If you use CGI scripts for error handlers and have your `ErrorDocument` directives access them through internal redirects like this, a bunch of additional environment variables, named `REDIRECT_*`, are available to you. (These environment variables are actually available any time a CGI script is invoked due to an internal redirect on the same server.) You can use these environment variables to figure out what went wrong, how your script was invoked, and what the original request was.

If you declare an error handler for code `401` and you want to use this means of redirecting to another document for handling, you *must* use this format. You cannot use the next format that I describe (which uses an external redirect) because `401` is an error having to do with authorization — and authorization is very URL-specific. Redirecting the client to a different URL interferes with the way that Web authorization is designed to work.

The final type of *handler* value that you can give to an `ErrorDocument` directive is a full (absolute) URL string. The following handler would cause Apache to redirect the client to the new URL.

```
ErrorDocument 500 http://otherhost.com/server-error.html
```

The major disadvantage to using this format is that the invoked script has no way of telling how it was reached or what the original request was. As far as the script knows, the client asked for it by name.

Chapter 14

Virtual Hosts

· ·

In This Chapter

▶ Understanding what a virtual host is

▶ Getting to know the different types of virtual hosts

▶ Declaring a virtual host in your server configuration files

▶ Getting acquainted with the DNS Internet naming system

▶ Understanding what double lookup means

▶ Understanding how virtual hosts and default hosts interact

· ·

Although a recent survey revealed well over 1 million web servers on the Internet, the Internet doesn't necessarily contain an equal number of Webmasters and actual web systems. Fortunately, that number is still small enough for you to join the elite by becoming a Webmaster yourself. The actual number of web systems is considerably smaller than the total, and the illusion of more web sites existing than actual systems is created through the use of *virtual hosts*. ISPs (Internet Service Providers) that sell domain names and web sites as part of their business frequently use this technique.

Virtual host technology allows your actual Apache Web server system to wear a set of masks or alternate identities, and you too can use it to create the illusion that more systems exist than there really are. So get out your magic wand, because this chapter describes the secrets behind the magician's tricks.

What's a Virtual Host?

Like the word *configuration,* the phrase *virtual host* is not one that falls trippingly off your tongue — nor off your fingers. The usual abbreviation is *vhost,* and I use it when my fingers get tired or I think your eyes are.

I've mentioned before this strange penchant computers have for preferring to use numbers instead of names and only deigning to use names for the benefit of poor, benighted humans. This extends down to the level of how computers talk to each other. When one system wants to talk to another system, it can use the equivalent of a telephone book to find out what numbers to use.

You can take this analogy, limping, a few steps farther. Although each telephone number applies only to a single location, you can reach multiple people at that number, and a single house can have more than one telephone number. The same situation applies to those numeric network addresses that computers use: A single computer can have more than one address, and a single address can have more than one name.

This is what virtual hosts are all about — setting things up so you can talk to different people by using their names, even though they're all sharing the same telephone number. Likewise, you can talk to the *same* person by using different telephone numbers at the same location.

Okay, that analogy is just about dead. I'm going to give it a gold watch and send it on home and tackle this another way.

What's in a [virtual] name?

A single network address can have multiple names, just as you may be called by your first name, middle name, or nickname. And a single computer can also have multiple addresses, just as you may have more than one telephone line. How you respond to a call may have to do with how you're addressed or which telephone you answer. This whole business of web virtual hosts revolves around that last point. Sound confusing? Well, don't worry — it *is* confusing.

A virtual host is like a web nickname for your computer. It lets you tailor what your visitors see according to how they got to your system. It's called a *virtual* host because otherwise you'd have computers all over the place with multiple personalities; calling them virtual takes some of the stress out of it, so it's more like a child pretending to be a superhero than someone really believing he or she is another person.

Apache provides two different types of virtual hosts: *name* virtual hosts and *address* virtual hosts. To drag that poor, tired analogy back in for a moment, these virtual hosts are like responding according to what you were called or which telephone you answered, respectively.

The rules behind virtual hosts

The entire topic of web virtual hosts is pretty complicated and confusing, so let me try going through it another way. If you feel you already understand the basics of virtual hosts, give yourself 20 Apache Guru Points and don't bother reading this section — except for amusement.

Here are the basic rules you have to work with:

✔ A single computer can have zero or more IP addresses

✔ A single IP address can have zero or more names

The normal rules of mathematics apply in this case, too, and from these rules, you can correctly deduce a third rule:

A single computer can have zero or more names

Of course, if you're going to be working with the network, addresses are a basic requirement — so all those *zeros* become *ones* instead:

✔ A single computer can have one or more IP addresses

✔ A single IP address can have one or more names

✔ A single computer can therefore have one or more names

The whole concept of web virtual hosts revolves around the *or more* clause.

Declaring a virtual host

You define a virtual host in your server configuration files with the `<VirtualHost>` container directive:

```
<VirtualHost host[:port]>
    [server-specific directives]
</VirtualHost>
```

The *host* argument can be either a host name, such as `WWW.Apache.Org`, or an IP address like `197.122.16.233`. You include the *:port* only if you're going to have your server working with port numbers other than the default value of 80.

Almost all the directives that can appear elsewhere in the configuration files can appear inside a `<VirtualHost>` container and would apply only to that virtual host. That includes things like `<Directory>` scoping containers, the `DocumentRoot` directive, and most of the other directives described elsewhere in this book.

Directives, scopes, rules, or whatever appears within a `<VirtualHost>` container apply *only* to that virtual host. Unless you duplicate them in another container or outside the container in the main server's definition, they don't apply to any other environment — they apply only to requests made specifically to that virtual host.

Each `<VirtualHost>` container should include a `ServerName` directive, and including a `ServerAlias` directive as well is a good idea. Apache uses the `ServerName` value for various identification purposes, including figuring out which vhost should handle a request and constructing a URL for a redirect. The `ServerAlias` value (which can actually be a list of names) tells the Apache Web server which other names may be used to access the virtual host. For example, people inside your organization may use either the full Internet name for your server or just the abbreviated host name; you can handle that with something like this:

```
<VirtualHost www.domain.com>
    ServerName WWW.Domain.Com
    ServerAlias WWW
</VirtualHost>
```

This allows Apache to recognize URLs like `<http://www/>` — as well as the more complete `<http://www.domain.com/>` — as being for this virtual host. (Naturally, other directives should appear inside the container in addition to the ones that I list; that's just for demonstration purposes.)

Your host for this evening will be. . . .

Because this topic is so confusing, I'm going to define a set of systems, names, and addresses that I use to illustrate the intricacies. These are in the following list.

Figure 14-1:
Rules of
the game:
systems,
names, and
addresses
for vhost
examples.

> 1. System *a* has one address assigned to it: 10.0.0.1.
> 2. Address 10.0.0.1 has a single name attached to it: A.Domain.Com.
> 3. System *b* has one address assigned to it: 10.0.0.2.
> 4. Address 10.0.0.2 has *two* names associated with it: B1.Domain.Com and B2.Domain.Com.
> 5. System *c* has two addresses assigned to it: 10.0.0.3 and 10.0.0.4.
> 6. Address 10.0.0.3 has a single name: C-A.Domain.Com.
> 7. Address 10.0.0.4 has a single name: C-B.Domain.Com.
> 8. System *d* has two addresses assigned to it: 10.0.0.5 and 10.0.0.6.
> 9. Address 10.0.0.5 has two names: D1-A.Domain.Com and D1-B.Domain.Com.
> 10. Address 10.0.0.6 has two names: D2-A.Domain.Com and D2-B.Domain.Com

I number the items shown in Figure 14-1 for ease of reference and to keep them separate — I list them in increasing order of complexity. I start stepping through them in the next section. Ready? All right, read on!

The simplest case: One address and one name

The first two items in Figure 14-1 describe the simplest kind of web server, the kind that I talk about in the earlier chapters of this book. Here are those two items again:

> **1. System *a* has one address assigned to it: 10.0.0.1.**
>
> **2. Address 10.0.0.1 has a single name attached to it:** A.Domain.Com.

With only one combination possible, no way exists to have the web server pretend to be more than host. This type of configuration is the easiest to manage, because all the configuration directives obviously apply to a single web presence: A.Domain.Com. The config files don't have any <VirtualHost> containers to complicate matters with issues of server-level scoping.

A case for name vhosts: One address, two names

In many cases registering Internet names is easier than acquiring IP addresses. As a result, a single IP address having multiple names is very common. The second case (items 3 and 4) shown in Figure 14-1 covers this. Here are those items again so you don't have to flip back and forth through the pages.

> **3. System *b* has one address assigned to it: 10.0.0.2.**
>
> **4. Address 10.0.0.2 has *two* names associated with it:** B1.Domain.Com and B2.Domain.Com.

In this case, system *b* has only one telephone number, but you can reach two different people by calling it. Because only one address exists, the only way that you can tell which one is desired is by knowing the name that the caller wants to reach — which is why the only way that this system can actually have multiple vhosts is by using the *name* virtual host method.

Apache 1.2 has only one way to set up this server to handle both names: with a `<VirtualHost B2.Domain.Com>` container (or for `B1.Domain.Com`) in the server configuration files, which defines the particulars for the second vhost. The configuration directives for the main server (the ones outside the `<VirtualHost>` container) define the particulars for the other virtual host.

In other words, in Apache 1.2 you need to pick one of the names to be described by a `<VirtualHost>` container. The directives inside the container define that virtual host's particulars, and the directives that *aren't* inside the container define the details of the other virtual host, as shown in Figure 14-2.

Figure 14-2:
Name-
based
virtual
hosts in
Apache 1.2.

```
#
# The "main" server is one of our name-vhosts
#
ServerName B1.Domain.Com
DocumentRoot /usr/local/web/htdocs/B1
#
# The second name-vhost is defined by the following
# container
#
<VirtualHost B2.Domain.Com>
    ServerName B2.Domain.Com
    DocumentRoot /usr/local/web/htdocs/B2
</VirtualHost>
```

With Apache 1.3, you can actually make sure that the main server is never a target and provide default values only for virtual hosts. That way you can actually have a `<VirtualHost>` container for each of the virtual hosts, and things are a little cleaner and easier to understand. You do this by using the `NameVirtualHost` directive, as shown in Figure 14-3, to let Apache know that the 10.0.0.2 address can be reached using multiple names.

```
#
# Take the "main" server out of the running as a
# selectable Web target
#
ServerName localhost
NameVirtualHost 10.0.0.2:80
<VirtualHost B1.Domain.Com>
    ServerName B1.Domain.Com
    DocumentRoot /usr/local/web/htdocs/B1
</VirtualHost>
<VirtualHost B2.Domain.Com>
    ServerName B2.Domain.Com
    DocumentRoot /usr/local/web/htdocs/B2
</VirtualHost>
```

Figure 14-3:
Using the
NameVir-
tualHost
directive in
Apache 1.3.

Doesn't the configuration in Figure 14-3 look easier to read and understand than the one in Figure 14-2?

Because these virtual hosts can be told apart only by name, the server won't be able to do much if the client doesn't give it a name as part of the request. This is actually the case for some older browsers.

A time for addresses: Two addresses, two names

In some environments, the Webmaster has access to lots of IP addresses, and assigning a few of them to a single web server machine is a simple matter. Items 5 through 7 from Figure 14-1, reproduced below, cover the situation where this is the case *and* each IP address has only a single name.

5. System *c* has two addresses assigned to it: 10.0.0.3 and 10.0.0.4.

6. Address 10.0.0.3 has a single name: C-A.Domain.Com.

7. Address 10.0.0.4 has a single name: C-B.Domain.Com.

The configuration directives for these two virtual hosts are pretty straightforward and are shown in Figure 14-4.

Because these two virtual hosts are *address* virtual hosts, the web server is immune to problems caused by older browsers that don't supply the name of their target host as part of the request header. The web server can tell which virtual host is the target from the IP address that was used to reach it.

```
#
# Take the "main" server out of the running as a
# selectable Web target - all of the real work
# goes through the virtual hosts, and the main server
# just supplies defaults
#
ServerName localhost
#
# Listing the containers with the names makes it
# easier for humans, but it makes things clearer
# that these are address-vhosts rather than name-vhosts
# if you use the addresses instead
#
#<VirtualHost 10.0.0.3>
<VirtualHost C-A.Domain.Com>
    ServerName C-A.Domain.Com
    DocumentRoot /usr/local/web/htdocs/C-A
</VirtualHost>
#<VirtualHost 10.0.0.4>
<VirtualHost C-B.Domain.Com>
    ServerName C-B.Domain.Com
    DocumentRoot /usr/local/web/htdocs/C-B
</VirtualHost>
```

Figure 14-4:
IP-based
virtual host
configuration.

The combo platter: Two addresses, four names

The server environments described in the preceding sections are simple
because they're just variations on a theme and deal exclusively with either
address-based virtual hosts or name-based vhosts. But what about a situation in which you want to mix up these types of hosts?

Suppose you have a system like *d*, described in items 8 through 10 of Figure
14-1. That single piece of hardware potentially can support up to four
different virtual web identities, but only by mixing and matching the two
different types of vhost. Here are those items from Figure 14-1 again:

   8. **System *d* has two addresses assigned to it: 10.0.0.5 and 10.0.0.6.**

   9. **Address 10.0.0.5 has two names:** D1-A.Domain.Com **and**
      D1-B.Domain.Com.

  10. **Address 10.0.0.6 has two names:** D2-A.Domain.Com **and**
      D2-B.Domain.Com.

If you're running Apache 1.2, you simply *can't* handle all four identities —
the software doesn't provide for it. The best that you can do is handle three
of the names, because of a simple rule built into that version of Apache:

The names of *all* name-based virtual hosts must resolve to the same IP
address as the main server's ServerName.

Huh? Okay, let me try again. The main server is defined by the directives
that aren't inside any <VirtualHost> containers, right? One of those
directives should be a ServerName directive. This server name is associated
with a particular IP address. If you're going to run any name-based virtual
hosts, they must be other names for that same IP address. If they are
associated with other IP addresses — even IP addresses for other vhosts
that Apache is using — they won't work. Name vhosts work only if they're
alternate names for the main server.

To support even three of the four names in the list, you need to fall back to
the trick of using the main server for one of them, as shown in Figure 14-5.

Figure 14-5:
Mixing
name- and
address-
based
vhosts in
Apache 1.2.

```
#
# The "main" server is one of our name-vhosts
#
ServerName D1-A.Domain.Com
DocumentRoot /usr/local/web/htdocs/D1-A
#
# The second name-vhost is defined by the following
# container; it shares the same IP address as the main host
#
<VirtualHost D1-B.Domain.Com>
    ServerName D1-B.Domain.Com
    DocumentRoot /usr/local/web/htdocs/D1-B
</VirtualHost>
#
# We have to pick either one or the other of the
# two names for the second address, since the rule
# doesn't permit name-vhosts on secondary addresses.
# Even though we're listing this by name, it's
# really an address-based vhost definition.
#
<VirtualHost D2-A.Domain.Com>
    ServerName D2-A.Domain.Com
    DocumentRoot /usr/local/web/htdocs/D2-A
</VirtualHost>
```

Apache 1.3 addresses this limitation (name-based vhosts only for the main server address). By using the NameVirtualHost directive, you can specify which IP addresses are allowed to have name-based vhosts associated with them. So I can rework the directives shown in Figure 14-5 to make all four of the listed names work as virtual hosts under Apache 1.3. The resulting directives are shown in Figure 14-6.

```
#
# The "main" server is once more marked as never
# selectable, since all of our accesses will come
# through one or another of the vhosts
#
ServerName localhost
#
# Mark the first address as allowing multiple name-based
# vhosts
#
NameVirtualHost 10.0.0.5
#
# Now list the two virtual hosts available on that address
#
<VirtualHost D1-A.Domain.Com>
    ServerName D1-A.Domain.Com
    DocumentRoot /usr/local/web/htdocs/D1-A
</VirtualHost>
<VirtualHost D1-B.Domain.Com>
    ServerName D1-B.Domain.Com
    DocumentRoot /usr/local/web/htdocs/D1-B
</VirtualHost>
#
# Repeat the process for the other IP address
#
NameVirtualHost 10.0.0.6
#
# List the virtual hosts available on that address
#
<VirtualHost D2-A.Domain.Com>
    ServerName D2-A.Domain.Com
    DocumentRoot /usr/local/web/htdocs/D2-A
</VirtualHost>
<VirtualHost D2-B.Domain.Com>
    ServerName D2-B.Domain.Com
    DocumentRoot /usr/local/web/htdocs/D2-B
</VirtualHost>
```

Figure 14-6:
Name- and
address-
based
vhosts in
Apache 1.3.

Multiple Hosts by Address

Separating your virtual hosts according to addresses used to be the only way to do it. You essentially gave each virtual host its own address, and you were never in any doubt — sort of like separating your personal telephone number from your business number(s).

Unfortunately, although this method is the tried-and-true one, it tends to require more persnickety attention to detail and management overhead because you have to keep track of both host names and addresses. However, it also has the advantage of working reliably regardless of the age of the client software — really old browsers just won't work with the name virtual host technique because it requires them to do something that they weren't created to do.

To use address virtual hosts, you need to fiddle (or have someone fiddle on your behalf) with the name and address registration system so requests for your hosts by name can be turned into the appropriate numbers and vice versa. You get a unique address for each of the virtual hosts and a unique name for each address. These names are how your visitors reference your system, and Apache internally figures out which virtual host's configuration applies.

You need one other thing in order to use multiple address virtual hosts: Your server system needs to answer to all the IP addresses. One way of making that happen is to have as many network cards or Ethernet boards as you have IP addresses; another way is to use fewer, and trick them into thinking they have multiple addresses.

Registration of system names and addresses

Because you can refer to systems in two basic ways — by name and by address — you also have two ways of translating things. When given a name, your computer needs to translate it into a number so your computer can actually use it; given a number, *you* want to be able to turn it into a name so it makes more sense to you. Quite reasonably, these activities are called *forward lookups* and *reverse lookups*. The forward lookup term refers to starting with a value that's meaningful to you (in other words, translating a name to a number).

This translation game has a number of basic rules and some special technobabble terminology for what goes on.

- ✔ Certain systems in the network are responsible for remembering the relationship between names and numbers. These systems are called *name servers*.

- ✔ The registered name of an IP address is called its *host name*. If an address has more than one registered name, each one is a host name for it.

- ✔ Internet names are broken into pieces called *components*, which are separated from one another by periods. For example, the name WWW.Apache.Org has three components.

- ✔ Internet names are *hierarchical*. For example, educational systems (.edu) are grouped together, and then departments at a particular university, and then systems within each department, and so on.

- ✔ Names in the Internet are read left-to-right when bandied about amongst humans but are read the other way (right-to-left) when actually being used by computers.

- ✔ Host names live within *domains*, which are used for grouping related systems together (for example, .com is used as the parent to most *com*mercial organizations on the Internet). The domain of a system consists of all the components of its Internet name to the right of its actual host name — in other words, its parent. The host name of WWW.Apache.Org is WWW, and it is in domain Apache.Org.

- ✔ A very limited number of *top-level domains* (abbreviated TLD) exist. These TLDs include the familiar ones like .Com, .Edu, and .Gov, but they also include the lesser-known two-letter per-country ones like .US (United States of America), .Au (Australia), and .Aq (Antarctica).

- ✔ The parent of all TLDs is . (pronounced like the word *dot* or sometimes called *the root*), which is usually not even included at the end of Internet names.

- ✔ A *subdomain* is any domain whose parent is anything other than . or one of the TLDs.

- ✔ If you combine a system's host name with its domain name, the result is called its *fully-qualified domain name* (abbreviated FQDN). A system's Internet FQDN allows other computers anywhere in the world to locate it. WWW may be a system's host name, but "WWW.Apache.Org" is its FQDN.

- ✔ No master registration system holding all the registration information exists on the Internet. Instead, the name servers are each responsible for a small piece or collection of pieces of the registration information, and they know how to reach each other to find out the rest.

✔ The pieces of the Internet naming system that a name server owns are called *zones*.

✔ The whole name/address registration system for the Internet is called DNS — Domain Name System. Sometimes it's mistakenly called BIND after the software that actually supports it — the Berkeley Internet Name Daemon.

But what does it all mean? Well, for starters, it means that to add a brand-new web server system to DNS, you have to register both sides of the translation: You have to tell DNS how to turn the name into an address and the address into a name.

Whereas multiple names can translate to a single address and a single name can even translate to multiple addresses, the process doesn't work both ways — each address must translate backward to one and only one name. If I dredge out the telephone comparison, by assigning multiple names to a single address, you're telling the telephone company how to reach each of those people, and the fact that they all use the same telephone number is unimportant. On the other hand, the telephone company requires a single name of the person who's going to pay the bills.

Because the two translation processes are separate (though related), some software packages — including the Apache Web server — do double-lookups to verify that both pieces of the translation match. That is, they start with the IP address and translate it into a name, and then they take that name and try to translate it into an IP address. If everything is set up correctly, the starting IP address and the ending IP address are the same; if they're not, something may be rotten in the state of Denmark.

So here are the basic rules about DNS that you should keep in mind when registering your web server's virtual hosts:

✔ Each IP address must translate to one and only one name.

✔ Each name must translate to at least one IP address.

✔ Each name can potentially translate to *more* than one IP address.

✔ Multiple names can translate to the same IP address.

Keep careful track of which IP addresses have multiple names and which ones have only single names, because they're used for the two different types of virtual hosts (name and address respectively).

Network boards with multiple addresses

In the world of TCP/IP networking, the circuit boards, modules, cards, or whatever connects you to the network are called *interfaces*.

If an interface is in use for TCP/IP networking, it has its own IP address. It can also have other addresses, like nicknames, to which it answers. These nickname addresses are called *aliases*.

How you tell your system that an interface has one or more aliases is extremely system-specific — each operating system has its own Deep Magic incantations that you need to perform. I describe two of the common methods, but you really need to check out your system's documentation for the correct procedure to use.

Using ifconfig: On many versions of UNIX, the ifconfig (interface configuration) command is what you use to control your network interfaces. The details vary from system to system, but the following example statements commonly do the right thing. For purposes of illustration, I call the interface that I'm twiddling eth0, and the two addresses (primary and alias) that I want it to have are 10.0.0.1 and 10.0.0.2.

```
# ifconfig eth0 10.0.0.1 netmask
    255.255.255.0 broadcast 10.0.0.255

# ifconfig eth0 alias 10.0.0.2 netmask
    255.255.255.0 broadcast 10.0.0.255
```

(Obviously you should alter the example statements to match your own environment and configuration!)

Some implementations allow you — or possibly *require* you — to combine the two statements into a single one.

Using RedHat Linux's ifup: If your system is running the RedHat Linux operating system,

here's how you can do the same thing as I described for the ifconfig method:

1. **Change your working directory to /etc/ sysconfig/network-scripts:**

   ```
   # cd /etc/sysconfig/network-
       scripts
   ```

2. **Figure out which of the ifcfg-* files refers to the interface that you want to add an alias to.**

3. **Copy the file to another name that ends with a colon and a number (for example, ":1"):**

   ```
   # cp ifcfg-eth0 ifcfg-eth0:1
   ```

4. **Edit the new file and make the DEVICE line match the name of the file — for the example, change DEVICE=eth0 to DEVICE=eth0:1. Also make any appropriate changes to the address, netmask, and broadcast values.**

5. **Tell the operating system to actually set up and activate the alias:**

   ```
   # ./ifup ifcfg-eth0:1
   ```

After you set up your aliases, you should verify that they're responding properly by pinging them from another system:

```
# ping -c 5 10.0.0.2
PING 10.0.0.2 (198.115.138.23): 56 data
    bytes
– 10.0.0.2 ping statistics –
5 packets transmitted, 5 packets received,
    0% packet loss
round-trip min/avg/max = 2.1/2.7/4.3 ms
```

If you get results that resemble the ones in the example, you have your alias! To make the alias last across reboots, check your operating system documentation on the subject of making permanent changes to your network configuration.

Multiple Hosts by Name

As an alternative to setting up a bunch of virtual host names with unique IP addresses, you can have them all use the same IP address. When you use these hosts in your server configuration, they're called *name* virtual hosts because the server can tell them apart only by name. The server can't distinguish between them by IP address because they all have the same address.

This can be a very useful technique, because you can use a single IP address to pretend to be a lot of separate systems and you don't have to be concerned about managing addresses and packet routing and all the stuff that goes along with using address hosts (which I describe in the previous section).

As with every alternative, though, you have advantages and disadvantages. I just described the major advantage, so here are the things that comprise the downside of using name virtual hosts:

✔ Name virtual hosts work only with relatively new browsers, such as Netscape Navigator 2.0, Internet Explorer 3.0, and Lynx 2.6 — or any of their descendants. The older browsers don't include the name of the server that they're trying to reach as part of the request header — and without that, the server can't figure out which named virtual host to use.

For the mordantly curious, the geek-speak for this is: Name virtual hosts work only with browsers that supply the `Host` header field as part of the request.

✔ Mixing name virtual hosts and address virtual hosts in a single server configuration can easily become confusing unless you document your server config files clearly.

✔ All name virtual host names must translate to the same IP address as the value of the default `ServerName` directive (that is, the one that isn't inside any `<VirtualHost>` containers).

As I describe a few sections ago, Apache 1.3 has removed this restriction, although you have to take extra steps to make it clear to the server what you're trying to do.

Within these restrictions, the configuration of a server that uses only name virtual hosts is generally simpler to set up and manage than one that uses address virtual hosts or a combination of the two types.

Listen: Do You Hear What I Hear?

By default, the Apache Web server uses *address wildcarding* — the server handles requests sent to any of your system's IP addresses. Also by default, Apache only listens to requests on a single port number (usually port 80). The Port directive changes which single port the server uses (see Chapter 4).

To make your server listen to *some* of your system's IP addresses, or *more* than one port, use the Listen directive. Listen statements take three forms. Listen IP-address tells Apache to listen to the specified IP address and the port from the Port directive in your server config files. Listen port-number tells Apache to listen to all requests that come in on the specified port number, regardless of the receiving IP address. Listen IP-address:port-number tells Apache to listen a specific IP address and port combination. The special IP address "*" tells the server to use address wildcarding; "Listen *:8000" has the same effect as "Listen 8000", but makes it a little clearer.

If you want your server to respond to all requests through ports 80 and 8100, for all of your system's IP addresses, use the following Listen statements: Listen *:80 and Listen *:8100. (The "*" tells the server to listen to all IP addresses for the listed ports.)

For your server to listen to *some* of your system's IP addresses, include a Listen statement for each address that you want the server to pay attention to. For example, if you only want the server to respond to Web requests that come in on port 80 through address 10.0.0.2, use this statement: Listen 10.0.0.2:80

The past few paragraphs boil down to two simple rules:

✔ For one port and all of your system's IP addresses, use the Port directive.

✔ For more than one port, or only some of your system's IP addresses, or both, use the Listen directive.

Special Considerations — Logging

You can use the various logging directives within <VirtualHost> containers. If you do that, the logging directives only log requests going to that particular virtual host, so you can keep all your virtual hosts' log files separate by putting a CustomLog directive inside each <VirtualHost> container.

But wait! A loophole is lurking here to snare the unwary! Remember that these log files are opened when the server is started and stay open until it's shut down. Each log file ties up an open-file slot, which detracts from the total number of log files that you have available for other purposes (like servicing requests). If you run a very big server with lots of virtual hosts (as some Apache users do — some of them with hundreds of virtual hosts per server), you're probably going to run into this limit with a loud splat.

Splitting up the access log

Running a separate set of log files is going to use up a lot of open file slots and may possibly interfere with your ability to service requests. What can you do? Well, traditional wisdom responds immediately with "So, don't do that!" but that advice is rather unsatisfying. A more palatable solution involves reducing the load on the server itself, at the cost of some extra work when you actually analyze the log files.

Here's how it works. Note that this works only if all your virtual hosts use the same logging formats.

1. **Make a note of the formats that you use in your** <VirtualHost> **containers for the** LogFormat **and** CustomLog **directives.**

2. **Add** CustomLog **directives to the global server scope (in other words, outside of any** <VirtualHost> **containers) that uses the formats that you recorded in Step 1.**

3. **Modify the** CustomLog **directives from Step 2 to include %v at the front of the format string. For example, change**

```
CustomLog access_log "%h %l %u %t \"%r\" %s %b \"%{Referer}I\""
```

to

```
CustomLog access_log "%v %h %l %u %t \"%r\" %s %b \"%{Referer}I\""
```

4. **Get rid of all the** LogFormat, TransferLog, **and** CustomLog **directives that you have inside** <VirtualHost> **containers.**

5. **Rename your access log (probably** logs/access_log **under the ServerRoot) to something else.**

6. **Restart your Apache Web server.**

7. **Put together something to break the single log file into separate ones for each virtual host.**

The net result of following these steps is that you have one set of log files for the entire server, all virtual hosts included, which frees up all those open file slots that the per-virtual host log files were using.

Figure 14-7 shows a sample Perl script that can split a combined log file into separate files, one for each virtual host. The script assumes that you used the "include a %v at the beginning of the format" suggestion. Feel free to modify it to meet your own requirements.

```perl
#!/usr/local/bin/perl
#
# This script will take a combined Web server access
# log file and break its contents into separate files.
# It assumes that the first field of each line is the
# virtual host identity (put there by "%v"), and that
# the logfiles should be named that+".log" in the current
# directory.
#
# The combined log file is read from stdin. Records read
# will be appended to any existing log files.
#
%is_open = ();

while ($log_line = <STDIN>) {
    #
    # Get the first token from the log record; it's the
    # identity of the virtual host to which the record
    # applies.
    #
    ($vhost) = split (/\s/, $log_line);
    #
    # Normalize the virtual host name to all lowercase.
    # If it's blank, the request was handled by the default
    # server, so supply a default name.  This shouldn't
    # happen, but caution rocks.
    #
    $vhost = lc ($vhost) or "access";
    #
    # If the log file for this virtual host isn't opened
    # yet, do it now.
    #
    if (! $is_open{$vhost}) {
        open $vhost, ">>${vhost}.log"
            or die ("Can't open ${vhost}.log");
        $is_open{$vhost} = 1;
    }
    #
    # Strip off the first token (which may be null in the
    # case of the default server), and write the edited
    # record to the current log file.
    #
    $log_line =~ s/^\S*\s+//;
    printf $vhost "%s", $log_line;
}
exit 0;
```

Figure 14-7:
A Perl
script to
separate
virtual-host
log records.

Other logging considerations

You can easily reduce the number of open file slots that your virtual hosts use by combining your access logs into a single file. This process is easy because you can control the format of the access log records to a fine degree. Unfortunately, you don't have this sort of control over the error log format — the error messages that the Apache Web server logs don't include the name of the server that incurred them.

This limits your options for reducing the use of open file slots for logging. You need to make a decision: Do you want to have a single default error log that contains all the errors for all the virtual hosts, or do you want to have a unique error log for each virtual host that contains only that host's errors? The first choice can make it difficult to debug problems, and the second uses up more open file slots.

Unless you're running a big server with lots of virtual hosts (more than 100), I recommend having a separate ErrorLog directive in each <VirtualHost> container. If you *are* running a humongous server, you probably need those slots and should use a combined access log *and* a combined error log.

The Default Server Again

In this chapter, I make a few sideways references to the main server, and I suppose that now is the time to devote a little more text to it.

The *main* server — which is also sometimes called the default server — is the server that is defined by configuration directives that are not inside <VirtualHost> containers. In some cases the main server is used to respond to requests that Apache can't determine a better target for, but in all cases its directives provide defaults for all <VirtualHost> containers.

For example, if you have a line such as

```
ScriptAlias /cgi-bin/ /usr/local/web/server/cgi-bin/
```

in your main server's definition, it applies to all virtual hosts as well — unless the virtual hosts override it with their own ScriptAlias /cgi-bin/ directive. And if you declare something like this in your main server directives:

```
<Location /server-status>
    SetHandler server-status
</Location>
```

the URL <http://hostname/server-status> invokes the status module regardless of which virtual host's name is used to access it.

On the other hand, directives that appear *within* a <VirtualHost> container apply *only* to that virtual host — they don't apply to any other hosts.

```
<VirtualHost A.Domain.Com>
    DocumentRoot /usr/local/web/htdocs/A
    <Location /server-status>
        SetHandler server-status
    </Location>
</VirtualHost>
<VirtualHost B.Domain.Com>
    DocumentRoot /usr/local/web/htdocs/B
</VirtualHost>
```

A request for <http://A.Domain.Com/server-status> would result in the status module display, but requesting <http://B.Domain.Com/server-status> would not — because it isn't defined for that virtual host.

The _default_ *Host*

In the event that the Apache Web server can't figure out which virtual host should handle an incoming request, it assigns the request to a special last-chance virtual host if you declared it. The name of this special virtual host is _default_, underscores and all, and it is never selected except under these circumstances.

```
<VirtualHost _default_>
    DocumentRoot /usr/local/web/htdocs/_default_
</VirtualHost>
```

You can include a ServerName directive within a <VirtualHost _default_> container; if you don't, the default virtral host inherits the ServerName value from the main server.

Using the _default_ virtual host allows you to continue to use the main server configuration strictly for supplying defaults and for it to never be treated as defining a real selectable server.

If you're using Apache 1.2 *and* you're using name vhosts *and* you have a _default_ vhost declaration, the _default_ vhost container *must* appear after all the name vhost definitions in the configuration files. If any name vhost containers appear after the _default_ declaration, they will never be assigned any requests. Apache 1.3 addresses this odd behavior.

Chapter 15

Serving by Proxy

● ●

In This Chapter

▶ Understanding the proxy server

▶ Building the Apache proxy module into the server image

▶ Opening the proxy for business

▶ Configuring the proxy as a separate virtual host

▶ Understanding proxy caching

● ●

*I*n general, a *proxy* is something or someone that does something on behalf of something or someone else. For example, if you can't make it to the shareholder's meeting, you can authorize someone else to vote your shares the way that you want; this arrangement is called voting by proxy.

The same meaning holds true for the use of the word proxy within the realm of the World Wide Web. A web proxy is a system that handles requests on behalf of clients that can't handle them directly; usually this is due to things like firewalls being in the way.

Although the Apache Web server software is not primarily a proxy server, it does include a module that permits it to act as one if you need it to. This chapter describes the ins and outs of taking advantage of this functionality.

What The Proxy Does

The Apache Web server proxy module can perform two main functions:

✔ Act as a proxy for client requests

✔ Act as a cache for documents and resources that pass through the proxy interface

The following sections describe these two functions in more detail.

Because the Apache Web server provides the ability to act as though it's multiple different Web sites (see Chapter 14), you can actually include proxy-server functionality in the same system and server configuration as your normal web stuff but make it look as though it's a separate system.

Here, let me do that for you

A web proxy server acts as a sort of intermediary for clients trying to reach systems on the other side of the proxy system. The clients need to be configured to recognize the proxy system as being in this role, which is about the only thing that's different for them, and the end user should hardly be affected.

"So what does the proxy do?" you ask. Well, what happens is that the end user or the client requests a particular URL — but rather than directly contacting the server that owns the resource, the client contacts the proxy instead and tells it, "Please go get this for me." The proxy then makes the actual request, gets the response, and then forwards the response back to the original client.

When dealing with proxies, the system that actually owns the resource is properly called the *origin server*.

Sounds rather pointless at first blush, doesn't it? But wait — there's more! One place in the network at which a proxy is particularly useful is at the periphery of an organization's network, which is the point where it connects to some other network (such as the Internet). The organization may not want to allow the whole wide world to be able to access its internal systems, so it installs a firewall.

Because a firewall system is already located on a *nexus* (connection point) between two or more networks and it's usually a pretty sophisticated system, you may want to install a web proxy server at the same location.

Although the use of a proxy server has some advantages in a firewall environment, the following list includes some of the negative aspects:

- A proxy server is a single point of failure (SPOF) for web clients trying to access the Outer World. That is, if the proxy server is down, the clients aren't going to be able to go through it.

- The use of proxy servers imposes some performance penalties. One reason is that you're involving yet another system in the transfer of information between the client and the system that owns the resource. Another reason is that many proxy servers won't pass along the response to the original client until they receive all of it from the source. This process can more than double the amount of time that end users sit twiddling their fingers while waiting for the results to appear on the screen, and sometimes the delay (especially when large files are involved) can cause one end or the other to think its counterpart has lost interest or failed somehow.

You have some options for working around these issues, but they generally involve throwing more resources (time, money, hardware, people, and so on) at the problem.

Let me see if I have that in stock. . . .

Because a proxy server is busy copying responses back and forth, it seems only natural to allow it to remember some of them so it doesn't have to repeat the process when asked for the same thing over and over again. This process is called *caching* (pronounced "cashing").

A properly configured caching proxy server can actually improve network performance. Here's how it works:

1. A client makes a request for an external resource and asks the proxy for it.

2. The proxy server checks to see if it has a valid copy of that resource in its cache.

3. If it does have a copy, it immediately sends it to the client and the transaction is over.

4. If it doesn't have a copy, it proceeds normally and requests the resource from the remote server that actually owns it.

5. When the proxy server receives the resource from the remote system, it stores the resource in its cache and then sends it to the client that originally asked for it.

As you can see if two or more clients ask for the same resource, Steps 4 and 5 — and all the extra network and disk activity that they entail — can be omitted.

The main problem with caching is that a lot of web resources exist, and if a proxy makes a copy of everything that passes through it, the disk space required is soon the biggest expense that the organization has. To keep this under control, caching servers allow the Webmaster to impose limits — such as "don't store more than 200 megabytes total" or "go through the cache every hour and throw out everything that hasn't been requested in the last 24 hours" — on what gets stored in the cache and for how long.

Firewalls and network boundaries

Talking about *boundaries* to a network may sound silly; lots of people envision The Network as being this big amorphous thing to which they're connected. This perception is almost universal, to the point that when you see a diagram that is used to show how things are connected, the network is always displayed as a big cloud.

Nevertheless, networks are made of wires, not clouds, and wires have definite attach-points to other wires. You can count the attach-points if you're patient and have a good calculator. At some point, the wires stop being *yours* and start being *theirs* (they belong to someone else) — and that point is a boundary between the two networks.

The places at which the wires connect are actually occupied by hardware boxes of some kind, just as the wires coming into your home and the wires within your home are connected by a fuse box. These connection boxes may be simple, or they may be quite complicated, depending on what they need to do.

One type of connection box is called a *firewall*, because it's intended to prevent things that are causing problems on one set of wires from spreading to the other side. Examples of the things that firewalls are supposed to stop appear in the news almost every day; remember the Morris, Father Christmas, and Wank worms? Because of their nature, those worms were actually more difficult to stop using firewall technology than the more recent (and obscure, though farther-reaching) Ping of Death and SYN Flooding attacks.

Regardless, a firewall is supposed to help prevent the nasties on the Other Side from polluting the network of the good guys on This Side.

Things that firewalls are typically asked to restrict include:

- ✔ Access to internal web servers by outsiders
- ✔ Interactive sessions (such as telnet) originating from the outside
- ✔ Mail traffic directly to internal systems

The usual vision of a firewall has it staunchly defending the Good Guys on the inside from the Bad Guys on the outside. Sometimes, however, it is also asked to help thwart potential abuse by insiders — such as preventing people on the *inside* from using mail, telnet, FTP, or the Web to directly access outside systems, thereby preventing them from easily transmitting trade secrets and the like. You may call this the Dark Side of firewall application (I do), because it's based on a limited — rather than unrestricted — trust of the people in the organization. Whatever; each organization must determine these policy issues for itself.

A firewall sitting on the boundary between two networks is only as good as the assurance that it's on the *only* path between them. If other connections exist between the internal network and external ones, and they aren't equally protected, the firewall is of limited usefulness because it can be bypassed and circumvented by simply going through one of the other connections. So one of the main tasks of network managers implementing firewall protection schemes is making sure that they cover all the bases and don't leave any backdoors or side doors open between their organization's network and the outside.

Configuring clients to use the proxy

To fulfill the first function (acting as a proxy for clients), the clients involved need to list the Apache server as their proxy server. Exactly how this task is done is extremely client-specific, but typically the user needs to set preferences that instruct the client about which proxy server to contact for the different schemes (such as HTTP, FTP, and so on). Figure 15-1 shows what such a preference selection form looks like in Netscape Navigator.

Establishing the Proxy

In order to have your Apache Web server function as a proxy server in addition to its normal function, you need to explicitly enable it — the proxy module is not included in the server by default. Here's what you need to do to enable it:

1. **Modify the** `src/Configuration` **file to include the proxy module by uncommenting the following line (remove the # from the front of the line):**

```
# Module proxy_module modules/proxy/libproxy.a
```

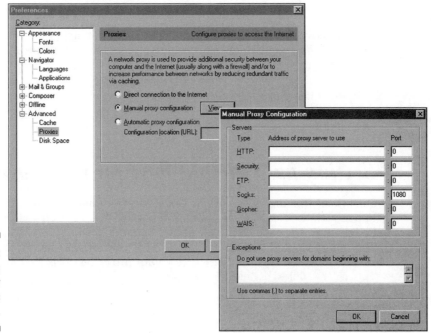

Figure 15-1:
Setting proxy preferences in Mozilla.

If you're using Apache 1.3, the line looks like this instead:

```
# AddModule modules/proxy/libproxy.a
```

2. Rebuild the `httpd` **image:**

```
% cd /usr/local/web/apache/src
% ./Configure
% make
```

3. Shut down the Apache server, put the new `httpd` **image into the right location, and then restart the server (see Chapter 4).**

After you complete these three steps, your server will be running with the proxy module built into it, and you can modify your configuration files to take advantage of the proxy's capabilities.

Turning the proxy on — And off

Before the Apache Web server can even think about performing any proxy-related functions, you must tell it to turn them on. The way that you do this is by including the appropriate directive (surprise!) in your server configuration files:

```
ProxyRequests on-or-off
```

This directive can appear only in the global environment or within `<VirtualHost>` containers — nowhere else. In fact, *all* the proxy directives fall under this same restriction.

Note that disabling the normal proxy operation with `ProxyRequests Off` does not stop the `ProxyPass` directive (described later in this chapter) from functioning.

Setting up a virtual host for the proxy

Sometimes thinking of the proxy as a separate virtual host — rather than tied in with the rest of your Apache Web server's operation — is easier to understand. The following code shows one way in which this can be done. Your proxy would be available on port 8080 of your web server; and if your server's host name is `A.Domain.Com`, your proxy server is therefore `<http://A.Domain.Com:8080/>`.

Add the following lines to your Apache Web server's configuration files (httpd.conf, srm.conf, or access.conf in the /usr/local/web/apache/conf directory). Make appropriate changes for the IP address of your server:

```
#
# Only do the following if the proxy is built into the
# server.
#
<IfModule mod_proxy.c>
    Listen 10.0.0.1:8080
    <VirtualHost 10.0.0.1:8080>
        ProxyRequests On
        CustomLog proxy_log "%h %l %u %t \"%r\" %s %b \"%{Referer}I\""
        DocumentRoot /usr/local/web/apache/htdocs/proxy
    </VirtualHost>
</IfModule>
```

Create the file /usr/local/web/apache/htdocs/proxy/index.html with the following contents:

```
<!DOCTYPE HTML PUBLIC "-//W3C//DTD HTML 3.2 Final//EN">
<HTML>
 <HEAD>
  <TITLE>No documents; proxy access only
  </TITLE>
 </HEAD>
 <BODY>
  <H1 ALIGN="CENTER">
   No Documents; Proxy Access Only
  </H1>
  <P>
  The server you have reached offers no documents of its
  own.  It functions strictly as a proxy server for
  forwarding Web requests.
  </P>
 </BODY>
</HTML>
```

"Cascading Proxies, Batman!"

Having firewalls nested within other firewalls may make sense in some situations — for example at a company that has one department working on highly secret stuff. Can you set up the Apache web proxy to point to another proxy, rather than go directly to the source for each document requested? The answer is — you guessed it — yes! In fact, you can have your proxy point to multiple other remote proxy systems depending on what's being requested.

You can do this with the `ProxyRemote` directive:

```
ProxyRemote request-type remote-proxy
```

The *request-type* indicates what requests should be forwarded to the remote proxy system, and the *remote-proxy* is the URL of the remote system itself. The request-type can be just a scheme name, such as ftp, in which case all FTP-type URL requests are forwarded to the specified remote system, or it can be a partial URL, in which case only requests that match the URL fragment are sent to the remote proxy. Consider the following examples:

- ✔ `ProxyRemote ftp http://other-system.com:8080`
- ✔ `ProxyRemote http://b.domain.com/ http://www-proxy.foo.com:8000`

In the first example, things occur as I previously described: Any request for an FTP operation that passes through the local proxy server is forwarded to the `other-system.com` proxy server for processing rather than directly to the FTP archive requested.

The second example indicates that requests should be forwarded to the `www-proxy.foo.com` remote proxy system *if and only if* the requested URL starts with `http://b.domain.com/`. All other requests pass directly to the system named in the request URL.

Forbidding proxy access

If you're installing a firewall and/or a proxy system for security reasons, you probably have an idea of some remote sites that you would like to consider to be off-limits. The Apache Web server's proxy module allows you to implement this sort of policy; you identify specific web locations that shouldn't be accessible either by name or by using a string that must not appear in the URL.

The directive that controls this functionality is the `ProxyBlock` directive:

```
ProxyBlock location-or-phrase [location-or-phrase. . .]
```

If the URL being requested through the proxy matches any of the items listed on the `ProxyBlock` directive line, the proxy refuses to forward it and returns an error indicating that the proxy was instructed not to process it.

The phrases used in the directive are not case-sensitive; a `ProxyBlock foo` stops both `http://www.foo.com/` and `http://www.domain.org/GlobalFOO.html`.

Using the proxy to connect web sites

One interesting thing that you can do with the Apache proxy module is make a remote web server's document space look like it's part of yours. You can do this with the `ProxyPass` directive:

```
ProxyPass local-Web-path remote-server-URL
```

When the Apache Web server receives a request for a document path that matches the *local-Web-path,* it secretly and silently turns it into a proxy request for the remote server.

Sound confusing? Here's an example on local server `A.Domain.Com`:

```
ProxyPass /six http://other-server.com/half-dozen
```

If a client requests the document <`http://a.domain.com/six/of-one`>, what it actually gets is the document located at <`http://other-server.com/half-dozen/of-one`>. Behind the scenes, your local server actually fetches the page and then forwards it to the client as though it is a local document. If you didn't need the example to understand what the directive does, give yourself 20 Apache Guru Points.

Naturally because multiple systems are involved, the potential exists for things to go awry if the remote system is inaccessible through network problems or hardware downtime. Also another issue is that the end user may perceive a deterioration in performance and response time, but you can't do much about that problem aside from making sure the document gets cached. But caching is another story, and I cover it in another section in this chapter.

Because the `ProxyPass` operation is concealed from the client and isn't dependent on the client's proxy settings, it continues to function even if you turn off normal proxy operation with a `ProxyRequests Off` directive.

Cache Me If You Can!

The second thing that the Apache proxy module can do is cache the requests and responses that pass through it. It doesn't cache them automatically, though — you need to turn on this function with the `CacheRoot` and `CacheSize` directives:

```
CacheRoot directory
CacheSize number-of-kilobytes
```

The directory named by the `CacheRoot` directive *must* be writable by the user as which the Apache server runs because it's going to be creating files in there as it handles requests.

The proxy module stores the cached information in a directory tree, and you use the `CacheRoot` directive to name the top of the tree. And you use the `CacheSize` directive to tell the proxy module the maximum amount of space that you want to permanently dedicate to the cached information. For example, the following directive settings

```
CacheRoot /usr/local/web/apache/cache
CacheSize 500000
```

inform the Apache Web server that requests and documents passing through the proxy should be stored under the `/usr/local/web/apache/cache` directory and that you don't want to permanently allocate more than 500 megabytes (500,000 kilobytes) of disk space to the files in the cache.

The cache may grow beyond the limit set by the `CacheSize` directive, but when the Apache garbage collector runs, it throws away older cached items until the total space used is less than or equal to the `CacheSize` value. See the next section for more information about the garbage collector.

The content of the cache directory is opaque — which means that you shouldn't expect to be able to browse through the directory tree and make sense of what you find. The cache directory's content is intended to be understood by the Apache Web server and its proxy module, and no one else should care about it. Under no circumstances should you *ever* modify any files under the `CacheRoot` directory!

You can exercise some control over the complexity of the cache directory structure with the `CacheDirLevels` and `CacheDirLength` directives:

```
CacheDirLevels depth
CacheDirLength number-of-characters
```

The `CacheDirLevels` directive tells the Apache Web server's proxy module how deep the cache directory tree should be. The default is three, meaning three levels of subdirectories, but you can select higher or lower values depending on your performance needs and the activity of your proxy. For example, if your proxy is pretty quiet and doesn't end up caching a lot of files, you're better off with a smaller value so the server doesn't have to keep hunting through the subdirectories. On the other hand, if your cache consists of thousands of files and hundreds of megabytes, you may want to increase the value slightly to spread the cached documents across more subdirectories.

The things that you're balancing against one another are the relative costs of finding a single file in a very large directory versus walking down a directory tree to find it in a less-crowded directory. The costs of these two operations are very system-specific and depend on how your operating system handles file operations, so I can't give you any guidelines other than trial-and-error. (You probably saw that coming, didn't you?)

The `CacheDirLength` directive tells the server how long each subdirectory name can be. Again, fiddling with this is only a task for the incredibly performance-conscious; the default value should be more than adequate. By increasing the length of each directory name, you allow for more subdirectories at each level — you can come up with more names that are two letters long than one letter long. If your proxy server is absolutely humongous, with tens of thousands of cached documents, increasing this value to 2 or 3 from the default setting of 1 may be worthwhile. Your mileage may vary.

Keeping undesirables out of the cache

Occasionally you may have certain web locations or documents that you *don't* want to have stored in your cache, maybe because they're really large, or they contain irrelevant content.

You can keep the Apache Web server from storing these undesirable elements in the cache with the `NoCache` directive:

```
NoCache location-or-phrase [location-or-phrase. . .]
```

Like the `ProxyBlock` directive described in an earlier section, the `NoCache` directive causes the proxy module to examine the URL being requested before storing anything in the cache. If the URL contains any of the phrases listed on the `NoCache` directive line or is for a host listed there, the result is not stored in the cache — every request causes the proxy to go all the way to the server that owns the resource. And just like the `ProxyBlock` directive, the `NoCache` directive doesn't care about upper-case versus lower-case letters.

The garbage collector

What would happen if you kept caching documents until the space was full? What about new requests made after that? Well, in order to keep things in the cache more or less relevant to recent requests (which is called keeping it *fresh*), the Apache Web server periodically runs something called a *garbage collector*.

The garbage collector's job is to weed through all the rubbish in the cache and throw out anything that's too old or takes up too much space. You control how often the garbage collector does its thing with the `CacheGC-Interval` directive:

```
CacheGCInterval  number-of-hours
```

The directive takes a single integer argument, which is the number of hours between clean-up attempts. Although it doesn't have an upper limit, you can't tell the garbage collector to run any faster than once an hour.

Decisions, decisions: How long to cache?

In addition to the preferred maximum size for the entire cache, which you set with the `CacheSize` directive, the proxy garbage collector uses some age-related attributes of the cached documents to determine when they're ripe to be thrown out. The garbage collector doesn't consider the actual age of the resource in the cache, but rather the results of a comparison of the document's expiration date against the current time.

If the cache is relatively quiet and cached documents don't get thrown away by virtue of something new needing their space, what prevents the proxy from keeping cached documents around forever — even if the master copies from which they were drawn get updated? If that scenario is allowed to happen, the clients that use the proxy may never see the updated documents at all — they would keep getting the old stale copies from the cache.

To prevent this from becoming a problem, the Apache proxy module provides the `CacheMaxExpire` directive:

```
CacheMaxExpire number-of-hours
```

The value on the directive line tells the proxy the longest amount of time (in hours) that a document in the cache is considered valid. If a request for a document is made and the copy of the document in the cache is older than this value, the proxy compares the validity of the cached copy against the master copy on the remote server. To put it another way, if a client asks for a document through the proxy and the proxy finds a copy in the cache that has been there for more than `CacheMaxExpire` hours, the proxy goes out to the master copy to see if it has changed. If it has changed, a new copy is made; if it hasn't, the existing copy is marked as good for another `CacheMaxExpire` hours. In either case, the copy in the cache that was made after the check is given to the client.

The default value for this directive is 24 hours.

How old is this thing, anyway?

Obviously if some of the proxy's decisions about the validity of a cached document are going to be based on a document's age, the proxy needs to have some sort of idea when the master document was last updated. In many cases finding out this information isn't a problem, because origin servers are encouraged to include a standard header field named `Last-Modified` in their responses.

Another recommended header field is the `Expires` field, which tells any system that receives the document *exactly* when it should throw the document away. The difference between the `Expires` and `Last-Modified` fields is subtle. The former directs any system that has a copy of the document to unceremoniously discard it when the expiration time passes, whereas the latter allows the system to make an estimate of how frequently it should check to see if a newer version is available.

However, the `Last-Modified` and `Expires` header fields are not required. So what's a proxy to do? Have no fear, the Apache Web server provides some more configuration directives (surprised? I didn't think so) to help deal with this exact situation.

The `CacheLastModifiedFactor` directive (now, there's a fingerful!) tells the Apache proxy what it should do if a cached document has a `Last-Modified` header field but no `Expires` field:

```
CacheLastModifiedFactor multiplier
```

For those types of documents, the proxy calculates its own value for the expiration time — when the proxy decides to throw the document out of the cache rather than being told to do it — by multiplying the given factor by the amount of time that has passed since the document's Last-Modified value.

Hmm. That explanation seems a little confusing, doesn't it? Let me give you an example. If the value of the CacheLastModifiedFactor directive is 0.1 (the default) and the proxy caches a document whose Last-Modified date is two days ago, the proxy sets the cached copy's expiration time to 0.1×48, or 4.8 hours from the time the document was put into the cache. If the document was last modified ten minutes before the request, the proxy sets the cached copy to expire in 0.1×10, or one minute later.

This gives a definite longevity skew to documents that haven't been modified recently — which makes sense, because they're evidently more stable and more likely to benefit from being cached.

This proxy-determined expiration time is calculated only when the document is first put into the cache.

In any event, the calculated expiration time is never longer than any value set by the CacheMaxExpire described in the previous section.

How about them other types of documents?

The previous section talks about setting how long a document is valid in the cache based on values of HTTP header fields in the response when the document was requested. But proxies can be used to access other types of resources besides the ones living on HTTP (web) servers — things like FTP archives, for example. *Those* don't have any header fields like that, so how does the Apache proxy figure out how long they should stay in the cache?

The answer lies with yet another configuration directive:

```
CacheDefaultExpire hours
```

Simply put, this directive causes the proxy to set the expiration time (the time when a cached document is thrown away) to the time that the document is loaded into the cache plus the specified number of hours. The default value for this directive is one, which means that FTP documents fetched through the proxy are kept in the cache for only one hour, by default. After that time passes, another request for the same resource results in a new copy being fetched and loaded into the cache.

Part V
The Part of Tens

The 5th Wave® By Rich Tennant

"ISN'T THAT OUR WEBMASTER? THESE PEOPLE ALWAYS FIND A CREATIVE WAY TO INTERFACE."

In this part . . .

Lists are very popular things, from your household's shopping list to the Ten Reasons Shakespeare Didn't Write the Plays. Almost any office or cubicle you peer into will have lists on the walls, on the desk, in the email, on the chair (if the occupant is out; possibly on the occupant otherwise), stuck to the screen. . . . Look around you: there's probably at least one list within ten feet of you *right this very minute!*

Even if lists are creations of the Borg, there's an idea that's almost as old as they are: "If you can't beat 'em, join 'em." So here's a set of lists for you to do with what you will. They purport to answer questions you might have that have been asked before, or point you to strange and wondrous areas of the Internet wherein lie riches of arcane lore, and who knows? They may actually *do* those things!

Lists, lists, lists . . . have I got lists for you! And wonder of wonders, there's ten things in each one!

Chapter 16

Ten Steps When You Have Problems

In This Chapter

▶ Verifying that you really have a problem

▶ Looking in various places to see if anyone else has reported the issue

▶ Asking other Apache Web server users if they've seen your problem

▶ Reporting your issue to the developers if it turns out to be a legitimate problem

*A*lmost every tool, application, or utility that touches the Internet in any way ends up being fairly involved. Maybe the concept is simple, maybe the actual program is simple, but one thing that you can always count on is that customers are endlessly inventive. You can be sure that someone is going to want you to do something or provide something that is not intuitively obvious and isn't covered in the documentation.

Even though that's true for simple applications, it's no less true for complicated ones — and a web server is a pretty complicated piece of work. The Apache Web server is no exception; the basic package provides over 150 separate configuration directives, and it's built from more than 60,000 lines of source code. With the Apache Web server a lot of potential exists for complex interactions leading to unexpected results.

So resign yourself to the fact that sooner or later you'll encounter a problem configuring or using the Apache software. This chapter describes ten basic things that you can do when a problem occurs.

The sections in this chapter appear more or less in the order that you probably find them the most useful, but having to skip around and do them in a different sequence is normal and expected. So get out your magnifying glass Watson! The game's afoot!

Make Sure It's a Problem

First of all, you need to make sure that what you *think* is a problem really *is* a problem and not just the result of some sort of mis-set expectations. You may find that the only way you can verify your problem is to cover most of the other points described in this chapter. However with such a complicated environment as the Apache Web server that is in use by so many people, the chances are good that someone else has already encountered the same issue.

If the problem has to do with the server misbehaving, you should double-check the documentation for the directives involved and make sure that some fine print isn't what's leaping up and biting you.

After you're pretty sure that you have a *bona fide* problem and it isn't just a spelling or configuration error of some type, check out the other options described in this chapter to see if it's a known issue with a known solution.

Reproduce the Condition

One thing that's *very* important is being able to reproduce the problem. Many issues require you to take the pulse of the Apache Web server while it is experiencing the problem. If you can reproduce the symptoms at will, you can be more hopeful about finding a solution than if the problem only happens sometimes.

Try to narrow down the conditions under which the problem occurs. Is the problem an error message at server startup that keeps the Apache server from even running? Does the problem occur only when Joe uses Internet Explorer to access the Personnel page about the company picnic? The more that you can refine the conditions, the easier it is to discover the cause and for someone else to reproduce the problem on another server, if that becomes necessary.

Get the Exact Symptomology

Symptomology is an expensive word that basically means "where it hurts." What it means in this case is figuring out *exactly* what's triggering the problem, *exactly* what the expected results should be, and *exactly* what's happening instead.

I cannot stress this too much. Hardly anything is more frustrating to a computer support person than a dialogue that goes like this:

```
Support: What seems to be the problem?
User: Apache isn't working.
S: Are you getting an error message? What does it say?
U: I don't know, it's just not working. It said something
   about "bogus."
S: Did it work before?
U: Yes.
S: Are you doing anything differently? Has anything been
   changed?
U: No.
S: What's the exact error message?
U: I don't remember.
S: Are you sure you didn't change anything?
U: No, I didn't touch anything. Oh, wait — MIS upgraded
   my PC and I have a different web browser now. But
   nothing's changed and everything else works just like it
   used to.
```

You see? Without a clear picture of what *should* be happening, what's *actually* happening instead, and the thing that's making it happen, you're just fumbling around in the dark. For example, in the preceding example dialogue, I'd take a stab at guessing that the change in the PC software had something to do with the problem — but that's no more than a guess.

You really need to get as many exact details as possible. Gathering this information may seem like a lot of work, but doing so actually makes identifying the cause and determining a solution a lot *less* work.

Check the Server Error Log

I can't stress this particular step enough; I can't count the number of reported Apache server problems that are clearly explained by messages in the server's error log.

Unless you've made changes, your server's error log file should be /usr/local/web/apache/logs/error_log; if your server is configured to run multiple virtual hosts and you defined a separate error log for each of them, obviously the names would be different.

Entries in the error log are time-stamped, so you should be able to narrow down which message refers to the problem that you're experiencing, even on an incredibly busy server.

Although messages in the error log can explain many problems, not all problems result in an entry being recorded. So don't despair if you look in the file and don't find anything; possibly the Apache Web server doesn't think it's an error or just isn't recording any information about it.

The server is particularly meticulous about recording messages in the error log that have to do with failed accesses, such as from file permission problems or user authentication or authorization failures. So if your problem falls into one of these categories, you would almost certainly find an explanation in the log file.

Verify Directive Syntax and Interaction

Syntax errors in the server configuration files are pretty easy to detect, because the server displays an error message and fails to start if it encounters any. However, errors in .htaccess files don't cause the server to fail, because they're geared toward specific directories and requests rather than the server at large — other areas of the server's Webspace can be healthy and accessible, so there's no reason for one unhealthy directory to cause the entire server to commit suicide.

If the Apache web server *does* encounter a syntax error of any kind in a .htaccess file, it reports the fact in the appropriate server error log. For example, you may see something like the following from a request for a document in a directory with a misconfigured .htaccess file:

```
[Thu Oct 16 19:34:58 1997] [alert] /usr/local/web/apache/htdocs/.htaccess:
                Invalid command BogusDirective
```

Because the server can't be sure what the unrecognizable directive was supposed to do, it simply reports an internal configuration error to the client and keeps running.

The server can't assume that giving the client the document that it requested is okay — what if the problem directive had to do with restricting access or checking user credentials? So the server has to just say "no can do" and give an indication of why.

If your visitors report server errors to you, be sure to check the error log where the causes are entered.

So much for syntax. What about directive interactions? This can cover anything from unexpected results from <Limit> directives to conflicting settings of overrides or options.

The sorts of directive interactions to check for here primarily have to do with scoping rules. Make sure that the directory or document in question isn't being affected by some directives applying to a higher scope, or a `<Files>` container, or perhaps a forgotten `.htaccess` file somewhere in the directory hierarchy.

Another common problem has to do with a misunderstanding about how `<Location>` containers map onto the filesystem; so if you're getting unexpected results (particularly having to do with authentication or authorization) when accessing documents, make sure that your `DocumentRoot`, `<Directory>`, and `<Location>` containers are all referring to the same filesystem locations that you think they should be.

Read the FAQ (Frequently Asked Questions) List

One time-honored institution of the Internet is a thing called a *FAQ* (pronounced *fak*). FAQ is an acronym for Frequently Asked Questions, and many applications and tools have FAQs. A FAQ is a list of the most common questions asked about a particular tool, particularly those questions that are asked over and over again, along with the answers.

The Apache Web server FAQ is included as a web document in your Apache kit in directory `/usr/local/web/apache/htdocs/manual/misc/FAQ.html` (assuming you use the directory structure convention described throughout this book). Of course, that FAQ is only going to be as up-to-date as the kit itself; so a master copy of the FAQ is available at the following URL:

```
http://www.apache.org/docs/misc/FAQ.html
```

This copy is guaranteed to have the latest information.

As with all the documentation available on the Apache web site, the FAQ is kept up-to-date with the current development effort — which means it may describe issues or provide answers that apply to a newer version of Apache than yours.

Search the Apache Bug Database

The Apache Group maintains a database of problem reports at the following URL:

```
http://bugs.apache.org/
```

This database is public and searchable, and querying it for keywords that apply to your problem is a very good idea. Figure 16-1 shows the search-criteria form for querying the database, or *bugdb* as it's sometimes called.

You should look for problems that are similar — or even identical — to the one that you're experiencing. Because the database is largely free-format (meaning not many restrictions are imposed on how things should be phrased or that special category words must be included), try phrasing your problem in several different ways before assuming that none of the entries describe your issue. One good trick is to use words from an error log entry and look for them in the body of the problem reports.

Even though the form says it can search the body of PRs (problem reports), it is actually searching both the reports themselves and the answers, too.

If the search finds any PRs in the database that match your criteria, it displays a list of them. Figure 16-2 shows a sample list of this sort.

The listing is pretty wide, so be sure to scroll left and right to see all the details. If you want to look more closely at a particular PR, you can click on the PR number that appears in the left-most and right-most columns. This PR number takes you to a detailed display of the report, the meat part of which looks something like that shown in Figure 16-3.

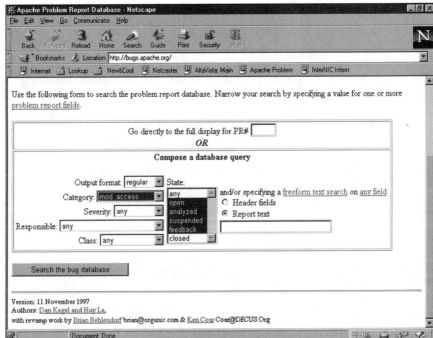

Figure 16-1:
The Apache problem report search screen.

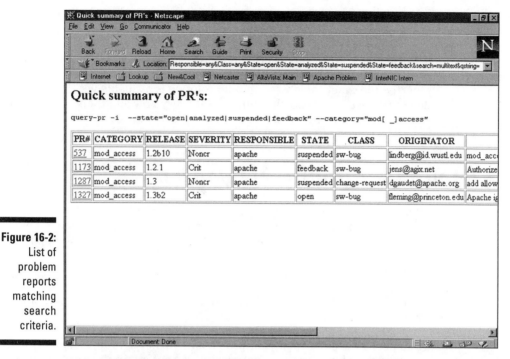

Figure 16-2:
List of problem reports matching search criteria.

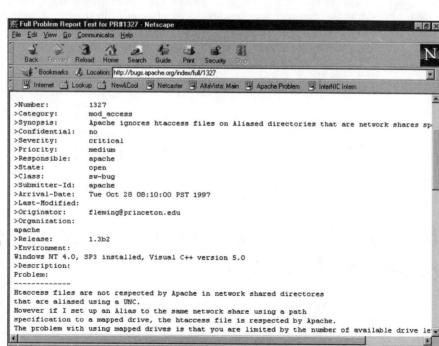

Figure 16-3:
Display of a sample Apache problem report.

The database includes several hundred problem reports, so if anyone else has encountered your problem, you have a good chance of finding it there.

If you find your problem described by an existing PR and a solution is also present, great! On the other hand, you may find that someone else has reported the exact same issue, but no solution is available yet. The thing to do in that case is to keep checking the PR every now and then, because you can't add your name to an interested party list for the case.

Check the Apache Newsgroup

Although no USENET newsgroup is dedicated to the Apache Web server, so many questions are asked about the Apache server in one particular newsgroup that it may as well be devoted to the software. That newsgroup is

```
comp.infosystems.www.servers.unix
```

and it may or may not be carried by your news server. If it isn't, ask for it by name!

If you post a description of your problem in the newsgroup, be sure to wait a couple of days for a response before you also enter it in the Apache bug database. Several Apache developers hang out in the newsgroup, and most questions get answered there in a fairly prompt manner. Issues reported in both places tend to get the developers irritated because they have to devote twice as much time to the problem. Time is a critical resource because minutes spent answering duplicate problem reports are minutes that *aren't* being spent on actually fixing problems or developing the software.

The newsgroup is a very active one, so you should check it frequently or request in your posting that people reply to you as well to the newsgroup. Otherwise, if you don't get back to the newsgroup for a few days, you may miss the answer because your news server has thrown out any answering articles to make room for new ones.

Verify File Protections and Check for Resource Exhaustion

Two of the most common causes of problems that you encounter are incorrect file permissions and inadequate resource settings for the Apache Web server process and its children.

Even though the permissions on the file that you're trying to access may be correct, or at least appear to be, don't forget that the Apache Web server's access to the file has to occur under the auspices of the username that the server is running as and that the server has to traverse the entire directory tree to reach the document. So make sure that the ownership of not only the file, but all of the directories in its parentage, is correct and that the server user has at least read and execute access to all of them, as well. Usually the Apache Web server is very good about reporting permission problems in the error log, but occasionally subtle interactions (particularly with symbolic links) can trip you up.

Remember way back when, early in the book, when I said that the server requires lots of open file slots? (Did you read that part yet? Give yourself 5 Apache Guru Points if you did. If you didn't, it's in Chapter 2.) File slots are the most commonly exhausted resource, and the Apache Web server really can't report them accurately in the error log.

Why? Because the file that can't be opened is usually not being opened by the server itself, but instead by some library routine or system call that the server invokes. And those are notoriously bad about reporting the exact details when something goes wrong for them. The most typical symptom of file slot exhaustion is CGI script problems.

Other resource problems can occur, too, and most of them suffer from the same inability of the server to report them. The next most common problem after file slots is memory, but you don't have any good way to identify memory as being the cause without extremely system-specific debugging steps. One thing to try is to increase the memory limits in the process that starts the Apache Web server; if your problem goes away, you've probably found the cause and you should make your increased limits a permanent part of the way that you start your server.

Report the Problem to The Apache Group

If you check and recheck and verify in all sorts of different ways that the behavior you're seeing is really and truly a bug, the appropriate thing to do is report it to The Apache Group so it can be examined and fixed.

Bugs are reported in a database accessible through your web browser. In fact, it's the same database that I describe earlier in this chapter. Entries are called problem reports, or PRs, rather than bugs; so if someone mentions PR#911 or whatever, you know what's being talked about. Figure 16-4 shows the top part of the problem report entry screen.

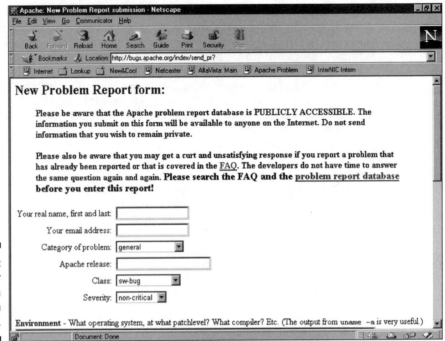

Figure 16-4:
Screen for
entering a
problem
report.

As the top of the form says, please be *very, very sure* that you check every-thing before reporting a problem. If you ask for help on something that has been reported — and solved — 40 times before or that's clearly described in the Apache FAQ, you're likely to get a very terse response from the developers.

Providing as much information as possible and being as accurate as you can is very important. Be sure to be specific; for example, if you're encountering the problem with Version 1.2.4 of the Apache server, be sure to say so — don't just say you're using the latest version.

If any messages in the error log pertain to the problem, be sure to include them, along with a description of what you did that caused them, in your problem report.

Notification of status changes and updates to problem reports is done through e-mail, so be sure to supply an e-mail address where you can be reached. Use an address that works anywhere on the Internet; in some cases in the past, reports have been submitted with addresses like joe or Susan, which doesn't help anyone. When the database system tries to send mail, it's not going to have a clue what the right address is, so joe or Susan never hear what's going on with their problems. The developers usually just close those types of reports without any investigation even taking place, because they have no way to contact the originator for additional information.

The developers in The Apache Group work on solving bugs as rapidly as they can, but please remember that none of them work on Apache as a full-time job. Therefore, you may have to wait days or even weeks before someone gets around to working on your problem. While you wait, pursuing other avenues of investigation is a good idea — even to the point of checking the source and seeing if you can identify the cause (and a fix) yourself.

After you enter a problem report into the database, you can no longer touch it directly. The only way that you can affect it is to reply to the e-mail message that you get from the database system. The text of your reply is attached to the existing PR text so you can update the case with additional information. Replying only to *that* mail message is important, because otherwise your reply may easily disappear and not get to where you want it to go.

Chapter 17

Ten Important RFCs

In This Chapter

▶ Understanding what RFCs are and why they're important

▶ Accessing RFCs through the Internet repositories

▶ Finding out details of The Rules to help you in your Web work

*W*ith the vast number of different kinds of systems out in the world, both hardware and software, the Internet couldn't possibly exist without some set of rules and conventions that all players agree to abide by.

Well, the Internet does exist (and no, I'm not going to get into solipsistic existentialism or start expounding about whether virtual things are real!), and a body of rules and conventions exists as well. They're (drum roll, please) . . . *The RFCs.*

RFC is an acronym for Request For Comments. Sounds funny, doesn't it? You may think that name means the rules are still in a state of flux. The name is an artifact from Ye Earlye Daze of the Internet, but it's still appropriate in a way — because the RFCs always are in a state of flux.

Well over 2,000 RFCs exist, with more coming out almost every week. Some of the new RFCs describe completely new topics, and quite a few of them provide corrections or enhancements to existing ones. When an RFC gets updated, the modified text is assigned its own number; the original text remains unchanged and accessible with the original RFC number so it's always available as a reference. You can access all the current RFCs, either directly or through a keyword search, at the following URL:

```
http://www.rfc-editor.org/
```

As you may expect from the name, an RFC goes through a review process during which anyone can comment on it. When the authors feel that all the issues have been addressed, they can advance the RFC to the final stage, at which point the RFC means "request for comments to go into a new RFC to modify this one."

The very nature of RFCs and the incredibly dynamic environment of the Internet virtually guarantee that the documents described in this chapter will someday become obsolete, superseded by newer, or more complete, or more correct versions. So don't take these RFC numbers as gospel — be sure to go out to the RFC repository and see if they've been updated. If they have been updated, feel free to mark the pages in this book with the newer RFC numbers — I don't mind. Really.

The RFCs are like the rules of the road or, perhaps, instructions for a complex machine. Software or systems that don't comply are like drivers who don't obey a red stoplight — they tend to crash or at least fail to get to where they want to go. If they actually *do* arrive safely, it's probably due to luck more than anything else.

Here, then, is a list of ten important instruction manuals for driving on the Internet. Some of them can be pretty dry to read, but they are the rules. (Ever try to read any of the laws and statutes under which you live? You'll find the RFCs easier to follow, I'm sure!) The software that you use should be coded to comply with these (or other) RFCs, but if you have any doubt, you now know where to look to get the ultimate answer. And if you don't like the answer you find — well, you can always write your own RFC and try to get it recognized and accepted!

Internet Primer: RFC2151

This RFC — formally titled *A Primer On Internet and TCP/IP Tools and Utilities* — is a sort of once-over-lightly treatment of many of the most commonly used utilities and tools.

It briefly describes the purposes and usage of things like `finger`, `whois`, `ping`, and `ftp`, and the cryptically named `archie`, `veronica`, and `jughead`, among others. If you're relatively new to the Internet or even to just the areas of Webmastering or system or network administration, this RFC is definitely worth a glance or two because you may have cause to use many of the applications that it describes.

RFCs about the Domain Name System

Remember the Domain Name System (DNS)? I talk about it a little bit back in Chapter 14. Oh, well — if you don't remember it or you haven't read that chapter yet (shame on you!), it doesn't really matter.

The DNS servers and hierarchy spread across the Internet are key to the Internet's function and operation. The DNS is how computers turn names into addresses and addresses into names, and determine the best way to send e-mail, and figure out who's the *real* authority behind a domain, and. . . . Well, just take it from me, the DNS is an incredibly crucial part of the Internet's structure.

Three useful RFCs describe the Domain Name System, its philosophy, implementation, and operation. If you're already a BindMaster, you probably either don't need to check out these RFCs or else you have their contents memorized. If you're a little fuzzy on the whole name/address/domain/FQDN/translation schtick, though, these RFCs can help shed some light in the DNS darkness.

Domain administrator's guide: RFC 1032

RFC 1032, the *DOMAIN ADMINISTRATORS GUIDE,* is more than ten years old and in many ways it's hopelessly out of date. Among other things, it describes the process of registering an Internet domain as you did it in the days when the U.S. government (specifically, the DDN, or Defense Data Network) was responsible for registering top-level domains.

Although it's rather quaint, it does provide some background about the issues involved in owning and managing an Internet domain name, and it provides some interesting glimpses into the history of the Internet and how we've come to be where we are.

Domain name concepts: RFC 1034

Although RFC 1034, *DOMAIN NAMES — CONCEPTS AND FACILITIES,* is as old as the RFC described in the previous section (about ten years old, if you haven't read that section), it treats the issues of the Domain Name System (DNS) in a more generic fashion. Therefore, most of the information that it contains is still pertinent to the current decade.

This RFC describes what DNS is, gives a high-level overview of how it works, and explains how it came to be. Then it goes into greater and greater detail. It's a medium-sized RFC — about 50 pages (that's $8^1/2$-x-11-inch pages) — and it's a very good introduction to the DNS system if you're not familiar with it.

If you're going to be managing any Internet domains as part of your Webmastering duties or if you're new to the area of DNS management, this RFC is definitely a good document to have on hand.

Domain name specification: RFC1035

Like the other two DNS-related RFCs described in the preceding sections, RFC 1035, *DOMAIN NAMES — IMPLEMENTATION AND SPECIFICATION*, is a decade old. Because it deals with technical details rather than political ones (like who's responsible for registering domain names), it is still relevant to the Internet of today.

DNS is an acronym for Domain Name System. Because the DNS is largely implemented by software called BIND (Berkeley Internet Name Daemon), originally developed at Berkeley, California, commonly you hear the naming system called BIND, and DNS name servers referred to as BIND servers.

Although some changes and enhancements to the DNS system have been made since this RFC was first published, this RFC is still an excellent resource for understanding the details of how your computer turns the names that you give it into the numbers that it needs. This RFC describes the process of locating the correct name server to ask about the name.

It also goes into what you may consider excessive detail about the format of the binary bits that the computers exchange. You can skip those parts unless you're a bit-head and find them intriguing; you don't get any Apache Guru Points if you read those parts, though — sorry.

DNS Aliases for Services: RFC2219

If you're going to have any input concerning the name of your web host or systems providing other network services, you may want to take a look at RFC 2219, *Use of DNS Aliases for Network Services*.

This document is quite new (October 1997) and discusses some of the naming conventions that have developed over the years for naming systems according to the functions that they perform — and the names that some software assumes service engines to have.

It also describes some of the ways in which you can use the DNS to help you keep your systems organized and in particular how you can easily migrate functions from one system to another.

If you're not responsible for any host-naming activities, you still may want to scan this document. At the very least, you can then be a back-seat driver in discussions concerning those issues.

The MIME Papers: RFCs 2045 through 2049

MIME is yet another acronym, this time for Multipurpose Internet Mail Extensions. Despite the name, the concepts defined by the MIME documentation have spread very widely into diverse areas — including web technology. One key attribute of a web resource, after all, is called its *MIME type*, and it is described using the format and rules put forth in the MIME RFCs.

As you may deduce from the name, MIME was originally developed with electronic mail in mind. The ideas were so neat, though, that other technologies started using them — and giving credit to the origin — so the term MIME is now as widespread as . . . well, RFC. And trying to change the name to get rid of or change the word *Mail* would be almost as difficult.

So the name MIME is probably here to stay, at least until some new set of definitions comes along that is so much better and different that *it* becomes the new standard. In the meantime, MIME is pervasive — get used to it.

A total of 5 RFCs describe different parts and aspects of the MIME concepts. The reason that MIME is broken up is not so much that it is so long and complicated; the underlying reason is to be able to update different aspects independently without having to release an entirely new RFC that changes only part of the old one. So the topic is broken into five logically separate portions for ease of maintainability.

Message body formats: RFC2045

Part 1 of the MIME series of RFCs is entitled *Format of Internet Message Bodies* and describes basically what the title says it does — how MIME-compliant documents (which include web resources) should be structured.

MIME documents are like web transactions — they consist of a header portion and a body portion. The header acts as a sort of envelope and contains information about the contents of the body portion. This RFC defines the different fields and attributes that can be part of a MIME document's header.

Internet media types: RFC2046

The second document in the MIME RFC series is called *Media Types*, and it describes and discusses the philosophy and practice behind the different types of data and content that MIME-compliant documents can contain. Internet Media Types (IMTs) are also called MIME types. In fact, you probably hear (or read) that term more frequently than you do the other.

Media types are actually two-part labels, with a slash (/) separating the two parts. The part that precedes the slash is called the *type,* and the portion that follows the slash is called the *subtype*. So a document labeled as `text/html` contains text, and the text contains HTML markup instructions. Similarly, a resource labeled as `application/octet-stream` is composed of application-specific data that is represented simply as a string of 8-bit bytes (octets).

A web resource's content is labeled according to the MIME typing scheme, even though the HTTP header field for the label is `Content-type` rather than `media-type`.

Want more information about this stuff? Read the RFC!

Non-ASCII headers in MIME: RFC2047

More and more of the e-mail messages, web transactions, and other information flowing across the Internet is becoming truly international in nature. This is good because it helps the world advance toward a common understanding and tolerance.

Unfortunately, this transition from English-centric transmission formats to international ones doesn't come without pain; one of the serious difficulties to overcome is the issue of the different alphabets and character sets used in the international community and how to represent them or provide for their use in places that were originally designed to handle only the U.S.-ASCII character set.

This RFC, *Message Header Extensions for Non-ASCII Text,* describes ways in which information from non-ASCII languages can be used in the header portion of MIME documents (and, by extension, web transactions as well). If you have to deal with a multilingual environment or one in which English isn't the preferred language, you may want to give this document a read.

Registering a MIME type: RFC2048

As more and more information is made available on the Internet, the spectrum of *types* of information is broadening, too. As applications that used to deal only with single desktop or workstation environments find their data files being shared or transmitted over the Internet, a way to clearly identify the application that can handle them is more and more urgent.

The MIME concept of Internet media types already provides this information. But what about applications that are just now seeing their documents hit the wire? How do the manufacturers get a definite, official, Internet-wide, recognizable media type with which these documents may be tagged?

You may find the answer to the "how" part of this question in this RFC, entitled *Registration Procedures*. The name sort of says it all. This RFC describes the process of requesting and registering a unique MIME type for a document content format. If you're an application developer, and your file format is unique to your application, and your application's documents are (or will be) flying across the Internet, you may want to read this RFC and see about registering a type for your stuff.

Conformance and examples: RFC2049

This RFC, *Conformance Criteria and Examples,* wraps up the series of MIME specification RFCs. This one includes the usual stuff that you find at the end of an involved document: examples, a bibliography, a review of the rules that determine whether a document is compliant, and the like. If you're going to be working on an application that generates MIME-compliant documents — such as sending a binary document via e-mail in response to a Web-based form completed by the user — this RFC is a good reference.

HTML Version 2.0: RFC1866

Although HTTP is the language that computers use to talk to each other in order to perform web transactions, HTML is the language that web documents are usually written in. The Web client knows how to turn the resource from HTML into something suitable for your reading pleasure — that's its job, after all.

This page-description language called HTML leads a very tempestuous life. Because it defines the instructions that the author uses to get the client to display things as he or she wants it to, huge surges of enhancements are made because authors decide that they want to do thus-and-such and manage to convince client developers to handle it. (Actually, a lot of the time the authors and the developers are one and the same, which doesn't hurt the process!)

RFC 1866, *Hypertext Markup Language — 2.0,* puts a stake in the ground for a particular set of capabilities and formats. Because it defines a standard, it provides a stable definition that authors can use as a reference — if author don't do anything that isn't described in the RFC, they can claim to be HTML/2.0-compliant and have a legitimate grievance if a client making the same claim doesn't handle their documents correctly.

Even though this is the latest standard version of HTML that is defined as an RFC, it still doesn't define the latest version commonly available. Version 3.2 is the latest version right now. It was developed by the World Wide Web Consortium (W3C) and code-named *Wilbur.* Wilbur contains a lot of commonly used and desirable features that HTML/2.0 doesn't define, such as tables, typeface sizes, colors, and so on. Whether Wilbur or any of its descendants would ever be made into an RFC is unclear; the responsibility for HTML development probably remains with the W3C.

However, even though you may write your documents according to the Wilbur definition or some other feature-set provided by your favorite browser, you should keep in mind that some older browsers just don't get it. But they probably *do* understand HTML/2.0, so if you at least write your HTML documents according to this RFC, you should be in pretty good shape.

Uniform Resource Names: 1737

URLs (Uniform Resource Locators) are used to find documents or resources on the Internet (specifically, through the Web). This RFC, *Functional Requirements for Uniform Resource Names,* describes some proposed requirements for providing resources with unique names as opposed to locations. You know, just in case the resource moves. If it does move, the URL changes, but the resource itself is the same, and its name should remain unchanged.

The whole issue of naming, characterizing, and locating Internet resources is an area that has a significant impact on the development of the Net and the Web in particular, so skimming this RFC just to keep up with things may be a good idea.

URL Definition: RFC1738

The whole point of the World Wide Web is to provide people with the ability to access information, documents, and other resources wherever they may exist on the Internet (or even on a private intranet). After you know that you want to access a particular resource, you need to be able to point your web client to it and say "go get it for me."

You do this is by telling your client where it can find the document — its Internet location. This location or Internet address needs to be in a format that your client and everyone else's clients can understand, which means that the syntax has to be pretty standard. RFC 1738, *Uniform Resource Locators (URL),* defines this standard syntax so that all the web software can use the same rules for locating web documents around the world. The URL that you use to access the Apache web site, for example, works just as well for anyone else on the Internet — it's a sort of global address.

There's actually quite a lot to it that most casual users of the Internet don't really see — such as how to represent special language-specific characters in Web addresses or how to pass information to a web resource that responds in real time. This RFC covers all those details. Well, most of them.

Although most web users probably don't know or care about these issues, if you're going to be a Webmaster, you need to care. So I highly recommend that you read this RFC so you are at least be familiar with the concepts. It's a medium-length RFC — only about 25 pages long.

RFC 1738 is probably going to be superseded soon by a new RFC that combines its rules with those of RFC 1808 (Relative URLs) and addresses some issues and shortcomings of the current documents. So keep an eye on the RFC repositories so you can make a new copy of the new RFC when it becomes available.

Relative URLs: RFC1808

When a web author is building a set of interlocking documents, you can hyperlink them to one another to insulate them from the vagaries of having to be relocated to another directory or web system. RFC 1808, *Relative Uniform Resource Locators,* describes the details of how embedded links of this sort can be used to manage this trick. It covers the details of the syntax involved in linking to a document relative to the current document's location and is almost required reading for page authors. As RFCs go, it's actually quite short — only about 16 pages long, in fact.

RFC 1808 is probably going to be superseded soon by a new RFC that combines its rules with those of RFC 1738 (which describes absolute URLs) and addresses some issues and shortcomings of the current documents. Keep an eye on the RFC repositories so you can make a new copy of the new RFC when it becomes available.

The HTTP/1.0 Specification: RFC 1945

HTTP is the language that web clients and web servers speak when humans aren't listening. The syntax of this language as originally released and deployed on the Internet is defined by RFC 1945, *Hypertext Transfer Protocol — HTTP/1.0.*

This document defines the grammar, syntax, and communication rules that govern web entities that are talking to one another in this dialect. It is currently the dialect with the widest penetration in the web, but it's already being superseded by the next version, HTTP/1.1 (see the next section).

However, HTTP/1.0 was the dialect used in over 95 percent of web transactions in 1997, so if you're going to get down into the issues of actually understanding and using the protocol (as you very well may if you fool around with CGI scripts very long), this document is a must-read.

Don't neglect the HTTP/1.1 protocol version, though, because soon it will be gradually replacing the HTTP/1.0 usage across the Web.

The HTTP/1.1 Specification: RFC 2068

After the first version of the HTTP protocol, Version 1.0 (see the preceding section), was defined, deployed, and came into general use across the World Wide Web, some unexpected deficiencies were discovered.

RFC 2068, *Hypertext Transfer Protocol — HTTP/1.1,* follows the time-honored practice of addressing shortcomings and adding enhancements to an existing definition by addressing the issues discovered after Version 1.0 went into widespread use. Many of the changes are intended to improve performance.

Although HTTP/1.1 isn't in widespread use yet, testing has already shown that web transactions that use this version of the protocol, rather than its predecessor, are vastly more efficient.

The Apache server 1.2 and later are fully compliant with *both* HTTP/1.0 and HTTP/1.1. The sole exception to this is the proxy module, which is not yet fully compliant with HTTP/1.1.

Chapter 18

Ten URLs for Web Authors

. . . .

In This Chapter

▶ Finding documentation for Apache topics

▶ Locating Internet standards documents (RFCs)

▶ Using the Apache problem report database

▶ Visiting the main Apache web site for more information

▶ Comparing numbers of users of web server packages on the Internet

. . . .

1 f you're going to be involved with the Apache Web server and you want more information, what better place to look than on the Web itself? You can find a lot of stuff on it; a couple of years ago, an estimated 30 million web pages were available — the count now is anyone's guess but probably a few more pages exist now.

This chapter points out ten web locations that are likely to be the most helpful to you when you're setting up and operating your web site using the Apache server software. Obviously these ten locations just scratch the surface of what's available, but if I gave you any more, this chapter wouldn't belong in The Part of Tens, would it? So polish up your web browser and get ready to surf — there's gold in that thar web!

The Apache Web Site

Of course, the best web site to keep in mind if you're going to be using a particular product is the site of the product's manufacturer, right? The Apache Web server software is no exception. I mention the URL for this site several times throughout the book, but here it is again — it should *definitely* appear here, even if it does show up elsewhere in the book:

```
http://WWW.Apache.Org/
```

As new releases of the Apache software become available or serious problems are discovered, they are prominently mentioned on the front page of the Apache site. In other locations on this site, you can also find

- Instructions describing how to access and download the Apache Web server software package

- Information about the people who comprise The Apache Group and actually develop the software

- Pointers to other Apache-sponsored or Apache-related projects, such as the module registry or the Java servlet integration effort

- Patches to fix various problems or add various bits of functionality (either because The Apache Group is between releases or because the enhancements aren't considered general-interest enough to be included in the main package)

- A list of pointers to web-accessible articles (such as from *PC Week*) that mention the Apache Web server project

- Pointers to several other places around the Internet where you can find Apache-related information

Of course, you can find other stuff on the site, too, but I'll leave that to you to discover.

The Latest Apache Documentation

The Apache web site is also the home of the master copy of the web server documentation. When you get an Apache Web server software distribution, it includes the version of the documentation and online manual that was current at the time the package was built. However, the master copy, located at

```
http://WWW.Apache.Org/docs/
```

includes any changes, additions, or corrections that have been made *since* your distribution kit was created.

This sometimes means that the documentation on the Apache site talks about features that aren't in your version of the software; places where you see this type of information should be clearly marked with notes like "Only available in Apache 1.3 or later," or whatever the proper version is.

The Apache Documentation Searcher

The online documentation for the Apache Web server is spread across several directories, and some topics may be described in multiple places. To help you find these scattered references or just quickly find a particular topic, you can use the documentation search script:

```
http://WWW.Apache.Org/manual-index.cgi/docs
```

This script allows you to access a very simple search engine that indexes the Apache master documentation files every night. It can only search for a single word at a time, and it doesn't do stubbing (like turning a search for `served` into one for `served`, `serve`, and `serving`), Boolean search (such as `foo AND bar`), or pattern-matching or regular expression processing (for example, `(address)|(ip)-based v(irtual )\{0,1\}host`). It just looks for documents that contain an exact match for the word that you enter.

This search engine is available only at the master Apache site and searches only the master copy of the Apache Web server documentation (see the previous section). However, it can help you locate things quickly — you just need to figure out how to properly phrase your queries (that is, the words that you want it to search for), just as you do with any search engine.

This tool can be particularly useful because the index includes documents that exist *only* at the main Apache site — that is, pages and documents that aren't included with the software kit.

The Apache Bug Database

The database of problem reports submitted by Apache users serves two functions: as a reference, when you're trying to find out if anyone else has ever had the same problem that you're having; and as a reporting mechanism, when you want to report a new problem that no one else has yet encountered. In either case, the URL for the database is

```
http://Bugs.Apache.Org/
```

This URL takes you to the form shown in Figure 18-1 and Figure 18-2; as these figures indicate, you can click on another button (shown in Figure 18-1) to add your own problem report, or you can fill in the fields (shown in Figure 18-2) to just search through the database of existing PRs (Problem Reports) for something that seems to match your issue.

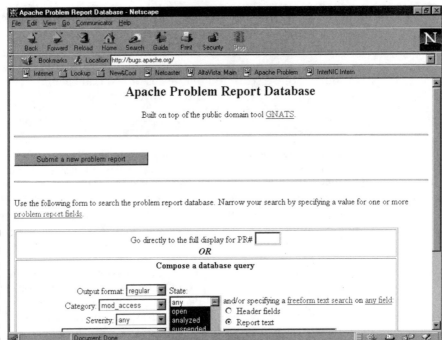

Figure 18-1:
The
Apache bug
database
page
(again).

If you decide that you want to enter a new problem report, *please* be sure that you check all the other possible places first to make sure your issue isn't already known. You should ask in the `comp.infosystems.www.servers.unix` USENET newsgroup, search through the documentation on the Apache site, check the Apache Web server FAQ, and especially search the existing bug reports. If you enter a new report that duplicates an existing one or describes an issue already covered in the FAQ or that the Apache server documentation clearly says is how things are *supposed* to work, the response to your PR is likely be very terse. Please remember that the two dozen or so Apache developers have other jobs and are supporting over a half million sites running the Apache Web server worldwide; help them out by doing your research first.

The ApacheWeek Electronic Magazine

A group of people at UK Web Ltd. in Great Britain publish a free weekly electronic magazine that talks solely about the Apache Web server. The URL for the magazine's site is

```
http://WWW.ApacheWeek.Com/
```

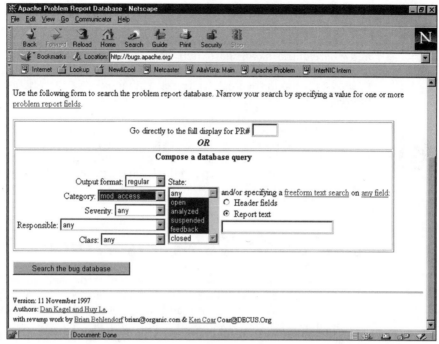

Figure 18-2:
The form for
searching
the Apache
bug
database.

You can sign up to receive weekly copies by e-mail, either in plain text or in full HTML (if you're using a full-featured mail agent such as Eudora or one of those agents that are built into Netscape Navigator or Internet Explorer).

In addition to giving you snippets about what happened with the Apache Web server development process last week, the online magazine include articles describing common tasks or confusing areas — such as handling page uploads from tools like Microsoft FrontPage or the intricacies of restricting access with authentication and authorization directives. You can search the site's index of past articles for topics that interest you. These articles are generally written in a clear, simple, and engaging style, with lots of hands-on instructions to help make their points.

The Apache Module Registry

Although the standard modules that are included with the Apache server kit provide a broad range of functionality, people have wanted the Apache Web server to do lots of other things that the standard modules don't cover. Due to the modular nature of the software's construction, adding new functionality is relatively easy, and a lot of people have taken advantage of this opportunity to enhance the server. The Apache Module Registry, located at

```
http://modules.apache.org/
```

provides a central location where all of these neat enhancements are listed and where authors can share their work with the Internet. So if you want to do something that doesn't seem to be available in the basic package, be sure to browse through the Registry to see if someone has already done it and offered it to the world.

The Apache Module Registry is maintained through volunteer efforts and has a tendency to occasionally fall behind the latest information. However, because the modules are maintained by their individual authors, all that you need to do is locate them through the Registry pages, and then you can find out the latest status directly from the source.

The World Wide Web Consortium

A few years ago, the CERN particle physics laboratory served as the hub for discussions and efforts about the World Wide Web technology. That wasn't the lab's main purpose, however, and subsequently the World Wide Web Consortium (the W3C) was formed to move the effort into a more general forum.

The W3C is a member-based organization, allowing various levels of participation. The discussion groups and conventions that it sponsors are where a lot of the ongoing development of the Web technology and philosophy take place.

You can find a lot of good stuff at the W3C web site, which is located at

```
http://WWW.W3.Org/
```

Anyone who is serious about being involved in the evolution of the Web should at least be familiar with some of the resources and efforts of the W3C. (You're reading this book, so this means *you*.)

The HTML/3.2 Standard

Although Version 2.0 of the HTML Web-page description language is described by an official Internet RFC, the evolution has been proceeding at a furious pace. The latest version that's clearly defined and widely deployed is described in a document from the World Wide Web Consortium at the following URL:

```
http://WWW.W3.Org/pub/WWW/TR/REC-html32.html
```

This is HTML 3.2, code-named *Wilbur*. (No, I don't know why.) It includes clarification of some details from the HTML/2.0 standard and defines a *lot* of new features beyond what's available in the previous standard — things like tables, font management, colors, text alignment, and so on.

If you're going to be a web author, you definitely should have this document bookmarked in your browser. Even if you're only (only!) going to be a Webmaster and not directly involved in content development, you should be aware of it so you can point your content providers to it as a reference.

The Internet RFC Repository

The cooperative environment of the Internet is driven by agreed-upon standards for communication between computers and computers, and computers and humans. (Extraterrestrial aliens too, I suppose.) Those standards are called RFCs, and they are developed and maintained by people interested in the topics that they cover. You can find a central searchable repository of all the existing RFCs at

```
http://www.rfc-editor.org/
```

These RFCs are the glue that holds the Internet together and define how hardware and software should work together in the Internet environment. Several Web-related topics are also defined by RFC documents, although the main focus remains on network-communication issues.

This site is a good one to be aware of because you can almost count on hearing someone say "it's doing thus-and-so according to RFC this-and-that." With the preceding URL, you can find the relevant RFC and see if that person really knows what he or she is talking about.

Over 2,000 RFCs are available, and most of them are more than two dozen pages long. So make sure you have a good supply of munchies if you plan a marathon RFC-reading session.

Chapter 17 describes some of the most important RFCs.

The Netcraft Web Survey

Okay, so you're interested in the Apache Web server, right? Why else are you reading this book? You've heard that the software is pretty popular, eh? Would you be interested in knowing just *how* popular it is? Because you can find out at the Netcraft web server survey page:

```
http://WWW.Netcraft.Com/Survey
```

Every month, the people at Netcraft scan the entire Internet for web servers and tally the ones that they find — including the software that they're running. More than a million web sites are on the Internet, and the number is doubling about every 18 months. The preceding URL shows a graph of the number of servers running the various web server software packages, and it's really quite interesting.

In addition, the Netcraft site allows you to poke at any particular web site and then tells you what software package that site is using for a web server.

I'll let you visit the site and draw your own conclusions from what you see on the graph.

Chapter 19
Ten Apache Answers

In This Chapter
▶ Preparing for difficulties
▶ Dealing with problems you're likely to encounter

*I*f you're going to be setting up the Apache Web server package on your system, there are probably going to be times when you'll stop, scratch your head, and ask yourself "Now why did it do *that?*" (If this never happens to you, don't worry about points — you're a certified Apache Guru. I should know; I'm one — or at least I play one in print! Heh-heh.)

The real Apache Web server Frequently-Asked Questions list has dozens and dozens of questions (and answers) in it, and it covers many pages. However, most of the responses are pretty terse, so I've tried to pick the ten issues Most Likely to Stump You and address them in a little more detail.

This was a pretty hard "top ten" list to pick; there are lots of questions asked over and over again. When I felt there was a tie, I chose the one that seemed to include the most frustration for the average Apache Webmaster encountering it. So get your medication ready, because one or more of these is likely to start gnawing on your ankle some day.

Why don't my virtual hosts work?

Oh, boy — is *this* a big one. It's actually a compilation of all the widely-varying vhost questions that come in; they all boil down to this basic question. The simple answer would be to say, "because they aren't configured right" — but despite being accurate, it's not a very satisfying answer, is it?

Most of the problems with virtual hosts stems from confusion about how the Apache Web server determines to which host an incoming request should be assigned. And if you thought it was confusing from the documentation, let me tell you that it's really hard to figure out from the source code, too.

The biggest source of confusion comes from the fact that address-based vhosts and name-based vhosts are declared by the same directive: `<VirtualHost>`. And during startup the Web server didn't tell you when it encountered something it thought would confuse it later.

In Apache 1.3, though, the `NameVirtualHost` directive was added. This has made configuration of virtual hosts a lot simpler, because you use it to tell the server *exactly* which IP addresses might have one or more name-based vhosts. Any IP address handled by your server which *isn't* identified in a `NameVirtualHost` directive is automatically treated as *never* being eligible for name-based vhosts. Requests that come in addressed to IP addresses that aren't named this way are assigned to the appropriate address-based virtual host.

Confusing? You bet! But you should have seen it before. . . . To put it another way, only IP addresses listed in `NameVirtualHost` directives are allowed to have multiple `<VirtualHost>` blocks. If you try to set up multiple containers for an address that *isn't* listed like this, Apache will inform you in no uncertain terms that it won't be able to tell them apart.

That's another thing that's new in Apache 1.3: conflict reporting at server startup. When the Apache Web server starts pre-figuring out the vhost setup, it tells you right up front when it finds things that are going to cause confusion.

If you're using name-based virtual hosts, your `<VirtualHost>` containers *must* contain a `ServerName` or a `ServerAlias` directive. Why? Because these are *name*-based virtual hosts, and those define the name. Without those directives, Apache won't be able to tell which virtual host is which.

If you're using address-based virtual hosts, make sure that you've only got a single `<VirtualHost>` container for each address.

If your virtual hosts all work correctly, give yourself 30 Apache Guru Points. If they worked right the first time you set them up, give yourself another 50. And if you're not using virtual hosts at all, give yourself 10.

How come people can see pages I put a <Limit> on?

The simple answer to this one is, "Because they're probably using a method you didn't list in your <Limit> statement."

Basically, the <Limit> container is used much too much, in places where it isn't needed or isn't appropriate. For instance, there's a common misconception going around (sort of like the flu — don't catch it, now!) that you need to put a <Limit> container around any authentication/authorization directives such as "Require valid-user" or "AuthUserFile."

Sorry, but that's rubbish. Put it right out of your mind. If what you want to do is protect a directory or set of files under all circumstances, include the appropriate directives as documented — but *don't* put them inside a <Limit> container.

<Limit> should only be used when you want to limit access to some methods (such as PUT or DELETE), but not others (like GET or POST). If you don't care what method is being used, you don't need — and shouldn't use — <Limit>.

See Chapter 6 for more information about this stuff.

Why don't my SSI directives work?

There are two ways this might be meant:

- ✔ SSI directives are being replaced with the text, "[an error occurred processing this directive]" in the document received by the client.
- ✔ SSI directives are being left in the HTML sent to the client; a "View Source" or the equivalent shows them in their original untranslated state.

The first one is easy to answer: that error message means that you're using the SSI directive incorrectly. Perhaps you've got the syntax wrong, or you're giving it invalid arguments. In any event, the solution is to verify that you've got it right, and then check the usual places (like the FAQ) to see if there's something subtle going on. The server error log should contain an explanation of what the server didn't like about the directive.

The second case is a bit harder to fix. Basically, this happens when the server either doesn't understand that it should parse the document, or else has been told not to do so. Here are some things to check:

- ✔ Is the `mod_include` module built into your Apache Web server image?
- ✔ Is the file extension (for example, ".`shtml`") listed as a candidate for parsing? In other words, do you have directives such as the following that cover the scope where the document lives?

```
AddHandler server-parsed shtml
AddType text/html shtml
```

- ✔ Are SSIs enabled for the scope where the document lives? That is, do you have an `Options` directive (such as one or more of the following) that should apply to the document's scope and allow the document to be parsed?

```
Options All
Options Includes
Options IncludesNoExec
```

Remember that each `Options` directive within a particular scope normally replaces the effect of any previous `Options` statements in that scope. That's why the preceding example statements have "+" in front of the keywords; the + tells the server "add this option to any existing settings, rather than replacing them."

- ✔ Is the relevant `Options` directive in a scope where it will be processed by the server? To wit, can you find one or more of the following applying to the directory or a near parent?

```
AllowOverride All
AllowOverride Options
```

- ✔ Is the document being accessed through a symbolic link which might change the scope?

These are the most common causes for this problem; it's almost always a scoping issue. Check out the inheritance and interactions of the above directives and you'll probably locate the source of the trouble.

Why can't I use SSI directives in my script output?

In the current design of the Apache Web server, there is no way for the output from one module to be passed along as the input of another. Specific to this case, there is no way the output from the mod_cgi module (which handles CGI scripts) can be passed along to the mod_include module (which deals with embedded server-side include directives).

Many (including me) would consider this a useful feature, but making it happen is going to require a major rework of a lot of how the Apache Web server does its thing. In other words, you're not going to see this happen before Apache Version 2.0. There are a lot of side-issues, too, like how to handle the response headers and how to keep processing time from building to the point that everything times out before the document is completely processed. Trust me, it's a very complicated issue.

This *is* on the Version 2.0 wish-list, however — so stay tuned.

How do I set up a password-protected page?

The simplest way to do this is to use the mod_auth authentication/authorization module. Here's what you do:

1. **Make sure that the directory containing the documents you want to protect (which might be all the files in the directory) is covered by a**

   ```
   AllowOverride AuthConfig
   ```

   directive, either directly or through inheriting it from some parent directory.

2. **Make sure that mod_auth is built into your server.**

3. **Decide upon the usernames and passwords you want to use, and create a file containing them using the htpasswd application:**

   ```
   % htpasswd -c .htpasswd User1
   [enter the password for username User1]
   % htpasswd .htpasswd User2
   [enter the password for username User2]
   ```

   Note that you only use the -c command option when creating the file the first time. The htpasswd utility is included in the support directory (Apache 1.2) or the src/support directory (Apache 1.3). You may need to compile it first.

4. **Put the newly-created .htpasswd file somewhere *outside* of the server's DocumentRoot area.**

5. **Put the following lines into an appropriate configuration file (such as a** `.htaccess` **file in the directory itself, possibly within a** `<Files>` **container if you only want to protect certain files rather than the whole directory; or put them inside a** `<Directory>`, `<Location>`, **or** `<Files>` **container in the server config files):**

```
AuthName MembersOnly
AuthType Basic
AuthUserFile .htpasswd-file
Require valid-user
```

Use the correct full filesystem location of your `.htpasswd` file on the `AuthUserFile` line.

6. **Make sure that the server user (the one the server *runs* as, not the one it *starts* as) can access the** `.htpasswd` **file — and, if you're using a** `.htaccess` **file for this, make sure the server user can access that, too.**

7. **If you're putting this stuff into the server configuration files, reload the server (see Chapter 4). If you're using a** `.htaccess` **file, you don't need to do this.**

8. **Try to access the page. You should be prompted for a username and password for the "MembersOnly" realm.**

Don't fool yourself into thinking that these pages are really secure, though. See Chapter 6 for more information.

How do I use /etc/passwd for Web authentication?

Another short answer: "You don't."

Seriously, this is one of the best ways you could choose to compromise your system's security. If you want to know why, go back and check out Chapter 6.

What, you're still reading this section? Shame on you! Subtract 5 Apache Guru Points.

{Sigh} Well, if you *must* know . . . simply set up a basic authentication realm (see the previous section) with "/etc/passwd" as the `AuthUserFile`. Note that this won't work if your system uses shadow passwords (if, for instance, the encrypted passwords are stored in a separate file, and not in the /etc/passwd file itself).

If you deliberately do this in spite of all warnings, sky-writings, and oracular pronouncements declaring it to be a Bad Thing, you automatically forfeit *all* accumulated Apache Guru Points, and are unable to earn more for a period equal to one month for each day you leave this idiocy in place. So there.

How do I enable PUT for Web publishing?

The PUT method is how web authoring tools like Netscape Communicator and Microsoft FrontPage allow users to upload their Web pages to the server. As you might expect, this is considered by many to be a feature to be enabled cautiously, with much fear, trembling, and fingers-on-the-Big-Red-Button. What, allow J Random Internet Person to upload and store files on my Web server? Are you mad?

It's a highly controversial area, and The Apache Group has chosen to finesse the issue by not building the ability directly into the server. Instead, you can turn it on yourself — the Apache Web server allows you to set up scripts to handle whatever methods you like that the server doesn't already deal with.

Rather than go into a long and involved description here, which would be flavored and colored by my own personal preferences and biases (didn't think I had any, did you? Hah!), I'll refer you to an excellent *Apache Week* article that covers the topic. Check out the following URL:

```
http://www.apacheweek.com/features/put
```

What are these "connection reset by peer" messages in my error log?

These messages in the server error log mean pretty much what they sound like: the other end of the client-server link got disconnected. Typically it means that the user pressed the "Stop" button on his browser, or turned off her computer, or otherwise interrupted the transaction before the server (or possibly the client) was finished having its say.

These errors are normal and harmless. If you see them a lot, it's probably due to impatience on the part of your visitors. If that doesn't seem to account for it, check with your network service provider to make sure your connectivity is still healthy.

What does "Premature end of script headers" mean?

You'll find these messages in the server error log if you find them at all — which you probably will.

When the Apache Web server starts up a CGI script, it also starts a timer ticking. The script has a limited amount of time to give some initial results back to the server — the header portion described in Chapter 12. If the server doesn't get this answer before the time expires something's wrong, reports an error to the client, and logs this message in the error log.

There are lots of things that can lead to this message, but by far the most frequent cause is that the script *sent* the header to the server, but hasn't flushed the buffer to make sure that it actually gets there. See Chapter 12 for more information about this, and make sure you flush your buffers. Ka-whoooosh-glurgle!

Another common cause is the script dying before it finishes sending the header — which is essentially the same thing, as far as the server is concerned. Try enabling the `ScriptLog` directive (if you haven't already) and checking the log file it creates to see if your script left a note explaining why it was dying.

Why do I get errors trying to compile Apache?

There are lots of reasons why you might get errors when you try to compile the Apache Web server. Sometimes the problem stems from your environment being untested or unverified, and you need a port that's tailored to your system (see Chapter 9). More often, there's a problem with your C compiler — such as it not being ANSI C compliant, or it was installed improperly, or it's having trouble finding files because of an incomplete or incorrect software installation. Sometimes you need to re-install your compilers after upgrading the operating system. And, less frequently, you'll get error messages because there are actual errors in the source code.

Use the usual means to track down the cause — check the bug database, FAQ, and newsgroup.

Chapter 20

Ten Common Error Messages

In This Chapter

▶ Understanding common error messages

▶ Recognizing important errors

*J*ust as there are frequently asked questions about the Apache Web server, there are a bunch of problems or confusions that are encountered over and over again as new users of the server (or even experienced ones) experiment with it and expand their understanding of its capabilities.

There's a lot of overlap between the common error messages and the frequently asked questions, as you might expect — lots of the questions are basically "why"s about the errors. I've tried to collect the ten most common error messages that *don't* fall into this overlap area; the results lie before you. Some of the errors aren't really errors, and some of them are — and some of them are subtle rather than obvious in their causes. Whatever, you'll probably run into some of these, so here's your chance to become prepared (and avoid having to look them up later).

By reading this chapter, you'll be able to say "Ah, yes" very wisely when you run across any of these, and your blinding insight will impress those around you. Ready? Here we go!

"Surf's Up!" — Normal Messages

Some of the messages that show up in the Apache error log aren't really errors, but are put there anyway you the server can keep you apprised of what it's doing in the normal course of events. The messages described in the following four sections fall into this category. They don't indicate any sort of problem, they're just there to let the Webmaster know the server changed state somehow — and why.

A server state change usually means that it started, stopped, or reloaded its configuration files and started over. These things don't happen by themselves; when they occur, it's because someone or something told the server to do them. If they seem to be happening unexpectedly, check for automatic maintenance tools or late-night staff.

"Server configured -- resuming normal operations"

This message is the most innocuous of all. It simply means that the server has come up, has loaded all of its configuration instructions, and is ready to serve the public.

Even though the message blathers about "resuming" normal activities, it says it even when it's starting for the first time and therefore not resuming anything. Don't let yourself be confused — the server can't tell whether it's just coming up or has just finished a reconfiguration request.

In Apache 1.3, you probably won't even see this message in your error log unless your logging level is set to `Notice` or lower with the `LogLevel` directive. Apache 1.3 also replaces the word "server" in the message with the actual server name and version, such as

```
Apache/1.3.0 configured -- resuming normal operations
```

This is followed by another message which indicates when the server image was built. The information in these two messages should be included when reporting problems.

"SIGHUP received. Attempting to restart"

This message lets you know that someone or something told the Apache Web server to break all its current links with clients and reload the configuration files *right now*. This is pretty common; if you change any of the server configuration file (*not* `.htaccess` files) you need to let the server know about it somehow. This message is harmless by itself — unless it's unexpected or is followed by other message indicating errors in your configuration directives.

A related message looks like this:

```
SIGUSR1 received.  Doing graceful restart
```

This means basically the same thing as the previous message, except that the server was told to let any current client activities finish before reloading the configuration.

See Chapter 4 for more information about restarting a running Apache Web server environment.

"httpd: caught SIGTERM, shutting down"

Like the messages in the previous sections, if you see this one in your error log it's no cause for alarm. It's just letting you know that the server was told to shut itself down, and it's recording the fact with a time-stamp just so you know *exactly* when it happened.

The only time when this message should raise your eyebrows is if it appears unexpectedly. (*Any* unexpected error should raise your eyebrows.) Usually this means that either some automatic maintenance task goofed and did it at the wrong time, or that some staffperson was correcting a problem or was just overzealous.

Of course, the next message you want to see is the "server configured" message described a couple of sections ago. If you don't see that, or there's a big gap between the shutdown message and the startup message, it means that your web server is or was out of operation for probably longer than you wanted.

"server seems busy, spawning n children (you may need to increase StartServers, or Min/MaxSpareServers)"

In Chapter 2, I describe how the Apache Web server works, creating children processes and handing them work as it comes in. I also mentioned that the server would automatically create more children if the traffic started getting really heavy; when it does this, it mentions the fact in the error log with a message like this. (The n in the message indicates how many extra children the parent created.)

If it only happens every now and then, it's nothing to worry about. If you see it a lot, though, you should probably take the implicit advice and add a line like the following to your server config files:

```
StartServers 50
```

Choose a number that's good for your environment; "50" is just an example. As a reference, if you don't have a `StartServers` line anywhere in your configuration files, the default value is 5. You can make a pretty good guess about how many you need from that fact and the numbers being shown in the "spawning" messages.

Whoops! SEGV, the Fatal Apache Error

The Apache Web server is a complex beast, and it's possible that there are genuine bugs here and there in the code. The probability of this is also affected by the number of third-party modules you've got linked into the server (if any). When one of these bugs is tickled, it often causes the current child process (the one that encountered the bug) to die. A sort of last-chance error handler reports the fact in the error log with a message like the following:

```
httpd: caught SIGSEGV, attempting to dump core in directory location
```

"Dumping core" means that the server is going to try to create a file containing a complete picture of what it was doing at the time of the problem. The `location` in the error message names the directory where the server is putting the file.

Some versions of the UNIX operating system consider it dangerous to write such a file if the process that had the problem was running under the superuser account. If yours is one of these operating systems, you can look and look for the file and never find it, because the system wouldn't permit it to be created. You need to consult your system's documentation to see how to get around this; there are also a couple of tips in the Apache FAQ, available at the URL below:

```
http://www.apache.org/docs/misc/FAQ.html
```

The information in this "core-dump" file is very meaningful to people like the Apache developers, who can use it to find out what went wrong. Don't try to look at the file with a text editor or anything else that expects it to contain regular text, though, because that won't work — it's in a special format.

A fatal error of this type *only* affects a single child process, and is usually triggered by one specific request or request syntax — which means that the server is almost certainly still running and handling other requests. You want to fix the problem, of course, but don't panic — because your server is still *mostly* in good health.

The Generic "Internal Server Error"

This isn't an error message that shows up in the Apache Web server's error log, but rather appears on the screen of your web site's visitors when something goes wrong.

The cause of the display may or may not be an actual problem with the web server itself; the client *will* get an error like this if the requested resource tickled a bug and triggered a SEGV error (as described in the previous section), but lots of less harmful things can make this show up, too.

If people complain about this to you, the first thing you should do is look at the server's error log — because the *real* cause of the problem will be described there. The details don't show up in the display the client sees because Apache tries to be helpful to you by keeping your dirty linen private.

Here are two of the most common causes of this problem:

✔ An error in a `.htaccess` file

✔ A misbehaving CGI script

Both of these are clearly explained by the messages you'll find in the server's error log file.

SSI Parsing Failures

This isn't an error message that shows up in the Apache Web server's error log, but rather appears on the screen of your web site's visitors when something goes wrong.

This is another set of errors that your visitors will probably see before you do, and will show up on their screens as a generic problem. It gets manifested by the following text showing up in a browser display of a web document:

```
[an error occurred processing this directive]
```

This means that the server recognized that it was supposed to parse the document for server-side include directives, and actually tried to do so, but ran into some sort of problem.

As with the "internal server error" issue described in the previous section, the Apache Web server's error log holds the keys to figuring out what went wrong. If there was a syntax error in one of your SSI directives, or the directive tried to do something illegal, or something else went wrong, or whatever — the details are in the error log, and usually describe the problem very clearly. Check the error log, correct the problem it shows, and the problem *should* go away.

"You can't make me talk!" When the client stops talking

The whole point of web activity requires cooperation between the thing asking for the information (the client) and the thing which is handing it out (the server). They pretty much take turns speaking their pieces — but sometimes the transaction gets cut off in mid-conversation, due to power failures, network glitches, or maybe just user impatience.

When it's the client's turn to talk, the server listens politely until it's done. If the client breaks off in the middle of a sentence, though, the server will eventually notice, at which point it figures the conversation was abruptly terminated. When this happens, the server write a message like the following to the error log:

```
read request . . . timed out for host
```

The exact details of the message vary, but they indicate how far along the conversation got before things went wacky. The identity of the client system is always listed, to help you figure out if it's a problem with a specific set of clients.

This happens quite a bit, and usually shouldn't be anything to worry about — the network is a big and chancy place, and people are notoriously impatient and intolerant of delays. If you see a dramatic upsurge in this sort of message, though, you should verify that your network connection is still healthy.

"Nobody's hearin' nothin'!" When the client stops listening

Like the issue described in the previous section, another common error crops up when there's a communication problem between the client and the server. If you find messages like the following in your server's error log,

```
send . . . lost connection to client host
```

it means that in the conversation between the server and the client, it was the server's turn to talk — but the client stopped paying attention. The error message gives details about what the server was trying to say, and the client to which it was trying to say it.

This is a really common error message, and usually occurs because the end-user got bored with waiting and pressed the "Stop" button on her browser or maybe even turned his computer off. For the most part these are harmless, so it's usually safe to ignore them. If they seem to come mostly from a single client, or occur when accessing a particular resource, though, you may want to investigate further. If not, don't worry about them.

Slips betwixt cup and lip — or betwixt document and client

There are lots of reasons why the Apache Web server might not comply with a client's request for a particular document, including things like authorization issues, file permissions, misspelled names, and the like. In each of these cases (among others), the server will send the client some sort of explanation, but it saves the *real* details for you, its Webmaster.

Here's what the typical "I tried, but I couldn't do it" message in the error log looks like:

```
access to URI failed for host, reason: cause
```

It's pretty straightforward: it identifies the URL (minus the web server information) that the client was trying to access, who the client was, and why the server wasn't able to comply. The listed cause of the problem is usually so simple as to make you snap your fingers and cry "Aha!"

Here are some of the phrases you might see for `cause` in the message:

```
File does not exist
Permission denied
Client denied by server configuration
Symbolic link not allowed
Directory index forbidden by rule
user username: password mismatch
```

See what I mean about the causes being simple to understand and correct?

Part VI
Appendixes

The 5th Wave®   By Rich Tennant

"That reminds me – I have to figure out how to build the Apache proxy module into the server image."

In this part . . .

The Apache Web server is a pretty complicated bit of software; it's what is called "feature rich." This richness means you can do a lot with it, but it also means that it can be easy to get confused. Han Solo's *Millennium Falcon* (from the *Star Wars* motion pictures) was a fast starship, but would *you* know what to do if you were plonked down in the pilot's seat? The Web is a big place, and it's easy to get caught and find yourself struggling in its gossamer strands.

Two appendixes are here: one is a sort of cookbook to help you find and fix the cause when you're caught in the Web ("Use the Source, Luke!"), and the other is a detailed description of a specific Apache feature that can help you spin a fancy set of pages of your own. Neither is required reading, but here they are — just in case. . . .

Appendix A
Troubleshooting

In This Chapter

▶ Narrowing the search for problem causes

▶ Checking for problems with your scripts

▶ Finding out why your server isn't responding

▶ Turning `telnet` into a web client for debugging purposes

▶ Packet tracing — listening to computers talk to each other

*W*ith a package as complicated as the Apache Web server, in an environment as confused and chaotic as the Internet, you're almost guaranteed to run into some sort of problem from time to time. This chapter describes some of things you can do to track the causes back to their lairs. Some of the techniques in here are for the serious practitioner, but be not afraid — many Apache Guru Points await within!

Is It Just Me, or . . .? — Is It a Known Problem?

The first thing to do when you encounter some sort of problem with your Apache Web server is to . . . you guessed it, *NOT PANIC*. Save that for later, it's more fun that way and impresses people with your professionalism.

The second thing you should do is figure out whether anyone else has ever run into the same problem before, and how they dealt with it if they did. The steps you should follow are pretty clearly described in Chapter 16, *Ten Steps When You Have Problems*.

If you go through all that and are still coming up empty, chances are that you've either stumbled on to a new issue, or else tripped over one so old that most people consider it obvious and don't even talk about it. That doesn't make it any less obnoxious to *you,* though — you still have to deal with it.

Okay, so you're in *terra incognita* now (literally, "unknown ground") — how do you solve the problem? Start by treating it as you would any other sort of problem: try to narrow down the possible causes. Don't waste time on the far-out possibilities at this point; if your foot hurts, you usually don't waste time checking for insect bites on your ear.

Try to find some set of circumstances under which you can make the problem happen at will — and then pare away at those until you've got a sort of "least-common denominator." This is called "reducing" the problem. Try different sets of things, like this:

- ✔ If you're having trouble compiling the server, try compiling a little separate test program of your own

- ✔ If you're getting weird results with a browser, try accessing the same page with a different one and see if the problem keeps happening

- ✔ If visitors are having trouble reaching your server, see if they can reach your system at all — try having them `telnet`, `ftp`, or send mail to your Web server host — and try accessing it yourself from your own system, and using `telnet`, `ftp`, or mail to get to some *other* system

See what I mean? As rough first steps, these can help you figure out where to focus your attention.

Verifying the CGI Environment

If the problem you're having (or your visitors are, which is the same thing) has to do with executing a CGI script, then the error they're getting is almost certainly an *Internal Server Error* display like that shown in Figure A-1.

If the document being accessed is a CGI script, but you're getting unexpected results but *not* an error page, the problem is with your script itself. Sorry, but you're on your own fixing that.

If you get the "Internal Server Error" page, then either the Apache Web server of your operating system is having trouble getting the script to run. Check the server error log; there should be meaningful information there

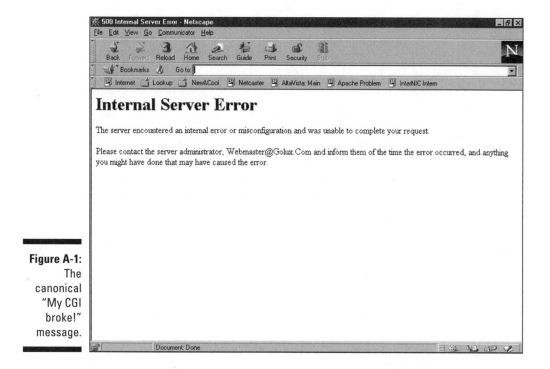

Figure A-1:
The
canonical
"My CGI
broke!"
message.

about what's wrong. If the message in the error log doesn't seem to be detailed enough, check the `ScriptLog` file (or configure it and restart the server) — *that* should give you enough information. Try running your script by hand, too, in an interactive session rather than under the web server.

If the source of your CGI script gets displayed rather than the script itself being run, that means that the web server isn't recognizing that it's a script. That either means that there's something wrong with your `ScriptAlias` directives (if the script lives in one of those directories), or that the file type (such as `.cgi`) of the file isn't enabled for script-like handling in the scope where it lives. Make sure that some higher-level scope hasn't disabled the `FileInfo` override. (See Chapter 12 for more information.)

Finding the Pulse of an Unresponsive Server

If visitors are having trouble specifically reaching your web server (for instance, `telnet` and the like work just fine), maybe your Apache processes aren't running properly. Here's a series of steps you can try:

1. Before anything else change your current directory to the place where the Apache process identification file (httpd.pid) is stored:

```
% cd /usr/local/web/apache/logs
```

2. Check to see if they're even running with the UNIX ps command:

```
% ps -aux | grep " `cat httpd.pid` "
```

(The exact syntax of the ps command may be different for your operating system.)

3. If the server isn't running, go ahead and try to start it normally. Watch for errors during the startup, and go back to Step 2. If it won't start up, you've almost certainly got a configuration problem — check the error log to see what's making the server choke.

If the server *does* appear to be running, try to get it to restart gracefully:

```
# kill -USR1 `cat httpd.pid`
```

If you get any error messages, it's probably confused — so go to Step 5. Otherwise, check it again with the browser and the ps command.

4. If it's still there but isn't responding, tell it more forcefully to re-initialize itself:

```
# kill -HUP `cat httpd.pid`
```

Did you get error messages? Go on to the next step if so, or else try to access it again with the browser, and make sure it's running with ps.

5. If it's *still* not doing what it's supposed to be, shut it down altogether and then restart it from scratch:

```
# kill -TERM `cat httpd.pid`
[keep checking with ps until it's gone]
[start Apache up the way you usually do]
```

6. If the ps command shows that the Apache processes aren't dying, then it's confused and hung (the technical term is "wedged"). In this case you need to bring out the heavy guns and manually terminate each Apache process with extreme prejudice:

```
# ps -aux | grep " `cat httpd.pid` "
# kill -KILL pid pid [pid. . .]
[the PID is the first number displayed in each line of ps output. Put all
of them (except the "ps" line itself!) on this "kill" line]
```

That should break things loose!

If you've gone through all this and it still isn't working (and you're still not getting error messages when you start up the server), there's probably some sort of configuration error. If you haven't yet, check the error log and see if there's anything revealing mentioned there. If not, try the ideas in the next section.

Don't forget — the server error log should be one of the *first* things you look at. The Apache Web server tries very hard to let you know about the pains it feels, and that's where it mentions them.

Checking Communication by Playing Computer

If your web server is up and running, and restarts without any complaints, but *still* won't answer when spoken to, it's time to snoop a little deeper. Roll up your sleeves, because we're starting to play with some Deep Magic here. If you get into this stuff, give yourself 30 Apache Guru Points on general principles.

Try pretending to be a client by using your telnet application to connect to the server:

```
% telnet localhost 80
```

"80" is the port number your server is using (from the Port directive in the server config files). This *should* connect you to your web server, which ought to be patiently waiting (for 30 seconds or so) for you to tell it what you want.

This debugging technique *will not work* if you're working with an SSL-enhanced (Secure Sockets Layer) version of Apache. If you are, you need to consult your vendor for assistance.

If you immediately get something like this:

```
% telnet localhost 80
Trying 127.0.0.1. . .
telnet: Unable to connect to remote host: Connection refused
%
```

then I can tell you right away that either your server has stopped running, or else it isn't paying attention to port 80. Either you misspelled (or forgot to include) the value on the `Port` directive, or there's some confusion between your `Listen` directives or virtual host configurations. Anyway, you've got an error in your server config files, so go poke around in them until you spot (and fix) the problem.

If your telnet session is waiting for you to type something, go ahead — let's send a request for the main page as shown in Figure A-2.

(Note that the "Enter" or "Return" key is being explicitly shown in Figure A-2. It's important that you press that key where you see "**[ENTER]**" in the text.)

Figure A-2:
Using
telnet as
a web
client.

```
% telnet localhost 80[enter]Î
Trying 127.0.0.1. . .Î
Connected to localhost.Î
Escape character is '^]'.Î
HEAD / HTTP/1.0[enter]◄
[enter]
```

The complete dialog between you and the computer *should* look something like that shown in Figure A-3. If it doesn't, use the response you *do* get to figure out what's going wrong. If there's nothing in the response that's helpful, check out the next section in this chapter: "Following the Packet Trail."

(Note that the "Enter" or "Return" key is being explicitly shown in Figure A-3. It's important that you press that key where you see "**[ENTER]**" in the text.)

If your little conversation directly with the server looked like that shown in Figure A-3, then your server is up and healthy — so your problem is probably that it's not giving you the pages you're expecting. That can only be due to configuration error (or a genuine bug, though that's unlikely), so double-check your error log and `<VirtualHost>` containers to make sure you haven't run afoul of one of the confusing aspects. There's a lot of documentation about the virtual host stuff included in the HTML files in the server kit on the CD.

```
% telnet localhost 80[enter]Î
Trying 127.0.0.1. . .Î
Connected to localhost.Î
Escape character is '^]'.Î
HEAD / HTTP/1.0[enter]◄┘
[enter]Î
HTTP/1.1 200 OKÎ
Date: Wed, 29 Oct 1997 23:57:19 GMTÎ
Server: Apache/1.3b3-devÎ
Connection: closeÎ
Content-Type: text/htmlÎ
Î
Connection closed by foreign host.Î
%
```

Figure A-3:
A chat
between
telnet
and
Apache.

Following the Packet Trail

Sometimes the only way to figure out what's going on is to actually watch what's being sent over the network. This is called "packet tracing," and is generally considered to be well into the realm of Deep Magic. If you get to this point and have to start messing about with packet traces, give yourself 50 Apache Guru Points.

One reason you might need to perform a packet trace is if you can't reproduce the problem yourself using telnet (as described in the previous section), and you have to actually trap the network traffic flowing between your server and the client.

The way you trace packets is by telling your system (or another one on the same local-area network) to "write down" all the bits and pieces of network conversation in a file. Most networks are pretty busy, and eavesdropping on everything will make your disks explode (figuratively speaking, of course) in record time, so you tell the system to only listen to a particular conversation, or only to certain topics.

You may need to twiddle your system in order to enable packet-tracing. Because of the privacy concerns, some operating systems don't allow eavesdropping without the superuser's explicit consent. For instance, on the DIGITAL UNIX operating system, you need to use the pfconfig (packet filter configuration) command to turn on eavesdropping mode.

Recording network conversations

The most common general-purpose packet tracing utility used in web debugging is called `tcpdump`. Your operating system probably has a copy already; if it doesn't, there's one on the CD-ROM that accompanied this book. You tell `tcpdump` which "conversations" to monitor using fairly obvious instructions like the following:

```
# tcpdump tcp port 80 and host www.mydomain.com
```

By default, the `tcpdump` utility will only record a small portion of each sentence, and it's usually *too* small to debug web transactions. You tell it to record more with the `-s` switch:

```
# tcpdump - 1514 tcp port 80 and host www.mydomain.com
```

This tells it to save up to 1514 bytes per sentence (less if the sentence isn't that long).

I recommend using a setting of 1514 bytes because that's the standard size of a packet transmitted on an Ethernet-based network. This setting allows you to grab all the information that might be contained in any single packet.

The next switch for `tcpdump` is `-w`, which instructs it to record the packets in a file, rather than spitting them out on your screen. This is useful if you need to send the recording to someone else to help you debug the problem, or if you want to analyze it using some other tool. Here's how you'd use the `-w` switch to make `tcpdump` save the recording in the file `/tmp/tcpdump.raw`:

```
# tcpdump -w /tmp/tcpdump.raw -s 1514 port 80 and host www.mydomain.com
```

The `tcpdump` utility will normally try to translate IP addresses into names, which means that it will be generating some network traffic itself as it asks the DNS (Domain Name System) servers for the translation. You can tell `tcpdump` to just leave the IP addresses alone by adding the `-n` switch (for "numbers only") to the command line like this:

```
# tcpdump -n -s 1514 tcp port 80 and hostwww.mydomain.com
```

The last switch of importance for the `tcpdump` utility is `-c`, which tells it how many sentences (or sentence fragments) to record before stopping automatically. If you don't include this switch, `tcpdump` will happily keep recording until you hit it on the head with something.

```
# tcpdump -c 10 -w /tmp/tcpdump.raw -s 1514 port 80 and host www.mydomain.com
```

A final recommendation: to record a conversation between a particular client system and your Web server, issue the following tcpdump command on your Web server system itself:

```
% tcpdump -n -p -s 1514 -c 50 tcp port 80 and host
```

This command instructs the tcpdump utility to record 1514 bytes of each of the first 50 sentences in the TCP (*Transmission Control Protocol*) conversation between the client system and port 80 on your Web server system. Because you're running tcpdump on one end of the conversation (the Web server end) rather than somewhere else in the network (which would be like a wiretap), you can add the "-p" switch — which tells tcpdump that it doesn't need any special privileges (like a court order for a wiretap) to listen to the conversation.

Playing back the recording

The tcpdump tool described in the previous section can be used to display the contents of the packets it's captured, but the results can look kind of messy, as shown in Figure A-4.

```
# tcpdump port 80 and host www.mydomain.comÎ
tcpdump: listening on eth0Î
23:41:12.000000 myclient.mydomain.com.1099 > Î
Î      www.mydomain.com.http: S 14384116:14384116(0) win Î
Î      8192 <mss 1460> (DF)Î
23:41:12.000000 www.mydomain.com.http > Î
Î      myclient.mydomain.com.1099: S Î
Î      2988295590:2988295590(0) ack 14384117 win 31744 Î
Î      <mss 1460>Î
23:41:12.200000 myclient.mydomain.com.1099 > Î
Î      www.mydomain.com.http: . ack 1 win 8760 (DF)Î
23:41:12.310000 myclient.mydomain.com.1099 > Î
Î      www.mydomain.com.http: P 1:229(228) ack 1 win 8760 Î
Î      (DF)
```

Figure A-4: A packet trace as displayed by tcpdump.

Another tool which can analyze a tcpdump packet trace file and tell you what's in it is the tcpshow utility. Unlike tcpdump, tcpshow probably *isn't* standard on your operating system, which means you have to install it. But that's okay — there's a copy on the book's CD.

The main switch for use with tcpshow is -data, which tells it to just display the actual contents of each packet, and none of the accompanying rubbish. Figure A-5 shows what a combination of tcpdump's recording and tcpshow's playback can tell you.

```
# tcpdump -w /tmp/tcpdump.raw -s 1024 -c 10 host
www.mydomain.com and port 80Î
# tcpshow -data < /tmp/tcpdump.rawÎ
10.0.0.2.1105 -> 10.0.0.1.http over TCPÎ
          GET / HTTP/1.0.Î
          Connection: Keep-Alive.Î
          User-Agent: Mozilla/4.03 [en] (Win95; U).Î
          Pragma: no-cache.Î
          Host: www.mydomain.com.Î
          Accept: image/gif, image/x-xbitmap, image/jpeg,
image/pjpeg, */*.Î
          Accept-Language: en.Î
          Accept-Charset: iso-8859-1,*,utf-8.Î
          .Î
---------------------------------------------------------------Î
10.0.0.1.http -> 10.0.0.2.1105 over TCPÎ
          <No data>Î
---------------------------------------------------------------Î
10.0.0.2.1106 -> 10.0.0.1.http over TCPÎ
          <No data>Î
---------------------------------------------------------------Î
10.0.0.1.http -> 10.0.0.2.1106 over TCPÎ
          <No data>Î
---------------------------------------------------------------Î
10.0.0.2.1106 -> 10.0.0.1.http over TCPÎ
          <No data>Î
---------------------------------------------------------------Î
10.0.0.2.1106 -> 10.0.0.1.http over TCPÎ
          GET / HTTP/1.0.Î
          Connection: Keep-Alive.Î
          User-Agent: Mozilla/4.03 [en] (Win95; U).Î
          Pragma: no-cache.Î
          Host: www.mydomain.com.Î
          Accept: image/gif, image/x-xbitmap, image/jpeg,
image/pjpeg, */*.Î
          Accept-Language: en.Î
          Accept-Charset: iso-8859-1,*,utf-8.Î
          .Î
```

Figure A-5:
A packet
trace as
displayed by
tcpshow
instead.

There, isn't that prettier than Figure A-4? The "no data" lines simply record places where the client and the server are making sure the conversation is going correctly.

As you can see, packet tracing lets you actually see what's going on between the client and the server, which can be a big help when it comes to trying to figure out which one's actually having the problem.

For more information about other tcpdump and tcpshow switches and options, consult the relevant documentation — because it may be different for the system you're using.

Appendix B

About the CD

· ·

*H*ere's some of what you can find on the *Apache Server For Dummies* CD-ROM:

- A complete source kit for the latest officially-released version of the Apache Web server package

- Binary kits of the latest official version of the Apache Web server software for several popular versions of UNIX

- A complete source kit of the latest released beta-test version of the Apache Web server software, along with pre-built binary executables for several versions of UNIX

- A copy of the latest released beta-test version of the Apache Web server for Windows NT 4.0 and Windows 95

- The GNU ANSI C compiler, and various utilities and tools for debugging your Web server

- Reference materials for working with the Internet and the World-Wide Web

System Requirements

Make sure your computer meets the minimum system requirements listed below. If your computer doesn't match up to most of these requirements, you may have problems in using the contents of the CD.

If you're using UNIX

- Any UNIX system. If the CPU is Intel-based (that is, it's an "x86" processor), it should be a 486 66MHz or faster processor. If it's not an Intel CPU, it should be of at least comparable speed.

- At least 32MB of total RAM installed on your computer. For best performance, the more RAM the better.

✔ At least 50MB of hard drive space available to install all the software from this CD. (You'll need less space if you don't install every program.)

✔ A CD-ROM drive — your UNIX system must have it configured and be able to mount CDs on it. (See "man MAKEDEV" on your system for more information.)

If you're using Windows NT or Windows 95

✔ An Intel-based system running Windows NT Version 4.0 or later or Windows 95. The CPU should be a 486 66MHz or faster processor.

✔ At least 32MB of total RAM installed on your computer. For best performance, the more RAM the better.

✔ At least 50MB of hard drive space available to install all the software from this CD. (You'll need less space if you don't install every program.)

✔ A CD-ROM drive.

If you need more information on the basics, check out *PCs For Dummies*, 4th Edition, by Dan Gookin (IDG Books Worldwide, Inc.).

How to Use the CD with UNIX

To install the items from the CD to your hard drive, follow these steps:

1. **Insert the CD into your computer's CD-ROM drive and close the drive door.**

2. **Log onto your computer as the** `root` **user.**

3. **Mount the CD with a command such as**

```
# mount -r /dev/cd0 /mnt
```

The actual CD-ROM device path will differ according to your version of UNIX and your hardware configuration. For example, `/dev/cd0` may be `/dev/cdrom`.

4. **Create a directory under which the packages will be installed:**

```
# mkdir /usr/local/kits
```

5. **Create the directory for the Apache Web server software, and unpack it there:**

```
# mkdir /usr/local/web
# cd /usr/local/web
# tar xf /mnt/ASFD/apache/kits-1.2.4/apache.tar
```

If you're going to install the 1.3b3 beta-test version, change the "1.2.4" to "1.3b3" in this step and the following step.

6. **Rename the software directory to the one used in this book:**

```
# mv apache_1.2.4 apache
```

To install a pre-compiled binary executable, see Chapter 4 for instructions.

7. **To install another package (such as** `lynx-2.7.1`**):**

```
# cd /usr/local/kits
# tar xf /mnt/ASFD/apache/tools/lynx-2.7.1.tar
```

Follow the instructions in the `README` **or** `INSTALL` **file in the new** `lynx-2.7.1` **directory.**

8. **To install additional packages, repeat step 7 for each one.**

9. **When you're done installing programs, dismount the CD-ROM:**

```
# umount /mnt
```

10. **You can eject the CD now. Carefully place it back in the plastic jacket of the book for safekeeping.**

How to Use the CD with Windows NT and Windows 95

To install the Windows items from the CD to your hard drive, follow these steps:

1. **Insert the CD into your computer's CD-ROM drive and close the drive door.**

2. **Click the Start button on the Task Bar and click Run.**

3. **In the dialog box that appears, type** `D:\ASFD\apache\kits-1.3b3\apache_win32.exe`**.**

You probably have your CD-ROM drive listed as drive D under My Computer in Windows 95 or Windows NT. Type in the proper drive letter if your CD-ROM drive uses a different letter.

4. **Click OK.**

   A license agreement window appears.

5. **Because I'm sure you'll want to use the Apache software, read through the license agreement, nod your head, and then click on the Accept button.**

   You'll have to accept the License Agreement every time you install the Windows version of the Apache Web server software.

6. **Follow the instructions on the screen, including choosing a directory for the Apache software. I** *strongly* **recommend that you choose "C:\Apache" for this.**

7. **After the main Apache installation is done, install the online documentation and the file icons. Click the Start button on the Task Bar and click Run.**

8. **In the dialog box that appears, type** D:\ASFD\apache\kits-1.3b3\apache_win32_ext.exe.

9. **Follow the instructions on the screen. Be sure to install this software in the same directory where you installed Apache in step 6.**

10. **When you've finished installing the software you chose, you can eject the CD. Carefully place it back in the plastic jacket of the book for safekeeping.**

What You'll Find

All of the items described in this appendix are under the ASFD/apache directory on the CD-ROM (/mnt/ASFD/apache if you've mounted the CD from UNIX, or D:\ASFD\apache if you're using Windows NT or Windows 95). Because the Apache Web server has only recently been made available on the Windows systems, most of what's on the CD-ROM is intended for use with UNIX systems.

All of the software under the apache directory on the CD-ROM is provided "as-is." With the exception of the Apache Web server software itself, all of the packages are provided without any official support. In most cases, the packages contain documentation that indicates where more information about them can be obtained.

Here's a summary of the software on this CD. If you use Windows, the CD interface helps you install software easily. (If you have no idea what I'm talking about when I say "CD interface," flip back a page or two to find the section "How to Use the CD with Windows NT and Windows 95.")

The Apache Web server package for Windows NT and Windows 95

For Windows NT and Windows 95 only. Only two files on the CD-ROM are directly intended to be installed in your Windows-based PC:

- ✔ The Apache Web server installation kit in `D:\ASFD\apache\kits-1.3b3\apache_win32.exe`
- ✔ The documentation kit in `D:\ASFD\apache\kits-1.3b3\apache_win32_ext.exe`

The GNU `gzip` *utility*

For UNIX only. Many of the packages and tools that you'll eventually end up downloading from the Net are *compressed* with the GNU `gzip` utility so they'll take up less space. Not all UNIX systems have this utility available, however, so a copy is included on the CD-ROM so you can install it if you don't have it.

The `gzip` package is in the `ASFD/apache/tools` subdirectory. To unpack it, use the following commands:

```
# mkdir /usr/local/kits
# cd /usr/local/kits
# tar xf /mnt/ASFD/apache/tools/gzip-1.2.4.tar
# cd gzip-1.2.4
```

Read the file `README` and follow the directions it contains.

The `gzip` and `gunzip` utilities (which are both part of this package) are covered by the GNU Public License. There's a copy of this in the file `LICENSE` in the directory you unpacked. *Please be sure to read this file.*

The GNU C Compiler

For UNIX Only. In order to build the Apache Web server software from scratch, you *must* have a C compiler that is ANSI-compliant. The compiler on your system may or may not be; if it isn't, you can use the GNU C compiler, `gcc`, which is included on the CD-ROM in the file `/mnt/ASFD/apache/tools/gcc-2.7.2.3.tar`.

If the compiler on your system is ANSI-compliant, it can successfully compile the Apache Web server package and you don't need to install GNU C.

To unpack the GNU C compiler, use the following commands:

```
# mkdir /usr/local/kits
# cd /usr/local/kits
# tar xf /mnt/ASFD/apache/tools/gcc-2.7.2.3.tar
# cd gcc-2.7.2.3
```

Once you've unpacked the kit, follow the directions in the file README.

The GNU C installation process can take a long time; sometimes more than an hour, depending upon the options you choose and the speed of your system. Just be patient; it will finish — eventually.

The GNU C compiler, gcc, is covered by the GNU Public License. There's a copy of this in the file LICENSE in the directory you unpacked. *Please be sure to read this file.*

The Lynx character-cell Web browser

For UNIX Only. Lynx is a Web browser that's designed to be used on terminals rather than fancy graphical displays. You can use it to surf when you're logged in to a system with Telnet, for instance. The apachectl script, which is part of the Apache kit itself and can be used to manage your Apache Web server, will try to use the lynx command if you ask for a status display.

If you don't need a Web browser for "dumb terminals," you don't need to install the lynx package.

To unpack the lynx browser package, use the following commands:

```
# mkdir /usr/local/kits
# cd /usr/local/kits
# tar xf /mnt/ASFD/apache/tools/lynx-2.7.1.tar
# cd lynx-2.7.1
```

Once you've unpacked the kit, follow the directions in the file README.

This version of the Lynx Web browser is covered by the GNU Public License. A copy of this is in the file LICENSE in the directory you unpacked. *Please be sure to read this file.*

Other tools and debugging utilities

For UNIX only. There are several freeware tools and applications to help you work with the Web or with your Apache Web server software. They're all on the CD-ROM in the /mnt/ASFD/apache/tools directory. Use the same steps to install them as are described for the GNU C compiler.

Reference documents and specifications

For UNIX and Windows. A number of RFCs and Web-related documents are in the ASFD/apache/ref directory on the CD-ROM. Some are in normal text format, some are HTML files you need to read with a Web browser, and some documents are provided in both formats.

The Internet and the Web in particular are rapidly evolving environments, and these documents may become dated quickly. Even if that happens, though, the copies on the CD-ROM should provide good basic and background information.

Appendix C: Server-side includes

Appendix C of *Apache Server For Dummies,* "Server-Side Includes," is only available from the *Apache Server For Dummies* CD-ROM. In the CD-ROM directory ServerSideIncludeApp, you'll find HTML and normal text format files of the appendix, plus a graphic file that illustrates one of the issues in the appendix.

If You've Got Problems (of the CD Kind)

I have tried my best to compile programs that work on most computers with the minimum system requirements. Alas, your computer may differ, and some programs may not work properly for some reason.

The two likeliest problems are

- Your version of UNIX isn't supported.
- You don't have enough memory (RAM) for the programs you want to use.

If you have trouble compiling any of the software under UNIX, make sure you're using an ANSI C compiler such as the GNU C compiler on the CD itself. If that doesn't seem to be the problem, check Appendix A, *Troubleshooting.* If you get error messages like Not enough memory or Setup `cannot continue` when working under the Windows NT or Windows 95 systems, try one or more of these methods and then try using the software again:

- ✔ Turn off any anti-virus software that you have on your computer. Installers sometimes mimic virus activity and may make your computer incorrectly believe that it is being infected by a virus.

- ✔ Close all running programs. The more programs you're running, the less memory is available to other programs. Installers also typically update files and programs. So if you keep other programs running, installation may not work properly.

- ✔ Have your local computer store add more RAM to your computer. This is, admittedly, a drastic and somewhat expensive step. However, if you have a Windows 95 PC, adding more memory can really help the speed of your computer and allow more programs to run at the same time.

Appendix C (on the CD-ROM)
Details of Server-Side Includes

●●●

In This Chapter

▶ Understanding what server-side includes are

▶ What SSI directives are available

▶ How to turn on server-side includes

▶ Using variables in server-side include directives

▶ Recognizing SSI problems when they occur

▶ Using server-side includes to customize documents when they're sent

●●●

*O*ne of the most powerful things your Apache Web server can do for you is to tailor the contents of documents before sending them along to the requesting client. One of the ways you can do this, the one that's described in this Appendix, is through the use of *Server-Side Includes* (SSIs).

This Appendix is on the *Apache Server For Dummies* CD-ROM in the directory ServerSideIncludeApp in .htm and .txt formats. You can view the .htm version in a standard Web browser. Any text editor or word processor should be able to view the .txt version of the Appendix.

Index

• Symbols •

& (ampersand), status module, 176
* (asterisk), scoping and wildcards, 57–58
? (question mark)
  scoping and wildcards, 57–58
  status module, 176

• A •

Acc information, statistics table (status module), 174–175
access, superuser. *See* superuser access
access checking, DNS enablement, 110–111
access logs
  combining, 247
  customizing, 88
  described, 84
  separating, 245–246
  virtual hosts and, 245–247
access rights
  CGI scripts, 202
  system requirements, 24
access to URI failed for host error message, 309–310
access_checker hook, modules, 122
access_checker phase, requests, 145
access.conf, security configuration file, 53
Action directive, content handlers, 225–226
AddEncoding directive, file types, 223
AddLanguage directive, file types, 223
  variable dimensions (client preferences), 186

AddModule verb, Configuration file, 158–159
addresses
  IP. *See* IP addresses
  loopback, 15
  network boards with multiple, 242
  registration of system, 240–241
AddType directive
  file types, 222–223
  FileInfo override, 225
administrator's guide, DNS (Domain Name System), 279
advertising and logging, 90–91
  agents, mod_log_agent management module, 138
aliases, 77–78
  defined, 77
  DNS (Domain Name System), 280
  redirection and, 180, 181
  ScriptAlias directive, 203
  ScriptAliased directories, 78
Allow directive, security-related directives, 100–101
ampersand (&), status module, 176
analog utility, log analysis tools, 86–87
Anonymous directives, mod_auth_anon module, 107–108
anonymous FTP, mod_auth_anon module, 107–108
ANSI C compiler, source code tools, 21
Apache documentation, 288–289
  Apache Group, reporting problems to, 273–275
Apache Manual, htdocs directory, 38
Apache Module Registry, resources for Web authors, 140, 291–292

Apache server
  authorization and authentication,
    97–113
  bug database, 269–271, 289–290, 291
  caching, 193–199
  CGI scripts, 201–215
  client preferences, 183–193
  commands, overview, 4–5
  computer systems and, 15–17
  configuration, 49–81
  configuration files, 17, 29–30
  content handlers, 224–226
  error handlers, 226–228
  error messages, 303–310
  file types, 221–223
  installing, 33–48
  Internet as optional, 14–15
  IP addresses, 12–14
  logs, 83–95
  Module Registry, 140, 291–292
  modules, 117–140
  monitoring, 165–178
  network requirements, 14
  newsgroup, 272
  origin of name, 2
  overview, 2–3
  porting to new platforms, 161–163
  proxy servers, 249–262
  rebuilding, 151–163
  redirection, 179–183
  requests, 141–148
  requirements, 12–30
  restarting, 76
  RFCs (Requests for Comments),
    277–286
  security, 67
  shutting down, 76
  skills required, 15–18
  source code, 21
  SSI (Server-Side Includes), 216–219
  starting, 75–76
  stopping, 76
  superuser access, 17–18, 24
  system requirements, 23–29
  systems and, 15–17
  tools required, 18–22
  troubleshooting, 313–322
  UNIX requirement, 12
  virtual hosts, 229–248
Apache Web site, resources for
  Web authors, 287–288
ApacheWeek electronic magazine,
  resources for Web authors, 290–291
arguments
  directives and, 49
  `FLAG` (directive rules), 53
  `ITERATE` (directive rules), 52
  `RAW_ARGS` (directive rules), 53
  `TAKE#` (directive rules), 51–52
asterisk (*), scoping and wildcards,
  57–58
`AuthAuthoritative` directive,
  `mod_auth` module, 106
`auth_checker` hook, modules, 121
`auth_checker` phase, requests, 146
`AuthGroupFile` directive, `mod_auth`
  module, 106
`AuthName` directive, security-related
  directives, 103
authorization and authentication,
  97–113
  authentication types, 98
  basic authentication, 99–100
  database management, 110
  databases and large user groups, 109
  DNS and, 110–111
  encryption and, 45
  `<Limit>` directive, 104–105
  methods, 104–105
  overview, 97–100
  `passwd` file, 112
  realms, 98
  request methods, 104–105
  security modules, 105–109

security-related directives, 100–104
tips, 110–112
trap-door functions, 99
AuthType directive, security-related
    directives, 102
AUTH_TYPE environment variable,
    CGI scripts, 204
AuthUserFile directive
  mod_auth module, 106
  passwd file and, 113
auto keyword, status module, 177
autopsy metaphor, requests, 142–143

• B •

backing up logs, 111
banner ads
  advertising and logging, 91
  privacy and logging, 92
BIG_SECURITY_HOLE switch,
    Configuration file, 154
binary files
  naming conventions, 80–81
  prebuilt server, 33–35
  unpacking kits, 43
block usage, scoping, 55
boundaries, firewalls and network, 252
Bourne Shell interpreter, source code
    tools, 21
browsers, 18–19
buffering CGI scripts, 213–215
bug database
  See also debuggers
  searching, 269–271, 289–290, 291

• C •

C compiler (ANSI), source code tools, 21
cache requests, proxy servers, 135
CacheDefaultExpire directive,
    proxy servers, 262

CacheDirLength directive, proxy
    servers, 259
CacheDirLevels directive, proxy
    servers, 259
CacheGCInterval directive, proxy
    servers, 260
CacheLastModifiedFactor directive,
    proxy servers, 261–262
CacheMaxExpire directive, proxy
    servers, 261
CacheRoot directive, proxy servers, 258
CacheSize directive, proxy servers, 258
caching, 193–199
  described, 193–194
  Expires date, 196–198
  ExpiresByType directive, 197–198
  ExpiresDefault directive, 197
  header fields, 195–196
  mod_expires, 196, 197–198
  mod_headers, 195–196
  negotiated resources, 198–199
  proxy servers, 194, 251, 258–262
  transaction copies, 194
  x-bit hack, 199
canonical, defined, 37
case sensitivity, naming conventions, 78
CGI environment, verifying, 314–315
CGI scripts, 201–215
  access rights, 202
  AUTH_TYPE environment variable, 204
  buffering, 213–215
  child processes, 202
  command-line arguments, 208–209
  Content-Length: header field, 213
  Content-Type: header field, 212
  DOCUMENT_ROOT environment
    variable, 205
  environment variables, 202–209
  error handlers, 228
  Expires: header field, 213
  GATEWAY_INTERFACE environment
    variable, 205

CGI scripts *(continued)*
  header fields, 210–213
  HTTP_* environment variable, 205
  Last-Modified: header field, 213
  Location: header field, 213
  naming conventions, 81
  NPH (Non-Parsed Headers), 215
  overview, 201–202
  PATH environment variable, 205
  PATH_INFO environment variable, 205
  PATH_TRANSLATED environment
    variable, 206
  QUERY_STRING environment
    variable, 205, 209
  REMOTE_ADDR environment
    variable, 206
  REMOTE_HOST environment
    variable, 206
  REMOTE_PORT environment
    variable, 206
  REMOTE_USER environment
    variable, 206
  REQUEST_METHOD environment
    variable, 206–207
  REQUEST_URI environment
    variable, 207
  ScriptAlias directive, 203
  SCRIPT_FILENAME environment
    variable, 207
  SCRIPT_NAME environment
    variable, 207
  security, 203
  separation of header and body,
    210–212
  server buffering, 213–215
  server communication, 209–213
  SERVER_ADMIN environment
    variable, 208
  SERVER_NAME environment
    variable, 208
  SERVER_PORT environment
    variable, 208

  SERVER_PROTOCOL environment
    variable, 208
  SERVER_SOFTWARE environment
    variable, 208
  Status: header field, 212
  UNIQUE_ID environment variable, 208
cgi-bin directory, 37
checksums, verifying installations, 44–47
check_user_id hook, modules, 121
check_user_id phase, requests,
    145–146
Child information, statistics table
    (status module), 175
child processes
  CGI scripts, 202
  status module, 171–175
  system requirements, 25
child_exit hook, modules, 123
child_init hook, modules, 122
CLF (Common Log Format), 85
client preferences, 183–193
  browsers, 183–193
  data-driven content typing, 190–191
  languages, 183–184
  multiviews, 191–192
  quality values, 187–189
  troubleshooting, 192–193
  type-map content handler, 190–191
  variable dimensions, 184–186
client requests. *See* requests
client specification of proxy servers, 253
client-side image mapping, mod_imap
    module, 127
client/server environment, described, 1
cmds hook, modules, 121
command-line arguments,
    CGI scripts, 208–209
command-line options, configuration,
    72–75
commands, overview, 4–5
comments, SSI (Server-Side
    Includes), 218

Common Log Format (CLF), 85
communications, troubleshooting, 317–319
compilation errors, troubleshooting, 302
compile-time server switches, Configuration file, 154–156
compressed files, uncompressing, 42–43
conditional HTML, SSI (Server-Side Includes), 219
conf directory, 37
config directive, SSI (Server-Side Includes), 219
configuration, 49
 aliases, 77–78
 command-line options, 72–75
 default server, 77
 directives, 49–53
 httpd.conf (server configuration file), 53
 minimal, 68–71
 mod_log_config management module, 138
 naming conventions, 78–81
 overrides, 61–62
 rebuilding Apache server, 151–163
 restarting Apache server, 76
 root directories, 62–68
 scoping, 54–60
 ScriptAliased directories, 78
 server-wide configuration files, 53–54
 shutting down Apache server, 76
 starting Apache server, 75–76
Configuration file (rebuilding Apache server), 151–160
 AddModule verb, 158–159
 BIG_SECURITY_HOLE switch, 154
 compile-time server switches, 154–156
 Configure script, 160
 DEFAULT_PATH switch, 154
 extra-setting lines, 152–154
 EXTRA_CFLAGS line, 153
 EXTRA_INCLUDES line, 153

EXTRA_LDFLAGS line, 153
EXTRA_LIBS line, 153
FD_SETSIZE switch, 154
HARD_SERVER_LIMIT switch, 154
HIGH_SLACK_LINE switch, 155
IRIXN32 rule, 157
IRIXNIS rule, 157
LOW_SLACK_LINE switch, 155
make utility, 153
MAXIMUM_DNS switch, 155
MINIMAL_DNS switch, 155
modules list, 158–159
mumble module, 158–159
NO_LINGCLOSE switch, 155
NO_SLACK switch, 155
PARANOID rule, 157
proxy servers, 253
rules, 156–157
SAFE_UNSERIALIZED_ACCEPT switch, 156
SERVER_SUBVERSION switch, 156
SHELL_PATH switch, 156
SOCKS4 rule, 157
STATUS rule, 157
SUEXEC_BIN switch, 156
USE_FCNTL_SERIALIZED_ACCEPT switch, 156
USE_FLOCK_SERIALIZED_ACCEPT switch, 156
USE_SO_LINGER switch, 155
USE_USLOCK_SERIALIZED_ACCEPT switch, 156
WANTHSREGEX rule, 157
XBITHACK switch, 156
configuration files, 29–30
 editing, 17
 error logs and, 29
 per-directory, 29–30
 server-wide, 29–30
 src directory, 39
Configure script, Configuration file, 160

Conn information, statistics table (status module), 175
connection reset by peer message, error log, 301
connections, lost, 309
constipation, defined, 39
containers, directive types, 50–51
content handlers, 224–226
  Action directive, 225–226
  error handlers, 226–228
  FileInfo override, 225
  modules and, 118, 224
  overview, 224
content negotiation
  defined, 184
  mod_negotiation translator module, 131–132
content types, mod_mime translator module, 131
content-handler phase, requests, 148
Content-Length: header field, CGI scripts, 213
Content-Type: header field, CGI scripts, 212
Content-types affected information, monitoring Apache server, 168
conventions, RFCs (Requests for Comments), 277–286
cookies, 88–90
  defined, 88
  mod_usertrack module, 89–90, 140
CPU cycles, system requirements, 26
CPU information, statistics table (status module), 175
create_dir_config hook, modules, 120
create_server_config hook, modules, 120
Current Configuration information, monitoring Apache server, 169
CustomLog directive, customizing access logs, 88

• D •

-d command, configuration command-line options, 72
data-driven content typing, client preferences, 190–191
databases
  authorization and authentication, 109, 110
  mod_auth_db module, 108–109
dbmmanage script, databases and large user groups, 109
deadly embrace, defined, 39
debuggers, 22
  See also bug database
decision-making modules, 133
declaring virtual hosts, 231–232
default server
  configuration, 77
  virtual hosts, 247–248
DEFAULT_PATH switch, Configuration file, 154
DefaultType directive, file types, 223
Deny directive, security-related directives, 101
diagnosis metaphor, requests, 146–147
directives, 49–53
  See also scoping
  arguments, 49
  containers, 50–51
  defined, 49
  monitoring, 167–170
  redirection, 182
  rules of, 51–53
  security-related, 100–104
  SSI (Server-Side Includes), 219
  <Directory> scope, 54, 55, 59
directory structures, choosing, 41
disk space, system requirements, 27–29
DLD (Dynamic LoaDing), mod_dld management module, 136
DLL files, script naming conventions, 81

DNS (Domain Name System)
  administrator's guide, 279
  aliases, 280
  concepts, 279
  host-based access checking, 110–111
  `MAXIMUM_DNS` **switch**, 155
  `MINIMAL_DNS` **switch**, 155
  registration of system names and
    addresses, 241
  RFCs (Requests for Comments),
    278–280
  specification, 280
DocumentRoot
  configuration and, 64–65
  minimal configuration, 68
`DOCUMENT_ROOT` **environment variable,**
  CGI scripts, 205

● *E* ●

eavesdropping, security and, 319
editing configuration files, 17
`encoding` **dimension, variable**
    dimensions (client
    preferences), 185
encryption, 45
environment context, modules, 119
environment variables
  `Allow` **directive,** 101
  CGI scripts, 202–208
  `mod_env` **management module,** 136
  `mod_setenvif` (decision-making
    modules), 133
error handlers, 226–228
  CGI scripts, 228
  `ErrorDocument` **directive,** 227–228
error log
  configuration files and, 29
  `connection reset by peer`
    message, 301
  described, 84
  `premature end of script headers`
    message, 302

server, 93–94
system requirements, 28
error messages, 303–310
See also troubleshooting
  `access to URI failed for host`,
    309–310
  `httpd: caught SIGTERM, shutting`
    `down`, 305
  `internal server error`, 307
  lost connections, 309
  SEGV (fatal), 306–307
  `server configured — resuming`
    `normal operations`, 304
  `server seems busy, spawning n`
    `children`, 305–306
  `SIGHUP received. Attempting`
    `restart`, 304–305
  SSI parsing failures, 307–308
  timeouts, 308
`ErrorDocument` **directive, error**
    handlers, 227–228
`ErrorLog` **directive,** 84
errors, troubleshooting. *See*
    troubleshooting
`etc/passwd` **file,** 300–301
  `AuthUserFile` **directive and,** 113
  caveat, 112
`example` **subdirectory,** `src/modules`
    directory, 40
EXE files, script naming conventions, 81
`exec` **directive, SSI (Server-Side**
    Includes), 219
expiration dates, `mod_expires`
    module, 134
`Expires:` **header field**
  CGI scripts, 213
  proxy servers, 261
`Expires` **date, caching,** 196–198
`ExpiresByType` **directive**
  caching, 197–198
  wildcards, 198
`ExpiresDefault` **directive, caching,** 197

extra-setting lines, `Configuration file`, 152–154

`EXTRA_CFLAGS` line, `Configuration file`, 153

`EXTRA_INCLUDES` line, `Configuration file`, 153

`EXTRA_LDFLAGS` line, `Configuration file`, 153

`EXTRA_LIBS` line, `Configuration file`, 153

• F •

`-f` command, configuration command-line options, 72

FAQs (Frequently Asked Questions), troubleshooting and, 269

fatal errors, SEGV, 306–307

`FD_SETSIZE` switch, `Configuration file`, 154

file protections, troubleshooting, 272–273

file types, 221–223
  `AddEncoding` directive, 223
  `AddLanguage` directive, 223
  `AddType` directive, 222–223
  `DefaultType` directive, 223
  `mime.types` file, 221–222
  naming conventions, 78–81
  `TypesConfig` directive, 222

`FileInfo` override, content handlers, 225

`<Files>` scope, 54, 56–57, 59

files, system requirements, 26

firewalls
  network boundaries and, 252
  proxy servers and, 250–251

`fixer_upper` hook, modules, 122

`fixer_upper` phase, requests, 147

`FLAG`, directive rules, 53

forward lookups, registration of system names and addresses, 240

FTP, `mod_auth_anon` module, 107–108

• G •

garbage collector, proxy servers, 260

`GATEWAY_INTERFACE` environment variable, CGI scripts, 205

GET method
  authorization and authentication, 104
  `REQUEST_METHOD` environment variable, 206

`getstats` utility, log analysis tools, 87

GIF files, images, 80

GNU C compilers, rebuilding Apache server, 161

GNU tools, unpacking kits, 42–43

graphics. *See* images

`Group` directive, minimal configuration, 68–69

groups, system requirements, 24–25

`gunzip` utility, uncompressing files, 42–43

• H •

`-h` command, configuration command-line options, 72–73

handlers
  content. *See* content handlers
  error. *See* error handlers
  modules and, 118

`handlers` hook, modules, 121

hard disk space, system requirements, 27–29

`HARD_SERVER_LIMIT` switch
  `Configuration` file, 154
  status module, 171

HEAD method, `REQUEST_METHOD` environment variable, 207

header fields
  caching, 195–196
  CGI scripts, 210–213
  proxy servers, 261

`header_parse` phase, requests, 145

`header_parser` hook, modules, 122

headers
  mod_headers module, 134–135
  premature end of script headers
    message, 302
helpers subdirectory, src directory,
    39–40
HIGH_SLACK_LINE switch,
    Configuration file, 155
hooks, 120–123
  access_checker, 122
  auth_checker, 121
  check_user_id, 121
  child_exit, 123
  child_init, 122
  cmds, 121
  create_dir_config, 120
  create_server_config, 120
  defined, 118
  fixer_upper, 122
  handlers, 121
  header_parser, 122
  init, 120
  logger, 122
  merge_dir_config, 120
  merge_server_config, 121
  post_read_request, 123
  translate_handler, 121
  type_checker, 122
host-based access checking,
    enabling DNS, 110–111
hosts, virtual. See virtual hosts
housekeeping records, modules, 119
.htaccess files
  overrides, 61–62
  scoping and, 60
htdocs directory, kit contents, 37–38
HTML
  naming conventions, 79–80
  RFCs (Requests for Comments),
    283–284
HTML/3.2 standard, resources for Web
    authors, 292–293

HTTP_* environment variable,
    CGI scripts, 205
HTTP headers, mod_headers module,
    134–135
HTTP (HyperText Transfer
    Protocol), 20–21
  RFCs (Requests for Comments), 286
  specification, 286
  tcpdump utility, 20–21
  tcpshow utility, 21
httpd: caught SIGTERM, shutting
    down error message, 305
httpd.conf
  minimal configuration, 70–71
  server configuration file, 53

• I •

icons in this book, 6–7
icons directory, kit contents, 38
ifconfig command, network boards
    with multiple addresses, 242
image mapping, mod_imap module,
    126–127
images
  defined, 34
  naming conventions, 80
include directive, SSI (Server-Side
    Includes), 219
information module, monitoring
    Apache server, 165–170
init hook, modules, 120
installing Apache server, 33–48
  directory structures, 41
  images, 34
  kit contents, 36–41
  kit types, 33–36
  platform support, 34, 35–36
  prebuilt server binaries, 33–35
  rebuilding and, 160–161
  source code and, 33
  unpacking kits, 42–43
  verification, 44–48

interfaces, network boards with multiple addresses, 242

`internal server error` error message, 307, 314–315

Internet, as optional for Apache server, 14–15

Internet Primer (RFC2151), RFCs (Requests for Comments), 278

IP addresses, 12–14

  loopback addresses, 15

  registration of system names and addresses, 241

  requests and, 142

  virtual hosts, 231–232

IRIXN32 rule, `Configuration` file, 157

IRIXNIS rule, `Configuration` file, 157

`ITERATE2`, directive rules, 52

`ITERATE`, directive rules, 52

• *J* •

JPEG files, images, 80

• *K* •

keywords, status module, 176–177

kit contents, 36–41

  `cgi-bin` directory, 37

  `conf` directory, 37

  `htdocs` directory, 37–38

  `icons` directory, 38

  `logs` directory, 38–39

  `src` directory, 39–41

  `support` directory, 41

  `tar` archive, 36

kits

  types of, 33–36

  unpacking, 42–43

• *L* •

`-l` command, configuration command-line options, 74

`language` dimension, variable dimensions (client preferences), 185–186

languages

  client preferences, 183–184

  quality values (client preferences), 187–189

`Last-Modified:` header field

  CGI scripts, 213

  proxy servers, 261

`<Limit>` directive

  authentication methods, 104–105

  troubleshooting, 297

`Listen` directive, virtual hosts, 244

`Location:` header field, CGI scripts, 213

`<Location>` scope, 54, 56, 60

`logger` hook, modules, 122

`logger` phase, requests, 148

logs, 83–95

  access, 84, 88

  advertising and, 90–91

  analysis tools, 86–87

  backing up, 111

  CLF (Common Log Format), 85

  cookies, 88–90

  error, 84

  `ErrorLog` directive, 84

  `mod_log_agent` management module, 138

  `mod_log_config` management module, 138

  `mod_log_referer` management module, 138–139

  overview, 83–85

  privacy and, 92–93

  protecting, 111

request, 84
rolling over, 95
server errors, 93–94
size management, 95
system requirements, 28
transaction, 85
TransferLog directive, 84
virtual host, 244–247
logs directory, kit contents, 38–39
lookups, registration of system names
    and addresses, 240
loopback addresses, IP addresses, 15
lost connections, error messages, 309
LOW_SLACK_LINE switch, Configuration
    file, 155

• *M* •

M information, statistics table
    (status module), 175
make utility
    Configuration file, 153
    source code tools, 21
management modules, 136–140
    mod_dld, 136
    mod_env, 136
    mod_info, 136–137
    mod_log_agent, 138
    mod_log_config, 138
    mod_log_referer, 138–139
    mod_status, 139–140
    mod_usertrack, 140
Manual (Apache), htdocs directory, 38
mapping images, mod_imap module,
    126–127
marketing, advertising and
    logging, 90–91
MAXIMUM_DNS switch, Configuration
    file, 155
MD5 hashing, checksums and verifying
    installations, 44, 45, 46–47
memory, system requirements, 26–27

merge_dir_config hook, modules, 120
merge_server_config hook,
    modules, 121
methods, authorization and
    authentication, 104–105
MIMEs (Multipurpose Internet Mail
    Extensions), 281–283
    conformance and examples, 283
    media types, 282
    message body formats, 281
    non-ASCII headers, 282
    registering types, 283
mime.types file, file types, 221–222
minimal configuration, 68–71
    DocumentRoot, 68
    ErrorLog directive, 69
    Group directive, 68–69
    httpd.conf, 70–71
    PidFile directive, 70
    Port directive, 69
    ServerAdmin directive, 70
    ServerName directive, 70
    ServerRoot, 68, 71
    ServerType, 68
    TransferLog directive, 69
    User directive, 68
MINIMAL_DNS switch, Configuration
    file, 155
mod_access module, security modules,
    105–106, 128
mod_actions, real-time processing
    modules, 125
mod_alias, translator modules, 130
mod_asis, protocol modules, 134
mod_auth module
    security modules, 106, 128
    setting up password-protected
    pages, 299–300
mod_auth_anon module, security
    modules, 107–108, 128
mod_auth_db module, security
    modules, 108–109, 128

mod_auth_msql module, security modules, 129

mod_autoindex, real-time processing modules, 125, 126

mod_cern_meta, protocol modules, 134

mod_cgi, real-time processing modules, 126

mod_digest module, security modules, 129

mod_dir, translator modules, 130–131

mod_dld, management modules, 136

mod_env, management modules, 136

mod_example module, 124

mod_expires
 caching, 196, 197–198
 protocol modules, 134

mod_headers
 caching, 195–196
 protocol modules, 134–135

mod_imap, real-time processing modules, 126–127

mod_include, real-time processing modules, 127

mod_info
 management modules, 136–137
 monitoring Apache server, 170

mod_log_agent, management modules, 138

mod_log_config, management modules, 138

mod_mime, translator modules, 131

mod_mime_magic, translator modules, 131

mod_negotiation, translator modules, 131–132

mod_proxy, protocol modules, 135

mod_rewrite
 redirection, 183
 translator modules, 132

mod_setenvif, decision-making modules, 133

mod_status, management modules, 139–140

Module Configuration Commands information, monitoring Apache server, 169

Module Groups information, monitoring Apache server, 168

Module Name information, monitoring Apache server, 168

Module Registry, 140, 291–292

modules, 117–140
 Apache Module Registry, 140, 291–292
 content handlers and, 118, 224
 decision-making, 133
 environment context, 119
 handlers and, 118
 hooks, 118, 120–123
 housekeeping records, 119
 management tools, 136–140
 miscellaneous, 123–125
 mod_example, 124
 module structure, 119
 mod_unique_id, 124–125
 monitoring Apache server, 165–166
 overview, 117–123
 protocol, 134–135
 real-time processing, 125–127
 Registry, 140, 291–292
 request context, 118–119
 security, 127–129
 translators, 129–133

modules list, Configuration file, 158–159

modules subdirectory, src directory, 40

mod_unique_id module, 124–125

mod_userdir, translator modules, 132–133

mod_usertrack
 management modules, 140
 tracking cookies, 89–90

monitoring Apache server, 165–178
 Content-types affected information, 168
 Current Configuration information, 169

directives, 167–170
information module, 165–170
kinds of information, 167–170
mod_info, 170
Module Configuration Commands
information, 169
Module Groups information, 168
Module Name information, 168
modules, 165–166
status module, 165–166, 171–178
MPEG files, images naming
conventions, 80
multiviews, client preferences, 191–192
mumble module, Configuration file,
158–159

● *N* ●

name virtual hosts, multiple
hosts by name, 243
names
registration of system, 240–241
virtual host, 234
NameVirtualHost directive,
234–235, 238, 296
naming conventions, 78–81
binary files, 80–81
case sensitivity, 78
HTML files, 79–80
images, 80
plain text, 78–79
scripts, 81
negotiated resources, caching, 198–199
Netcraft Web survey, resources for
Web authors, 294
network boards with multiple
addresses, 242
network boundaries, firewalls and, 252
newsgroups, Apache server, 272
NO_ARGS, directive rules, 51
NoCache directive, proxy servers,
259–260

NO_LINGCLOSE switch, Configuration
file, 155
NO_SLACK switch, Configuration
file, 155
notable keyword, status module, 177
NPH (Non-Parsed Headers),
CGI scripts, 215

● *O* ●

Order directive, security-related
directives, 101–102
origin servers, defined, 250

● *P* ●

packet tracing, 319–322
recording network conversations, 320
reviewing recordings, 320–321
tcpdump utility, 320–321
tcpshow utility, 320–322
pages, requests comparison, 141–142
PARANOID rule, Configuration file, 157
parsing
SSI, 216–219
x-bit hack, 199
parsing failures, SSI, 307–308
passwd file, 300–301
AuthUserFile directive and, 113
caveat, 112
password-protected pages, setting up,
299–300
PATH environment variable,
CGI scripts, 205
PATH_INFO environment variable,
CGI scripts, 205
paths, redirection and, 181–182
PATH_TRANSLATED environment
variable, CGI scripts, 206
peers, defined, 13
per-directory configuration files, 30
permanent redirection, 180

permissions, 65–68
  protecting Apache server, 67
  root user, 65–66
  ServerRoot, 66–68
PGP signatures, verifying installations
      with checksums, 44–46
phases, request, 143–146
PID information, statistics table
      (status module), 174
PidFile directive
  minimal configuration, 70
  shutting down Apache server, 76
PL files, script naming conventions, 81
plain text, naming conventions, 78–79
platform support, installing Apache
      server, 34, 35–36
Port directive
  minimal configuration, 69
  troubleshooting with, 317–318
PORTING file, rebuilding Apache server,
      162–163
POST method
  authorization and authentication,
      104–105
  REQUEST_METHOD environment
      variable, 207
post_read_request hook, modules, 123
post_read_request phase,
      requests, 144
prebuilt server binaries, installing
      Apache server, 33–35
preferences, client. *See* client
      preferences
premature end of script headers
      message, error log, 302
privacy and logging, 92–93
  See also security
processes, system requirements, 25
protection. *See* security
protocol modules, 134–135
  mod_asis, 134
  mod_cern_meta, 134

mod_expires, 134
mod_headers, 134–135
mod_proxy, 135
proxy servers, 249–262
  CacheDefaultExpire directive, 262
  CacheDirLength directive, 259
  CacheDirLevels directive, 259
  CacheGCInterval directive, 260
  CacheLastModifiedFactor
      directive, 261–262
  CacheMaxExpire directive, 261
  CacheRoot directive, 258
  CacheSize directive, 258
  caching, 194, 251, 258–262
  caching negotiated resources, 198–199
  client specification of, 253
  Configuration file, 253
  connecting Web sites with, 257–258
  enabling, 253–258
  Expires: header field, 261
  firewalls and, 250–251, 252
  forbidding access, 256–257
  functions of, 249
  garbage collector, 260
  header fields, 261
  Last-Modified: header field, 261
  mod_proxy module, 135
  NoCache directive, 259–260
  origin servers, 250
  overview, 249–253
  ProxyBlock directive, 257
  ProxyPass directive, 257–258
  ProxyRemote directive, 256
  ProxyRequests directive, 254
  turning on and off, 254
  virtual hosts and, 254–255
proxy subdirectory, src/modules
      directory, 40
ps command, troubleshooting
      unresponsive servers, 316
PUT method, enabling, 301

• Q •

quality values (client preferences), 187–189
  query arguments, 189
  scripts, 189
QUERY_STRING environment variable, CGI scripts, 205, 209
question mark (?)
  scoping and wildcards, 57–58
  status module, 176

• R •

RAM, system requirements, 26–27
RAW_ARGS, directive rules, 53
real-time processing modules, 125–127
  mod_actions, 125
  mod_autoindex, 125, 126
  mod_cgi, 126
  mod_imap, 126–127
  mod_include, 127
realms
  AuthName directive, 103
  authorization, 98
rebuilding Apache server, 151–163
  build phase, 160
  Configuration file, 151–160
  GNU C compilers, 161
  installing new server, 160–161
  PORTING file, 162–163
  porting to new platforms, 161–163
recording network conversations, packet tracing, 320
redirection, 179–183
  aliases and, 180, 181
  described, 179
  directives, 182
  mod_rewrite, 183
  paths, 181–182
  permanent, 180
  temporary, 180
  types of, 180

referers, mod_log_referer management module, 138–139
refresh[=n] keyword, status module, 177
regex subdirectory, src directory, 40–41
registering
  MIME types, 283
  system names and addresses, 240–241
Registry, Apache Module, 140, 291–292
regular expressions, scoping and, 58
relative URLs (Uniform Resource Locators), 285–286
REMOTE_ADDR environment variable, CGI scripts, 206
REMOTE_HOST environment variable, CGI scripts, 206
REMOTE_PORT environment variable, CGI scripts, 206
REMOTE_USER environment variable, CGI scripts, 206
Req information, statistics table (status module), 175
request context, modules and, 118–119
request log, 84
request methods, authorization and authentication, 104–105
REQUEST_METHOD environment variable, CGI scripts, 206–207
requests, 141–148
  access_checker phase, 145
  auth_checker phase, 146
  autopsy metaphor, 142–143
  check_user_id phase, 145–146
  content-handler phase, 148
  defined, 28
  diagnosis metaphor, 146–147
  fixer_upper phase, 147
  header_parse phase, 145
  IP addresses and, 142
  logger phase, 148
  pages comparison, 141–142
  phases, 143–146

(continued)

requests *(continued)*
  `post_read_request` phase, 144
  `translate_handler` phase, 144
  `type_checker` phase, 147
Requests for Comments. *See* RFCs
`REQUEST_URI` environment variable,
    CGI scripts, 207
`Require` directive, security-related
    directives, 103
resource configuration file,
    `srm.conf`, 53
resource exhaustion, troubleshooting,
    272–273
resources, caching negotiated, 198–199
resources for Web authors, 287–294
  Apache bug database, 289–290, 291
  Apache documentation, 288–289
  Apache Module Registry, 140, 291–292
  Apache Web site, 287–288
  ApacheWeek electronic
    magazine, 290–291
  HTML/3.2 standard, 292–293
  Netcraft Web survey, 294
  RFCs (Requests for Comments), 293
  W3C (World Wide Web
    Consortium), 292
restarting Apache server, 76
result files, `src` directory, 39
reverse lookups, registration of system
    names and addresses, 240
RFCs (Requests for Comments), 277–286
  DNS, 278–280
  HTML, 283–284
  HTTP, 286
  Internet Primer, 278
  MIMEs, 281–283
  overview, 277–278
  resources for Web authors, 293
  URLs, 284–286
rolling over logs, 95
root directories, 62–68
  DocumentRoot, 64–65
  permissions, 65–68

ServerRoot, 63, 64
`root` user, permissions, 65–66
rules
  Configuration file, 156–157
  directive, 51–53
  virtual host, 231, 233

• S •

`SAFE_UNSERIALIZED_ACCEPT` switch,
    `Configuration` file, 156
`Satisfy` directive, security-related
    directives, 104
scoping, 54–60
  See also directives
  block usage, 55
  defined, 54
  `<Directory>` scope, 54, 55, 59
  `<Files>` scope, 54, 56–57, 59
  `.htaccess` files, 60–62
  `<Location>` scope, 54, 56, 60
  regular expressions and, 58
  sequence of, 58–60
  wildcards and, 57–58
scoreboard (status module), 171–173
script headers, `premature end of
    script headers` message, 302
`ScriptAlias` directive, CGI scripts, 203
ScriptAliased directories, 78
`SCRIPT_FILENAME` environment variable,
    CGI scripts, 207
`ScriptLog` directive, server error log, 94
`SCRIPT_NAME` environment variable,
    CGI scripts, 207
scripts
  CGI. *See* CGI scripts
  naming conventions, 81
  quality values (client preferences), 189
  server error log, 94
search script, Apache documentation, 289
security
  Apache server, 67
  CGI scripts, 203

eavesdropping and, 319
privacy and logging, 92–93
protecting logs, 111
security configuration file,
  `access.conf`, 53
security files, avoiding Web
  access to, 111
security modules, 105–109, 127–129
  `mod_access` module, 105–106, 128
  `mod_auth` module, 106, 128
  `mod_auth_anon` module, 107–108, 128
  `mod_auth_db` module, 108–109, 128
  `mod_auth_msql` module, 129
  `mod_digest` module, 129
security-related directives, 100–104
  `Allow` directive, 100–101
  `AuthName` directive, 103
  `AuthType` directive, 102
  `Deny` directive, 101
  `Order` directive, 101–102
  `Require` directive, 103
  `Satisfy` directive, 104
SEGV (fatal) error message, 306–307
server buffering, CGI scripts, 213–215
server communication, CGI scripts,
  209–213
server configuration file,
  `httpd.conf`, 53
`server configured – resuming
  normal operations` error
  message, 304
server error log, 93–94
  scripts, 94
  troubleshooting, 267–268
`server seems busy, spawning n
  children` error message, 305–306
server status, `mod_status` management
  module, 139–140
server-side image mapping, `mod_imap`
  module, 127
Server-Side Includes. *See* SSI
server-wide configuration files, 29–30
`ServerAdmin` directive, minimal
  configuration, 70

`SERVER_ADMIN` environment variable,
  CGI scripts, 208
`ServerName` directive
  minimal configuration, 70
  virtual hosts, 237
`SERVER_NAME` environment variable,
  CGI scripts, 208
`SERVER_PORT` environment variable,
  CGI scripts, 208
`SERVER_PROTOCOL` environment variable,
  CGI scripts, 208
ServerRoot, 63–64
  `conf` directory, 63
  minimal configuration, 68, 71
  permissions, 66–68
  shortcuts, 64
  subdirectory access, 63
servers
  origin, 250
  troubleshooting unresponsive, 315–317
`SERVER_SOFTWARE` environment variable,
  CGI scripts, 208
`SERVER_SUBVERSION` switch,
  `Configuration` file, 156
ServerType, minimal configuration, 68
`sh` Bourne Shell interpreter, source code
  tools, 21
`SHELL_PATH` switch, `Configuration`
  file, 156
shortcuts, ServerRoot, 64
shutting down Apache server, 76
`SIGHUP received. Attempting
  restart` error message, 304–305
`SIGKILL` signal, shutting down
  Apache server, 76
`SIGTERM` signal, shutting down Apache
  server, 76
`Slot` information, statistics table
  (status module), 175
slots, scoreboard, 173
`SOCKS4` rule, `Configuration` file, 157
source code
  Apache server, 21
  installing Apache server, 33

source code tools, 21
source files, src directory, 39
specification
  DNS (Domain Name System), 280
  HTTP (HyperText Transfer
    Protocol), 286
src/Configuration file. *See*
    Configuration file
src directory, 39–41
  configuration files, 39
  file types in, 39
  helpers subdirectory, 39–40
  modules subdirectory, 40
  regex subdirectory, 40–41
  result files, 39
  source files, 39
src/PORTING file, 162–163
src/support/dbmmanage script,
    databases and large user
    groups, 109
srm.conf, resource configuration
    file, 53
Srv information, statistics table
    (status module), 174
SS information, statistics table
    (status module), 175
SSI (Server-Side Includes), 216–219
  comments, 218
  directives, 219
  overview, 216
  parsing, 216–217
  parsing failures, 307–308
  troubleshooting directives, 297–299
  x-bit hack, 217–218
standards, RFCs (Requests for
    Comments), 277–286
starting Apache server, 75–76
starvation, defined, 39
statistics table (status module), 173–175
  Acc information, 174–175
  Child information, 175

Conn information, 175
CPU information, 175
M information, 175
PID information, 174
Req information, 175
Slot information, 175
Srv information, 174
SS information, 175
STATUS rule, 176
Status: header field, CGI scripts, 212
status module (monitoring Apache
    server), 165–166, 171–178
  & (ampersand), 176
  ? (question mark), 176
  auto keyword, 177
  child processes, 171–175
  HARD_SERVER_LIMIT switch, 171
  keywords, 176–177
  mod_status management
    module, 139–140
  notable keyword, 177
  refresh[=n] keyword, 177
  scoreboard, 171–173
  statistics table, 173–175
STATUS rule
  Configuration file, 157
  statistics table (status module), 176
stopping Apache server, 76
storefronts, advertising and
    logging, 90–91
subdirectory access, ServerRoot, 63
SUEXEC_BIN switch, Configuration
    file, 156
superuser access, 17–18
support directory, 41
syntax, rules of directives, 51–53
syntax verification, troubleshooting,
    268–269
system names and addresses,
    registration of, 240–241

system requirements, 15–17, 23–29
  access rights, 24
  CPU cycles, 26
  disk space, 27–29
  error logs, 28
  files, 26
  groups, 24–25
  log files, 28
  memory, 26–27
  processes, 25
  superuser access, 24
  user IDs, 24–25

• *T* •

TAKE#, directive rules, 51–52
tar archive, kit contents, 36
TCP/IP, network boards with multiple
    addresses, 242
tcpdump utility
  HTTP, 20–21
  packet tracing, 320–321
tcpshow utility
  HTTP, 21
  packet tracing, 320–322
Telnet, 19–20
  terminal settings, 19
  testing for Apache use, 20
  troubleshooting with, 317–319
temporary redirection, 180
terminal settings, Telnet, 19
timeouts, error messages, 308
tools, 18–22
  browsers, 18–19
  debuggers, 22
  HTTP, 20–21
  log analysis, 86–87
  management modules, 136–140
  source code, 21
  Telnet, 19–20
tracing packets. *See* packet tracing

transaction copies, caching, 194
transaction log, 85
TransferLog directive, 84
translate_handler hook, modules, 121
translate_handler phase,
    requests, 144
translating URLs to files, 65
translator modules, 129–133
  mod_alias, 130
  mod_dir, 130–131
  mod_mime, 131
  mod_mime_magic, 131
  mod_negotiation, 131–132
  mod_rewrite, 132
  mod_userdir, 132–133
troubleshooting, 313–322
  See also error messages
  Apache bug database, 269–271,
    289–290, 291
  Apache Group reports, 273–275
  Apache newsgroup, 272
  client preferences, 192–193
  communications, 317–319
  compilation errors, 302
  determining nature of problem,
    313–314
  FAQs and, 269
  file protections and resource
    exhaustion, 272–273
  "Internal Server Error" page, 314–315
  <Limit> directive, 297
  <Location> scope, 269
  packet tracing, 319–322
  Port directive, 317–318
  ps command, 316
  reproducing conditions, 266
  server error log, 267–268
  servers, 315–317
  SSI directives, 297–299

(continued)

Troubleshooting *(continued)*
    symptoms, 266–267
  syntax verification, 268–269
  with telnet, 317–319
  ten steps when you have problems,
    265–275
  verification, 266
  verifying CGI environment, 314–315
  verifying installations, 47
  virtual hosts, 295–296
type dimension, variable dimensions
    (client preferences), 185
type-map content handler, client
    preferences, 190–191
type_checker hook, modules, 122
type_checker phase, requests, 147
TypesConfig directive, file types, 222

• U •

uname utility, system features, 16
uncompressing files, unpacking
    kits, 42–43
UNIQUE_ID environment variable,
    CGI scripts, 208
UNIX, Apache requirement, 12
unpacking kits, 42–43
  binaries, 43
  GNU tools, 42
  uncompressing files, 42–43
URLs (Uniform Resource Locators)
  defined, 285
  mod_log_referer management
    module, 138–139
  relative, 285–286
  resources for Web authors, 287–294
  RFCs (Requests for Comments),
    284–286
  translating to files, 65
USE_FCNTL_SERIALIZED_ACCEPT switch,
    Configuration file, 156

USE_FLOCK_SERIALIZED_ACCEPT switch,
    Configuration file, 156
User directive, minimal
    configuration, 68
user IDs
  mod_userdir translator
    module, 132–133
  mod_usertrack module, 89–90, 140
  system requirements, 24–25
USE_SO_LINGER switch, Configuration
    file, 155
USE_USLOCK_SERIALIZED_ACCEPT
    switch, Configuration file, 156

• V •

-v command, configuration
    command-line options, 75
variable dimensions (client
    preferences), 184–186
  AddLanguage directive, 186
  encoding dimension, 185
  language dimension, 185–186
  type dimension, 185
verifying CGI environment,
    troubleshooting, 314–315
verifying installations, 44–48
  checking documentation pages, 47–48
  checksums, 44–47
  encryption, 45
  MD5 hashing, 44, 45, 46–47
  PGP signatures, 44–46
  troubleshooting, 47
virtual hosts, 229–248
  access log combining, 247
  access log separations, 245–246
  combining access logs, 247
  declaring, 231–232
  default server, 247–248
  examples, 233–238
  IP addresses, 231–232

Listen directive, 244
logs, 244–247
multiple hosts by address, 239
multiple hosts by name, 243
multiple names and addresses, 233–238
names, 234, 243
NameVirtualHost directive, 234–235, 238, 296
network boards with multiple addresses, 242
overview, 229–231
proxy servers and, 254–255
registration of system names and addresses, 240–241
rules, 231, 233
ServerName directive, 237
splitting up access log, 245–246
troubleshooting, 295–296
virtual memory, system requirements, 26–27

• W •

W3C (World Wide Web Consortium), resources for Web authors, 292
WANTHSREGEX rule, Configuration file, 157
Web browsers. *See* browsers
Web pages, requests comparison, 141–142
Web sites, connecting with proxy servers, 257–258
Web storefronts, advertising and logging, 90–91
wildcards
ExpiresByType directive, 198
scoping and, 57–58
World Wide Web Consortium (W3C), resources for Web authors, 292

• X •

x-bit hack

caching, 199
SSI (Server-Side Includes), 217–218
-x command, configuration command-line options, 75
XBITHACK switch, Configuration file, 156

• Z •

zones, registration of system names and addresses, 241

NOTE: The GNU (General Public License) may apply to individual programs on the *Apache Server For Dummies* CD-ROM. Please see the individual programs for details.

IDG Books Worldwide, Inc., End-User License Agreement

READ THIS. You should carefully read these terms and conditions before opening the software packet(s) included with this book ("Book"). This is a license agreement ("Agreement") between you and IDG Books Worldwide, Inc. ("IDGB"). By opening the accompanying software packet(s), you acknowledge that you have read and accept the following terms and conditions. If you do not agree and do not want to be bound by such terms and conditions, promptly return the Book and the unopened software packet(s) to the place you obtained them for a full refund.

1. **License Grant.** IDGB grants to you (either an individual or entity) a nonexclusive license to use one copy of the enclosed software program(s) (collectively, the "Software") solely for your own personal or business purposes on a single computer (whether a standard computer or a workstation component of a multiuser network). The Software is in use on a computer when it is loaded into temporary memory (RAM) or installed into permanent memory (hard disk, CD-ROM, or other storage device). IDGB reserves all rights not expressly granted herein.

2. **Ownership.** IDGB is the owner of all right, title, and interest, including copyright, in and to the compilation of the Software recorded on the disk(s) or CD-ROM ("Software Media"). Copyright to the individual programs recorded on the Software Media is owned by the author or other authorized copyright owner of each program. Ownership of the Software and all proprietary rights relating thereto remain with IDGB and its licensers.

3. **Restrictions on Use and Transfer.**

   (a) You may only (i) make one copy of the Software for backup or archival purposes, or (ii) transfer the Software to a single hard disk, provided that you keep the original for backup or archival purposes. You may not (i) rent or lease the Software, (ii) copy or reproduce the Software through a LAN or other network system or through any computer subscriber system or bulletin-board system, or (iii) modify, adapt, or create derivative works based on the Software.

   (b) You may not reverse engineer, decompile, or disassemble the Software. You may transfer the Software and user documentation on a permanent basis, provided that the transferee agrees to accept the terms and conditions of this Agreement and you retain no copies. If the Software is an update or has been updated, any transfer must include the most recent update and all prior versions.

4. **Restrictions on Use of Individual Programs.** You must follow the individual requirements and restrictions detailed for each individual program in the "About the CD" section of this Book. These limitations are also contained in the individual license agreements recorded on the Software Media. These limitations may include a requirement that after using the program for a specified period of time, the user must pay a registration fee or discontinue use. By opening the Software packet(s), you will be agreeing to abide by the licenses and restrictions for these individual programs that are detailed in the "About the CD" section and on the Software Media. None of the material on this Software Media or listed in this Book may ever be redistributed, in original or modified form, for commercial purposes.

5. **Limited Warranty.**

   (a) IDGB warrants that the Software and Software Media are free from defects in materials and workmanship under normal use for a period of sixty (60) days from the date of purchase of this Book. If IDGB receives notification within the warranty period of defects in materials or workmanship, IDGB will replace the defective Software Media.

   (b) IDGB AND THE AUTHOR OF THE BOOK DISCLAIM ALL OTHER WARRANTIES, EXPRESS OR IMPLIED, INCLUDING WITHOUT LIMITATION IMPLIED WARRANTIES OF MERCHANTABILITY AND FITNESS FOR A PARTICULAR PURPOSE, WITH RESPECT TO THE SOFTWARE, THE PROGRAMS, THE SOURCE CODE CONTAINED THEREIN, AND/OR THE TECHNIQUES DESCRIBED IN THIS BOOK. IDGB DOES NOT WARRANT THAT THE FUNCTIONS CONTAINED IN THE SOFTWARE WILL MEET YOUR REQUIREMENTS OR THAT THE OPERATION OF THE SOFTWARE WILL BE ERROR FREE.

   (c) This limited warranty gives you specific legal rights, and you may have other rights that vary from jurisdiction to jurisdiction.

6. **Remedies.**

   (a) IDGB's entire liability and your exclusive remedy for defects in materials and workmanship shall be limited to replacement of the Software Media, which may be returned to IDGB with a copy of your receipt at the following address: Software Media Fulfillment Department, Attn.: *Apache Server For Dummies*, IDG Books Worldwide, Inc., 7260 Shadeland Station, Ste. 100, Indianapolis, IN 46256, or call 800-762-2974. Please allow three to four weeks for delivery. This Limited Warranty is void if failure of the Software Media has resulted from accident, abuse, or misapplication. Any replacement Software Media will be warranted for the remainder of the original warranty period or thirty (30) days, whichever is longer.

   (b) In no event shall IDGB or the author be liable for any damages whatsoever (including without limitation damages for loss of business profits, business interruption, loss of business information, or any other pecuniary loss) arising from the use of or inability to use the Book or the Software, even if IDGB has been advised of the possibility of such damages.

   (c) Because some jurisdictions do not allow the exclusion or limitation of liability for consequential or incidental damages, the above limitation or exclusion may not apply to you.

7. **U.S. Government Restricted Rights.** Use, duplication, or disclosure of the Software by the U.S. Government is subject to restrictions stated in paragraph (c)(1)(ii) of the Rights in Technical Data and Computer Software clause of DFARS 252.227-7013, and in subparagraphs (a) through (d) of the Commercial Computer–Restricted Rights clause at FAR 52.227-19, and in similar clauses in the NASA FAR supplement, when applicable.

8. **General.** This Agreement constitutes the entire understanding of the parties and revokes and supersedes all prior agreements, oral or written, between them and may not be modified or amended except in a writing signed by both parties hereto that specifically refers to this Agreement. This Agreement shall take precedence over any other documents that may be in conflict herewith. If any one or more provisions contained in this Agreement are held by any court or tribunal to be invalid, illegal, or otherwise unenforceable, each and every other provision shall remain in full force and effect.

Installing the *Apache Server For Dummies* CD-ROM

● ●

*H*ere's some of what you can find on the *Apache Server For Dummies* CD-ROM:

- ✔ A complete source kit for the latest officially-released version of the Apache Web server package
- ✔ Binary kits of the latest official version of the Apache Web server software for several popular versions of UNIX
- ✔ A complete source kit of the latest released beta-test version of the Apache Web server software, along with pre-built binary executables for several versions of UNIX
- ✔ A copy of the latest released beta-test version of the Apache Web server for Windows NT 4.0 and Windows 95
- ✔ The GNU ANSI C compiler, and various utilities and tools for debugging your Web server
- ✔ Reference materials for working with the Internet and the World-Wide Web

For details about the *Apache Server For Dummies* CD-ROM, refer to Appendix B, "About the CD-ROM." Chapter 3 and Chapter 4 cover the most important issues for getting Apache up and running on your system.

IDG BOOKS WORLDWIDE BOOK REGISTRATION

We want to hear from you!

Visit **http://my2cents.dummies.com** to register this book and tell us how you liked it!

- Get entered in our monthly prize giveaway.
- Give us feedback about this book — tell us what you like best, what you like least, or maybe what you'd like to ask the author and us to change!
- Let us know any other *...For Dummies*® topics that interest you.

Your feedback helps us determine what books to publish, tells us what coverage to add as we revise our books, and lets us know whether we're meeting your needs as a *...For Dummies* reader. You're our most valuable resource, and what you have to say is important to us!

Not on the Web yet? It's easy to get started with *Dummies 101*®: *The Internet For Windows*® *98* or *The Internet For Dummies*®, 6th Edition, at local retailers everywhere.

Or let us know what you think by sending us a letter at the following address:

...For Dummies Book Registration
Dummies Press
10475 Crosspoint Blvd.
Indianapolis, IN 46256

BESTSELLING BOOK SERIES